Christ in Job and Career

Daily Devotions for Christians at Work

Foreword by Jimmy Davis, Jr.

Editors
Kevin J. Cooney
William (Bill) Dudley
Tammy L. Peavy
Stephen Pincus
Greg Smith
James D. Slack

EMETH PRESS
www.emethpress.com

Christ in Job and Career: Daily Devotions for Christians at Work

Copyright © 2017 James D. Slack
Printed in the United States of America on acid-free paper

All rights reserved. No part of this book may be reproduced, or stored in a retrieval system or transmitted in any form or by any means, electronic, mechanical, photocopying, recording, scanning or otherwise, except as permitted by the 1976 United States Copyright Act, or with the prior written permission of Emeth Press. Requests for permission should be addressed to: Emeth Press, P. O. Box 23961, Lexington, KY 40523-3961. http://www.emethpress.com.

Library of Congress Cataloging-in-Publication Data

Names: Cooney, Kevin J., editor.
Title: Christ in job and career : daily devotions for Christians at work / Kevin J. Cooney, William (Bill) Dudley, Tammy L. Peavy, Stephen Pincus, Greg Smith, James D. Slack,
editors ; foreword by Jimmy Davis, Jr.
Description: Lexington : Emeth Press, 2017. | Includes index. Identifiers: LCCN 2017054768 | ISBN
9781609471194 (alk. paper)
Subjects: LCSH: Employees--Prayers and devotions. | Devotional calendars. | Employees--Religious
life.
Classification: LCC BV4593 .C47 2017 | DDC 242/.68--dc23
LC record available at https://lccn.loc.gov/2017054768

Dedication

This book is dedicated to all public servants everywhere and to the glory of God. All praise goes to Him.

His mercies begin afresh each morning.

—*Lamentations* 3:23(b) [NLT]

Contents

Foreword / vii

Preface / ix

Acknowledgements / xi

About the Editors / xiii

Daily Devotionals (Week 1, Day 1 through Week 52, Day 5) / 1 – 348

About the Contributors / 349

Subject Index / 361

For we are God's masterpiece. He has created us anew in Christ Jesus, so we can do the good things he planned for us long ago.

    —*Ephesians* 2:10 [NLT]

Foreword

I live on Alabama's death row. When I arrived in 1994, I was angry. Angry at those who testified against me. Angry at those who lied. Angry at those who told the truth. Angry at my attorney. Angry at the jury. Angry at my family. Angry at my so-called friends. Angry at the correctional officers in prison. Above all, I was angry at myself – what I did and who I was. You would not want to know me back then. For the first ten years on death row, I was not a nice person.

Almost 15 years ago, I gave my anger to God. I surrendered my life to Jesus. I asked for His forgiveness of my sins, and I repented.

Then miracles happened. Death row became Life Row. It became a place where I lived, not waited. God began pulling me out of my comfort zone time and time again. I stopped hanging with old friends. I found Christian friends. Then He told me to minister to both inmates and correctional officers. Then He pulled me further out of my comfort zone and showed me how to be a leader in the Life Row church. God then used a free-world brother to get me to write a devotional in *The Christian Public Servant* – a daily workplace devotional that is sent to thousands on six continents through a blog and Facebook. At first, I was afraid. I was also ashamed because I could not write well. But my free-world friend said just "follow Him. He won't ask you to do anything you can't do with His help." And so, I did. And now, for nearly four years, I write each Friday's workplace devotional in *The Christian Public Servant*.

God has a way of pushing me out of my comfort zone and into His comfort zone. And each time, I am blessed. What was once death row is now Life Row, and it has become my workplace. You see, I don't just <u>wait</u> on death row anymore; I <u>work</u> for Christ on Life Row every day!

Christ in Job and Career includes this past year's devotionals from the electronic version called *The Christian Public Servant*. Each devotional is written by a volunteer – someone called by God. The editors are also volunteers – brothers and a sister called by God. As you read this book, perhaps God will call <u>you</u> out of your comfort zone to write a devotion for the next issue. You will bless thousands across the world – especially that one person who needs to read what God has placed in your heart on that particular day.

If you wish to write a devotional, please contact one of the editors. They will send you a "tip sheet" on how to write one, and they will edit so the words God places on your heart will truly glorify Him in the words sent out electronically and then published in the next hard copy edition.

I am so blessed when I read these devotions. I know you will be blessed, too.

Jimmy Davis, Jr.
Z-557 Unit N-10
Death Row (now, Life Row!)
Holman Correctional Facility
Alabama Department of Corrections
Atmore, Alabama USA

Preface

This ministry began in 2012 with the introduction of an electronic workplace devotional called *The Christian Public Servant*. Through this ministry, people receive work- and career-devotionals five mornings a week. Eventually growing to nearly 20,000 readers on six continents, *The Christian Public Servant* is found on our blog and on our Facebook page. If you would like to receive the electronic weekday devotional, find and "follow" us at: https://christianpublicservant.com.

This volume is a collection of the best from the electronic version – ones that have never been published in print. Each devotion, by design, is intimate – written informally as if you are talking with a close friend over a cup of coffee or tea. Each one follows a simple and short format that allows ample fit in your busy workday.

We pray the daily devotionals bless you at work and throughout career!

Pax Christi,

Kevin J. Cooney
kjcjapan@gmail.com

William (Bill) Dudley
bbssongs@gmail.com

Tammy L. Peavy
tammy.peavy@mid.ms.gov

Stephen Pincus
scpincus@gmail.com

Greg Smith
greg@kelseysarmy.org

James D. Slack
jslack0229@live.com

Acknowledgments

This book is dedicated to the glory of God. Without our Lord, this project could not have been accomplished. All praise goes to Him.

We also dedicate this book to our loving families who inspire us each day. The Cooney family – wife Atsuko, children Aiyana and Kian; the Dudley family – wife Annette, children Stephen, David, Tiffany, and Faith; the Peavy family - parents Grady and Kathren Robbins; the Pincus family – wife Amy and sons Stephen, Jr. and Mark; the Smith family – wife Missey, children Zach, Stevie, Lindsey, Codie, and Kelsey (home with our Lord); the Slack family – wife Janis, children Sarah, Samuel, and (son-in-law) Brandon.

This book of the law shall not depart out of thy mouth; but thou shalt meditate therein day and night, that thou mayest observe to do according to all that is written therein: for then thou shalt make thy way prosperous, and then thou shalt have good success. Have not I commanded thee? Be strong and of a good courage; be not afraid, neither be thou dismayed: for the LORD thy God is with thee whithersoever thou goest.

    — *Joshua* 1:8-9 [KJV]

About the Editors

Kevin J. Cooney, Ph.D., worships our Lord at the Church on the Ridge in Snoqualmie, Washington, where his family lives. He is a Visiting Professor at Ritsumeikan Asia Pacific University in Beppu, Japan. He previously served as the Director of the Pacific Rim Center at Northwest University where he held a dual appointment as Professor of Business and Political Science. He was also on the faculty at Union University and Arizona State University. Kevin earned the Ph.D. in political science from Arizona State University, which was followed by a post-doc certification in marketing and management from the University of Florida. He is the author of several books and numerous academic papers on East Asian security and economics. After over twenty years of teaching, Kevin left full-time academic work in 2014 to pursue writing and consulting.

William (Bill) Dudley, MPA, worships our Lord and is a singer/songwriter and Worship Pastor at Beacon Baptist Church in Virginia Beach, Virginia, where his family lives. He earned the Master of Public Administration (MPA) Degree from the Robertson School of Government at Regent University in Virginia Beach. Bill is a retired 32-year Naval Officer and ordained minister. He works for the U.S. Department of Defense.

Tammy L. Peavy worships our Lord at Crossgates Baptist Church in Brandon, Mississippi. She is a Fire Safety Education Officer for the Mississippi State Fire Marshal's Office in Jackson, Mississippi, and she has taught fire prevention in Katete, Zambia, Africa. She also assisted in the delivery of a fire truck to the citizens of Katete. Tammy resides in Pearl, Mississippi.

Stephen Pincus, M.A., worships our Lord at St. Vincent's Catholic Church in Newport News, Virginia. He earned the Master of Arts (MA in public administration) Degree from the Robertson School of Government at Regent University in Virginia Beach, Virginia. Stephen is a retired firefighter for the City of Newport News, Virginia, where he rose to the rank of Public Affairs Chief. His family resides in Yorktown, Virginia.

James D. Slack, Ph.D., Ph.D. worships our Lord at Bluff Park United Methodist Church in Hoover, Alabama, where his family lives. He is a professor at Jackson State University in Jackson, Mississippi. Jim follows our Lord into prisons, and he routinely visits Jesus on death row. He is a member of the Emmaus Community and the Kairos Prison Ministry.

Greg Smith worships where ever the Lord leads him. Missey and Greg are looking for a new church-home in their community of Overland Park, Kansas. He earned the BA (cum laude) in history and the MA in education, both degrees from Avila University. Greg is a former state representative and state senator in Kansas, as well as a police officer and deputy sheriff. He currently works for the Johnson County (Kansas) Sheriff's Office, and he is the executive director of the Kelsey Smith Foundation. This Foundation is named for his deceased beloved daughter, Kelsey, who at the age of 18 was kidnapped, sexually assaulted, and murdered on June 2, 2007. The Kelsey Smith Foundation works to prevent youth and young adults from being victims of violent crime. He and Missey give seminars on "safety awareness" throughout the U.S.

Week 1, Day 1

believe it, see it, and feel it

Reading

Isaiah 43:18-19 [NLT] But forget all that—it is nothing compared to what I am going to do. For I am about to do something new. See, I have already begun! Do you not see it?

Reflection

Wow! Can you **believe it, see it, and feel it**?

As you prepare for work today, forget the past. What went wrong last week, last month, or last year. What should have happened, but didn't. What shouldn't have happened, but did. And even forget the good things that happened in the past. Keeping your job. Getting that new job. That promotion. That raise. All the whatever's.

As you travel to work today, believe in all the changes only God can make. Changes in relationships with coworkers. The attitude of your supervisor. Changes in your job. Advancements in your career.

As you enter your building today, know He has already begun making changes!

So as you sit down to work today – **believe it, see it, and feel it**.

Yes – **believe it, see it, and feel it** this day. For He is about to do something new!

Prayer

Father God, I am grateful for what You have done for me in the past. But I am so blessed knowing You are doing something for me in the future! I already **believe it, see it, and feel it** – for You are my God. In Jesus' name, I pray. Amen.

Kevin J. Cooney
William (Bill) Dudley
Tammy L. Peavy
Stephen Pincus
James D. Slack
Greg Smith

Week 1, Day 2

everything will work out

Reading

Proverbs 16:3-4(a) [NIV] Commit to the LORD whatever you do, and he will establish your plans. The LORD works out everything to its proper end

Reflection

Like most college graduates, I celebrated as if I was done forever with school. I had learned what was needed, and I was ready for the real world. And shortly I found my first professional job!

But that was before I met my future bride. See, education in her family is a big deal. Even when I asked for her father's blessing to marry his daughter, part of *that conversation* entailed my commitment to earn a master's degree one day. For several years now, even after finding a better job, my wife has been urging me to do as she did and earn that second degree.

It's funny how things work. You think something happens as irony or a coincidence, but God's plan unfolds right in front of you daily. It wasn't long ago I found myself reading scripture that spoke a little louder than normal. My quick skim changed to a slow read and, in that moment, everything clicked. I need more education because of the door He wants to open for me. All I need to do is commit to Him – to *pledge to sacrifice on His behalf* – and go back to school for Him and not just for myself or for my family. If I commit to Him, **everything will work out** to its proper end.

So here I am, preparing to go back to school – four years after *that conversation* with my (now) father-in-law, two years after my wife started mentioning it, and several months after I learned where my Lord fits in. Yes, I have doubts and face plenty of stress. What if I can't do it? What about my full-time job? Will I have time for family? But in addition to a supportive family, I am committed to Him – I have *pledged to sacrifice on His behalf* – and I know **everything will work out** to its proper end. I have God on my side, and I'm excited to continue seeing His plan unfold!

Are we in the same boat? Are you going back to school while working full-time? Are you worried about how everything will fit together? Commit to Him – *pledge to sacrifice on His behalf*. Watch His plan unfold, and know **everything will work out** to its proper end.

And after work each night next semester, maybe we'll see each other in an online course!

Prayer

Dear Lord, give me strength to commit to You and to pledge to sacrifice for You. Give me courage to follow Your plan for me. Bless me with comfort knowing You are in charge of my life – including my work, my family, and my education. In Your name, I pray. Amen.

Brandon Miller

Week 1, Day 3

go beat myself up

Reading

Psalm 130:3 [KJV] If You, Lord, kept a record of our sins, who, O Lord, could ever survive?

1 John 1:9 [KJV] If we confess our sins, he is faithful and just to forgive us our sins and to cleanse us from all unrighteousness.

Reflection

I did it again. I messed up. I gave into my flesh. I did what I knew was not Christ-like. I SINNED. There I said it. I admit it. I don't know why I have trouble admitting it. I know, as a Christian, I am supposed to be the example. So because I think I need to be perfect, I'll **go beat myself up** until I feel I have punished myself enough to feel like maybe Christ will now forgive me. Yet Christ has never told me to **go beat myself up** in the process of forgiveness. He said I just need to confess it, and He will be faithful to forgive and remember no more.

So why do I take something so easy and complicate it to where the result is I **go beat myself up**? Maybe it's because I don't comprehend the depth of His love and forgiveness. I am thankful He doesn't keep a record of my sins; He does forgive; and I really do not have to **go beat myself up**. I just need to run to Him for forgiveness, receive His mercy and then, through the power of the Holy Spirit, set my sights again on pleasing Him.

What happened in your job so far this week that makes you say "I need to **go beat myself up**?" Maybe you got mad at a coworker and said the wrong thing. Maybe you were short with a citizen you serve. Maybe you slacked off on your responsibilities. If you're like me, you could make a list of things you messed up as you aim at perfection.

However, there is only one person who achieved perfection. Thankfully, because He did achieve perfection, He relieved you of having to achieve perfection. So you don't need to murmur "I need to **go beat myself up**." You just need to go to Him for forgiveness, and then receive His wisdom and strength to do better in the future.

Something to think about as you go to work this morning.

Prayer

Father, I am so thankful You do not remember my sins, but You provide mercy and strength for me to overcome them. So this workday, Father, forgive me for my trespasses as I forgive those who trespass against me, and lead me not into temptation but deliver me from evil. For thine is the kingdom and the power and glory forever. Amen.

Bill Dudley

Week 1, Day 4

this kind of workplace violence

Reading

Leviticus 19:18 [NIV] Do not seek revenge or bear a grudge against anyone among your people, but love your neighbor as yourself. I am the LORD.

Isaiah 41:10 [NIV] So do not fear, for I am with you; do not be dismayed, for I am your God. I will strengthen you and help you; I will uphold you with my righteous right hand.

Reflection

A friend called last night. He's stressed about coworkers not treating him, well, like they do other at work. A group of guys mock and ridicule him constantly. They make unpleasant jesters, thinking he doesn't see, whenever he enters the breakroom, comes out of the restroom, or sits in his cubicle. One of the guys was supposedly his friend, but he started **this kind of workplace violence**.

My friend also confessed he sometimes thinks of coming to work and hurting others, including himself. To get even, he thinks of escalating **this kind of workplace violence**!

I told him not to seek revenge. Just trust God, and pray He will touch his situation. I told him God will protect him and give him the courage to find the appropriate channel for remedy. God also will place in his heart forgiveness and an opportunity to end the hostile environment.

Well, my friend prayed all night. He found the courage go to the supervisor. Understanding the situation, the supervisor called a meeting. The guys apologized, my friend forgave, and things got back to normal.

Do you experience **this kind of workplace violence**? You know, the subtle and sometimes not-to-subtle kind? Whispering. Mild mocking. Signals. God will give you the courage to seek justice and a remedy. But God does not want you to seek vengeance.

Today at work, rely on God to guide you to an appropriate remedy. Rest assured, He does not want you in **this kind of workplace violence**. After all, He is God.

Prayer

Lord, thank You for always being there for me, especially when I think I am all alone. Thank You for the workplace experiences that build up my faith in You. At work and elsewhere, thank You for blessing me with Your goodness, wisdom, and courage. In Your name, I pray. Amen.

William Waples

Week 1, Day 5

show someone the kindness of God

Reading

2 Samuel 9:3(b) [KJV] And the king said, Is there not yet any of the house of Saul, that I may shew the kindness of God unto him?

Reflection

One day a brother talked to me about a correctional officer facing a big challenge in his life. His wife needed an operation, which meant he would have to take care of her. He was worried about how he could do both – take care of his wife and be at work.

The brother and I went to the officer and told him we would be praying for him and his wife. We would be praying the Lord would find some way to take care of his wife and for him to keep working. We told him his worries are with God now, and he should not worry. Everything will work out.

Well, that officer's face went from showing anxiety and fear to showing peace and joy. Knowing two condemned men on Death row would pray for him and his wife helped him put things into perspective. He and his wife will survive, and the Lord will take care of both – just as He takes care of my brother and me. Yes, he started showing peace and joy on his face.

Today at work, go out of your way to **show someone the kindness of God**. A coworker? Your boss? Someone you serve? Someone on the street on your way to or from work? Don't worry, God will lead them to you – just as He led that correctional officer to two condemned men.

When you **show someone the kindness of God**, you will feel His kindness, and you will be blessed!

Prayer

Father, in the name of Jesus, I pray. Open and clear my spiritual heart, eyes, and ears today so I can be bold to show Your kindness and build up peace and joy! Amen.

Jimmy Davis, Jr.

Week 2, Day 1

looking for a job

Reading

Proverbs 3 5-6 [NKJV] Trust in the Lord with all your heart, and lean not on your own understanding. In all your ways acknowledge Him, and He shall direct your paths.

Reflection

Some time ago, a close friend unexpectedly got laid off from her job. Although devastated, she picked herself up and began searching for open positions. In no time, my friend applied to over 20 jobs! Well, she had a few interviews here and there, but nothing seemed "right" and each one declined to hire her. She just continued **looking for a job**.

Now, my friend is a Christian. She kept trusting in the Lord – even though she did not understand why she was laid off in the first place, let alone why she could not find a new position. She just kept leaning on the Lord.

And then it happened. Suddenly God opened the right doors, and she received three job offers within one week!!

Are you laid off? Are you **looking for a job**?

Acknowledge the Lord with all your heart in your search for a new position – even if you don't understand why certain things are happening to you or around you. God will guide you down the right path.

So today, know God is **looking for a job** – the right job just for you!

Lean on Him, not yourself.

Prayer

Dear Lord, I trust You with all my heart. Give me courage of faith to acknowledge and praise Your marvelous works throughout this day. I know You will guide my paths. In Your name, I pray. Amen.

Phoenecia Hill

Week 2, Day 2

do anything to help

Reading

James 2:14-17 [ESV] What good is it, my brothers, if someone says he has faith but does not have works? Can that faith save him? If a brother or sister is poorly clothed and lacking in daily food, and one of you says to them, "Go in peace, be warmed and filled," without giving them the things needed for the body, what good is that? So also faith by itself, if it does not have works, is dead.

Reflection

A friend called today, stressed over his job situation. It's beginning to have a negative impact on his family life. His current job does not pay enough, and he must spend a lot of time away from his three-year-old daughter and his wife. He's trying to get a job in a neighboring state that would pay more and give him more time with his family. He has an interview lined up for the following week but does not have a car worthy of the trip.

As I listened, I began to wonder, "Can I **do anything to help**?" Of course, I would pray for my friend. Yet the Spirit kept nudging me and tugging at my heart to do more. In fact, toward the end of the conversation, my friend asked if I could drive him next weekend to that neighboring state for the interview.

Now I don't know about you, but my weekends are rather full. Taking an out-of-state trip would be inconvenient. But then I began to think of how the drive would not only help my friend but also help his family. I could also share my faith and love for Christ. So I said I would drive him.

Have you found yourself in the middle of a situation where the Spirit nudged you to act and **do anything to help**? Today at work, remember God puts you in the pathways of people who have a lot of burdens – citizens you serve, coworkers, and people you pass in the lobby. Quite often, they need someone who will **do anything to help**. Today, won't you give of yourself and share your faith and love of the Lord by sharing your works? Today, won't you **do anything to help**?

Prayer

Lord, thank You for always watching over me in dismayed times. Let me be Your hands and Your feet. Let me live my faith through Your action so I may fulfill the needs of others. I ask this in Jesus' name. Amen.

William Waples

Week 2, Day 3

frail human biases

Reading

1Timothy 5:21(b) [NKJV] maintain these principles without bias, doing nothing in a spirit of partiality.

Leviticus 19:15(b) [NKJV] you shall not be partial to the poor nor defer to the great, but you are to judge your neighbor fairly.

Reflection

For the past two years, a friend has been applying for in-house jobs as a social service worker. Yet every time, she's turned down. Oh, she has experience and never applies for a position where she lacks qualifications. But she doesn't get the job.

So what is the problem? Why does she get passed over? Based on a rumor about Human Resouces, my friend suspects applicants are selected before the search. Positions are posted only to follow protocol! Have you ever experienced an unjust situation at work?

My friend knows first-hand it's hard being treated unfairly in the workplace. She wants to retaliate – get even somehow. My advice is "don't." Instead, she must use this unpleasant experience to demonstrate she <u>will</u> follow Christian principles and not let her own **frail human biases** get in the way. Like you and me, my friend must demonstrate her faith to coworkers and supervisors – even to Human Resources!

Today at work, you may experience injustice, but don't let your own **frail human biases** get in the way of treating others fairly – regardless of how you are treated. Maintain Christian principles in everything you do. If you do nothing in the spirit of partiality, others may follow and the organization's culture may change. Remember don't retaliate through **frail human biases**. Others are watching, and so is our Lord!

Prayer

Father in Heaven, please help me maintain Your values at work. Let me show You through my actions, and empower others to do what is right and just. In Your Son's name, I pray. Amen.

Barbara Hill

Week 2, Day 4

be strong and stay focused

Reading

Proverbs 16:16 [ESV] How much better to get wisdom than gold! To get understanding is to be chosen rather than silver.

Reflection

Although you must go to work today to earn the "gold" necessary for survival, what makes your work – your productive activity – worth living for? Is it money alone?

Fellowship with Jesus, coupled with one's tangible mission in Christ for the Kingdom of God, brings the necessary love, peace, and joy from the Holy Spirit to make life more than hand-to-mouth. As you work today, **be strong and stay focused**. There is wisdom and understanding out there – His wisdom and His understanding – and they are more valuable than gold and silver.

So **be strong and stay focused** throughout this workday. After all, His return is closer today than it was yesterday! And all the gold and silver in your paycheck will not help.

Prayer

Lord, it is so easy to get confused over work and career. Gold and silver – a good salary – is needed, but You are needed more than money. Let me **be strong and stay focused** on You. In Your name, I pray. Amen.

Chris Summers

Week 2, Day 5

try to please someone

Reading

1 Corinthians 10:33 [NLT] I, too, try to please everyone in everything I do. I don't just do what is best for me; I do what is best for others so that many may be saved.

Reflection

I have a friend in the free-world, someone I consider my brother. I don't "just" mean a Christian brother, I mean we are as close as if we are brothers in the same worldly family. He is going through some big challenges at his workplace. He is not in trouble, but I sense worry in his letters, and I see fatigue on his face when he visits. He doesn't talk about it much, probably concerned about burdening me. You see, he tries to please <u>me</u> and keep <u>me</u> at peace. He wants to do what is best for <u>me</u>.

In my letters to him, I now search for the very best scriptures, ones that will give my friend a special peace. And in those letters, I try to make him laugh a bit while assuring him God is with him. When he visits, I try to get him talking about sports or something that will make him laugh. I try to show him the humor God carries around.

And suddenly my friend realizes what I am doing. As he tries to please <u>me</u>, I am trying to please <u>him</u>! We are both doing the best for each other so we both may be saved and continue our brotherly love in heaven.

Today at work, **try to please someone**. Not in some worldly way, but in a godly way. <u>Please</u> for the right reasons – showing God's love, protection, and grace. It doesn't matter how long that person has claimed to be a Christian – he may not yet be truly saved. <u>Please</u> that person in ways that will save him by restoring faith in our Lord. Yes, at work today, **try to please someone**. Who knows, that person may try to please you in return!

Prayer

Father, in the name of Jesus, I pray. For so many years, my selfish attitude led me to have an empty life. Then I gave my life to your Son, and I was born again with a new attitude. Father, help me please others in ways that please You. Give strength and confidence to do my best for others so many will be saved. Amen.

Jimmy Davis, Jr.

Week 3, Day 1

bring love to work

Reading

1 Corinthians 13:4-6 [NIV] Love is patient, love is kind. It does not envy, it does not boast, it is not proud. It does not dishonor others, it is not self-seeking, it is not easily angered, it keeps no record of wrongs. Love does not delight in evil but rejoices with the truth

Reflection

This scripture is typically used at weddings to remind the bride and groom of God's expectations in their relationship. But does God expect any less in your workplace relationships?

It doesn't matter if you are a supervisor or coworker. If you **bring love to work**, look at all you gain. You do not lose patience with people you serve or tasks you do. You celebrate the accomplishments of others without boasting about your own. Selfishness is left in the parking lot, and rumors are absent in the breakroom. If you **bring love to work**, honesty beats gamesmanship and is good for the organization's culture and productivity.

It may be hard to quantify, but love really has an impact on the bottom line. While it may take some time to root, it cannot be planted without you.

So as this workweek begins, **bring love to work**. Love will never fail any organization.

How might love help you today at work?

Prayer

Father, thank You for the opportunity to serve Your purposes. Help me love today as I work with everyone I serve and serve with. In the mighty name of Your Son, my Lord and Savior, Jesus Christ, I pray. Amen.

David Boisselle

Week 3, Day 2

make it grow

Reading

1 Corinthians 3:6-9 [NIV] I planted the seed, Apollos watered it, but God has been making it grow. So neither the one who plants nor the one who waters is anything, but only God, who makes things grow. The one who plants and the one who waters have one purpose, and they will each be rewarded according to their own labor. For we are coworkers in God's service; you are God's field, God's building.

Reflection

Recently I had the privilege of visiting Romania on a mission trip. There I was reminded again God is always at work and our job is to serve faithfully and leave the rest to Him. In one village, our team has worked for some years planting seeds by running a Bible school in an open field. Others watered the seeds planted some years past, and today that village has a church shining a bright beacon of God's love in an otherwise challenging and difficult environment. But it is God who continues to **make it grow**.

So as you go about today's work, do not get discouraged. Yes, it's true some days seem to be more productive than others. And yes, you often plant and water projects and ideas, but it's easy to get dispirited when setbacks occur. And it's too easy to grow impatient because you don't see immediately the desired long-term result. Just understand God has a divine plan for you and your work and He will take your labor to further His kingdom.

Today at work, plant the seeds. Or water the planted seeds. Remember you are His field. You are His building. You are a coworker in God's service.

But let Him **make it grow**.

Prayer

Dear God, on this workday, help me remain diligent in my tasks. When I face adversity, help me recognize my labor is not in vain for surely You will bless the seeds I plant. Also, bless the efforts of my team in serving as coworkers for our community in ways that bring honor and glory to You. In Christ's name, I pray. Amen.

Lou Lassiter

Week 3, Day 3

that which has no wisdom

Reading

Proverbs 8:1-4 (KJV) Doth not wisdom cry? And understanding put forth her voice? She standeth in the top of high places, by the way in the places of the paths. She crieth at the gates, at the entry of the city, at the coming in at the doors. Unto you, O men, I call; and my voice is to the sons of man.

Reflection

My coworker believes everything he reads on the internet. Even "news" that seems so irrational, he considers truthful. He wants to think exactly like all those around him. And he doesn't seek God's direction. He only seeks the opinions of others. And he fears only what others may think if he disagrees with the popularity of current rumors and conspiracies found on the internet.

Too many people believe in what they read or hear without thinking about it.

Do you know someone who fits this bill?

Especially right now, the internet overflows with so-called fact and truth. And the world seems quite hip with believing **that which has no wisdom**.

Before you go to work today, as you read the "news" on your phone, remember this: All good things come from God, and that includes wisdom.

So starting today, search for the true voices of wisdom around you. Don't be content with the rumors and innuendos you read from a variety of unknown sources. Wisdom is crying out to you. Understanding is lending her voice. She is at the entry of every discussion. She is at the door of every debate.

Today in the break room, do not listen to **that which has no wisdom**.

Prayer

Lord, help me look for Your voice of wisdom. Help me seek You and Your word in my deliberations. Help me remember it is Your wisdom that counts, not the world's. In Jesus' name, I pray. Amen.

Noah M. Griffing

Week 3, Day 4

sin in the situation

Reading

1 John 2:9; 11(b) [ESV] Whoever says he is in the light and hates his brother is still in darkness... and does not know where he is going, because the darkness has blinded his eyes.

Luke 23:34(b) [ESV] Father, forgive them, for they know not what they do.

Reflection

Have you ever encountered jealousy at work? Maybe someone has sabotaged your project, slandered you in the break room, or dressed you down in front of your supervisor. Being hurt by someone's unintentional carelessness or being run over in competition is bad enough. But an intentional wound out of jealousy – now that's a whole different thing.

This once happened to me. A supervisor inflicted acts of hate on me each time I accomplished a significant goal. I sought advice from a Christian friend, and this was his advice. I had to examine myself for jealousy! I needed to check myself for **sin in the situation** – sinning against someone because of the sin received. I had to become aware I have blind spots to my sin and it is my own sin that causes those blind spots. And guess what? He was right!

The Bible reminds you and me we are not above hurting those we know – including people at work. And while you think a coworker knows exactly what she is doing to hurt you, you are walking in the darkness – and the darkness blinds your eyes to further sin – if you sin in return.

It's always a good idea to step back when actions are directed at you or when you are directing your actions at a coworker. Examine the motive of your behavior and response. And then recall our Lord dying on the cross and how it seemed those crucifying Him knew exactly what they were doing. And remember He forgave them. He chose not to leave the light and fall prey to **sin in the situation**. Can you do the same?

So at work today, be aware of the blind spots caused by your own sin. Go to Him, and He will help you avoid **sin in the situation.** He will help you get back to loving your coworker as yourself, regardless of your coworker's intent and action.

Yes, today at work, walk in the light, do not be blind, and know where you are going.

Prayer

Kind heavenly Father, we praise You for shining Your light into our work-life and rescuing us from darkness. We want the same for all our coworkers. When we are hurt by someone, show us how to rise above it and act with Your sufficient grace. We ask in the name of Your Son, Jesus. Amen.

Jonathan Waugh
Linda Waugh

Week 3, Day 5

well able – no matter what

Reading

Numbers 13:30 [NLT] But Caleb tried to quiet the people as they stood before Moses. "Let's go at once to take the land," he said. "We can certainly conquer it!"

Reflection

There are brothers on Life Row I call my prayer warriors. Their prayers and the way they live for Christ give me confidence to believe I am **well able – no matter what** – to do Jesus' will every day.

We need people like Caleb in our lives – those who take God at His Word and give strength to you and me to do the same. But we all need to be Caleb ourselves. You and I need to be **well able – no matter what** – to do God's will.

But sometimes we fail by not responding, not loving, not forgiving. We fail by not moving in compassion toward others. You and I fail because we do not act as if we are **well able – no matter what**.

Caleb did not fail because of what God told him. As you prepare for work today, God is telling you the same thing He told Caleb and everyone else who follows Him. He has already given you everything you need to do His work – in your workplace, in your community, and in your life.

Now, go to work today knowing He has made you **well able – no matter what**!

Do not fail Him.

Prayer

Father, in the name of Jesus, I pray. Thank You for equipping me every day so I can be **well able – not matter what** – to carry out Your will. Amen.

Jimmy Davis, Jr.

Week 4, Day 1

even when it causes division

Reading

Luke 12:51 [NIV] Do you think I came to bring peace on earth? No, I tell you, but division.

Reflection

We've all heard the phrase "that's <u>not</u> Christian." But *what <u>is</u> Christian* – especially when it comes to making management decisions, setting agency policies, or finding workplace solutions?

Are we to act like others? You know, make decisions with passivity and tolerance just to avoid discontent. Are we to embrace all ideas and actions – just for the sake of peace?

If I am obedient to Christ, biblically-based workplace decisions may well cause some division. Keep in mind, Christ said He did not come to bring peace, but division. So as a *Christian public servant,* I should expect others may react negatively when I apply lessons taught in the Bible. Yes, some will want to define *what <u>is</u> Christian* in ways that render a temporary peace that restricts the power of the Holy Spirit. In fact, some might accuse me of <u>not</u> being Christian when I do otherwise.

So at work today, your task is to remain obedient in Christ – knowing in Him all things work together for His glory – **even when it causes division**. Your task is to strive for a consistent faith that demonstrates Jesus is Lord of your life.

It's difficult to do, I know, especially in the workplace. But in all matters remain obedient to Him. Show *what <u>is</u> Christian* – **even when it causes division**.

Prayer

Lord, prepare me for the divisions caused by showing and applying Your word at work and throughout my day. Help me be obedient to You. I know true peace will come only when You return to take ownership of Your kingdom here on earth. In Your name, I pray. Amen.

Stan Best

Week 4, Day 2

forgive even without an apology

Reading

Ephesians 4:31-32 [NIV] Get rid of all bitterness, rage and anger, brawling and slander, along with every form of malice. Be kind and compassionate to one another, forgiving each other, just as in Christ God forgave you.

Reflection

It seems like the workplace is a convenient setting to hurt someone's feelings and get away with doing so without ever apologizing. There are too many ways to "keep going" at work – too many ways to pretend like nothing happened. This makes it hard to forgive a coworker who hurts you, especially when there is no "I'm sorry."

Have you ever been hurt by a coworker who did not apologize?

Well, for a moment try to imagine he just didn't know any better. Or maybe no one taught her about kindness or compassion. Or maybe no one loved that particular coworker when he was a child – or still doesn't love him as an adult. Maybe the person comes to work from a place of hurt and she brings a heart filled with hurt. After all, *hurt people often hurt other people.*

As you reflect on that coworker, remember Christ wants you to **forgive even without an apology**. Only He knows what is going on in that person's heart, and rest assured, He is working on that heart. So as a *Christian public servant*, do what Christ wants – respond with His love and not with your own hurt feelings.

Today at work, there may be times when someone will do and say things to hurt you. And the coworker may do this and never say "I'm sorry." You have a choice to make. You can hold on to that hurt, become bitter, and lash out to retaliate or even hurt others. Or you can follow scripture, obey God, and be a reflection of Christ.

Which will it be?

Today at work, **forgive even without an apology** and open the way for God to do some healing.

Prayer

Dear Heavenly Father, soften my heart today so I might forgive others as You forgive me. Help me understand an apology may never come, but I must be willing to forgive – with or without it. Help me model Your Son's example of forgiveness. In Jesus' name, I pray. Amen.

Dawnielle Ballard

Week 4, Day 3

with intentional words

Reading

Psalms 19:14 [NLT] Let the words of my mouth and the thoughts of my heart be pleasing in Your eyes, O Lord, my Rock and the One Who saves me.

Reflection

There is an art to legislative writing. On a small level, I see the careful efforts of our City Clerk and City Attorney as they draft legislation for our City Council meetings. Ultimately, they want to avoid presenting vague or unenforceable language in the various ordinances presented to the Council to vote on. So the language must be clear **with intentional words**.

Speaking deliberately is important to many public sector jobs. What you say bears weight with people. Yet, as a *Christian public servant,* how often do you apply that principle to your walk with God as you serve others in the workplace? And how often do you pray **with intentional words**?

Life is quite hectic – and so is the job. I know mine is. There is always plenty to keep us busy and distracted. Sometimes that translates into my prayer life. In fact, sometimes I pray for the sake of praying rather than for the sake of seeking His intervention.

What about you?

Today at work, I want to be intentional with my communication with God. I want to speak and pray **with intentional words**. I want Him to know His direction is crucial to my life and my work-life.

I want Him to be the center of my workday. Don't you want the same?

So today, as this workweek begins, speak and pray **with intentional words**.

Prayer

Savior, I lead my efforts today for Your kingdom. Let me be a light to my colleagues and the public. Grant me wisdom in my speech. Anoint my countenance that I glorify You. In Your name, I pray. Amen.

Courtney Christian

Week 4, Day 4

a perfect workday

Reading

Psalm 37:5-6 [NIV] Commit your way to the LORD; trust in him and he will do this: He will make your righteous reward shine like the dawn, your vindication like the noonday sun.

Reflection

A good workday. That means many things to many people. For some, a good workday is actually no workday – time off for vacation. For others, it is a workday free from stress. Still, others view a good workday when certain tasks need not be done.

But shouldn't we envision a bit more than just a good workday? After all, we are children of God. Shouldn't we expect **a perfect workday**?

For me, **a perfect workday** doesn't entail a vacation. It's not necessarily stress-free. It may even include the most distasteful tasks. No, for me **a perfect workday** begins when I rise early and commit my thoughts, my actions, and my life to the Hand of God. Then I take on my workday with faith that *His fingerprints will be all over it* – as His righteousness shines through me to those in my workplace. It entails me trusting Him for protection and for peace with coworkers, supervisors, and those I serve.

It is my prayer you and I will have more than just a good workday. I pray we will have **a perfect workday** – now and forever!

Prayer

Good morning, God! I know You have my day already figured out. I commit to You as I rely on Your grace and will in making this **a perfect workday**. Tonight, long after the setting of the noonday sun, I want to reflect and know You were with me in my workplace. In Jesus' name, I pray. Amen.

Deanna Alexander

Week 4, Day 5

blessed enough to know

Reading

1 Samuel 16:17-18(a)(c) [MSG] Saul told his servants, "Go ahead. Find me someone who can play well and bring him to me." One of the young men spoke up, "I know someone. I've seen him myself… And GOD is with him."

Reflection

Here I am in prison. Facing a sentence of death. Limited in all aspects of life since I got here. And like my life in the free-world, for most of my time in here, I just sat and did nothing. It wasn't until someone saw something in me that I began to realize I had a gift from God.

And I am now **blessed enough to know** to use that gift. I use it in letters and writings. In phone calls. With brothers and correctional officers. With free-world people who visit.

Oh, I know it is not my gift. I did not create it. I did not buy it at the prison store. I did not even see it at first. Someone had to point it out. It is a gift from God. And so I am now **blessed enough to know** God gave me this gift for a reason – to use with whoever God sends to me.

In so many ways, God has changed where I live to *where I work*! And like David, using that gift has opened countless doors. Yes, He advances me because I use that gift in my workplace.

How about you? Are you **blessed enough to know** He has given you a gift? Or do you need someone to point it out? And do you think your workplace is just inside that building you go to each morning? Or do you realize your workplace is wherever God sends you?

Today at work, don't be like me and waste most of your time. Be **blessed enough to know** He has given you at least one special gift. And be **blessed enough to know** to use that gift throughout the day. When you leave your worldly workplace, be **blessed enough to know** He also wants you to think of everywhere you go as His workplace.

So use that gift *everywhere* and with *everyone*. And like David and me, He will surely advance you!

<u>Prayer</u>

Father, in the name of Jesus, I pray. Thank You for giving a gift to someone like me! Help me use that gift to bring glory to Your name. Amen.

Jimmy Davis, Jr.

Week 5, Day 1

joy in the work

Reading

Ecclesiastes 3:22(a) [NLT] So I saw that there is nothing better for people than to be happy in their work. That is our lot in life.

Reflection

For many years I have volunteered as a swimming referee in my country. There is no pay, just the joy of seeing children do well and helping them to do better. This last summer as watched my country's Olympic trials on TV I saw on the pool deck a friend who has trained me and mentored me as a swimming official over many years. You know what? She had the biggest smile I have ever seen. She has been volunteering for decades and now she was on deck with some of the greatest swimmers in the world. She had joy and everyone could see it! But what I and her other friends know is that she also has the same joy working with little children just starting out in swimming when the Olympics are just a faraway dream. The reason for this is that she puts **joy in the work**.

Finding joy in our workplaces can be hard at times. There is the cranky boss or co-worker. There is the customer who will not stop complaining. There is even the coach who thinks you made the wrong call. We can think that the whole world is against us and it is easy to get depressed. God wants us to have joy in this life. We should take the time to enjoy what we do. We spend a third of our lives working, more or less, why not find the joy in what we do? God created us for work and He wants us to find **joy in the work** He created us for.

Today, when everything comes flying at you and you just want to scream, think of God and the joy He has in His children when they are following Him. God takes joy in us and our work so we should reach for the joy of our heavenly Father when things come at us hard. Today be like my friend and have joy in the work in the great days and in the little days. Do this and each day you will be more like Him. Today at work, be like my mentor and put **joy in the work** – whatever the task.

Prayer

Lord, help me put **joy in the work** I do today – no matter how large or small, major or minor my tasks may be. And help me be like You, Lord – loving those around me who struggle to find Your joy. In Your name, I pray. Amen.

Kevin Cooney

Week 5, Day 2

hamster wheel

Reading

Galatians 6:4-5 [NLT] Pay careful attention to your own work, for then you will get the satisfaction of a job well done, and you won't need to compare yourself to anyone else. For we are each responsible for our own conduct.

Colossians 3:23-24 [NLT] Work willingly at whatever you do, as though you were working for the Lord rather than for people. Remember that the Lord will give you an inheritance as your reward, and that the Master you are serving is Christ.

Reflection

One of the greatest tools used by Satan is *comparison envy*. We compare ourselves to others all the time – using the wrong standards and lenses. We become "green with envy" when a coworker gets the promotion or raise that obviously was "due" to you and me. We despair and become bitter when Jane receives all the kudos from the boss – leaving us with the crumbs. But then, when we are the "teacher's pet," we believe we deserve the rewards because our work is "obviously" so much better–and this leads to a dangerous form of pride.

Yes, Satan uses comparison envy to keep us in bitter bondage to our emotions – up one day and down the next – depending on the comparison scorecard. And it gets us nowhere. It's kind of like being on a **hamster wheel**. It spins and your legs move, but you never advance.

How can you free yourself from this trap? The only solution is to keep your eyes on your own work – recognizing who your true Boss is – the Lord. When your goal is to please Him first, you know He is proud of you when you overlook the offense. He is joyful when you uncover hidden pride and repent.

So at work today, get off that comparison **hamster wheel**. It takes you nowhere. Just keep your eyes on the Lord for He is the Master you serve. And begin to earn your inheritance!

Prayer

Lord, grant me the courage to give up my toys of ego and pride. Let me embrace Your standards of success. I cannot do this on my own strength. In Your name, I pray. Amen.

Gary E. Roberts

Week 5, Day 3

asking then listening

Reading

Acts 13:36 [NASB] For David, after he had served the purpose of God in his own generation, fell asleep, and was laid among his fathers and underwent decay.

Reflection

Ever wonder why you have your current job? Or just what is the purpose of your career?

Ever ask other questions like: Should I work here or apply there? How do I handle this difficult and annoying citizen? Should I help my coworker, or is this an opportunity for her to grow? How do I confront my boss when he is not being fair?

Do you ask these questions to just yourself? Maybe you ask family and friends. But do you take these questions to God? If you're like me, you probably can't begin to count the times you ask God questions about job and career.

Now it's important to ask God questions, but it's also important to listen for His answer. Yes, **asking then listening** are both necessary if you seek the Father's guidance. And only by **asking then listening** can you do exactly what He wants you to do – turn everything over to Him.

This work week, make certain you approach each job and career situation with a focus on God's purpose. By **asking then listening**, you will better serve your workday.

By **asking then listening**, you will better serve His kingdom.

Prayer

Father, God, I want to serve Your purpose in my job and career – in my life – during my short time in this world. Give me wisdom to ask You and listen to You so, before I fall asleep, I waste not a moment of my life. In Your Son's name, I pray. Amen.

Ronald Wilson

Week 5, Day 4

be more like Him

Reading

Matthew 6:14-15 [NLT] If you forgive those who sin against you, your heavenly Father will forgive you. But if you refuse to forgive others, your Father will not forgive your sins.

Reflection

Have you ever been wronged in your workplace? Hurt? Really offended? Intentionally? Unintentionally? It has happened to me a couple of times. And I'm sure it has happened to you at least once. The longer you work, the greater the chance it's going to happen again.

From an early age, I was taught to forgive people – no matter what they had done to me. Yet as an adult, forgiveness seems a much harder task. But nothing's changed – I know He wants me to forgive others – and that includes in my professional life.

As a public servant, you are expected to serve. But as a *Christian public servant*, you are expected to **be more like Him**. You can't hold grudges, and you can't retaliate. To **be more like Him**, you have no choice but to forgive.

So as you prepare for work and all the stress that awaits, remember what you must do if you are wronged today. You must forgive. It will be a difficult task, for sure, but it is the only way you can **be more like Him**.

And it is the only way He will forgive you.

Prayer

Lord, be with me today as I work with people. Help me reflect You. Teach me to forgive. Help me to ask forgiveness of those I have wronged. Help me be like You, not me. In Your name, I pray. Amen.

Meredith Pulsford

Week 5, Day 5

drink from His cup

Reading

Luke 22:42-43 [KJV] Saying, Father, if thou be willing, remove this cup from me: nevertheless not my will, but thine, be done. And there appeared an angel unto him from heaven, strengthening him.

Reflection

For the first 15 years here, I did not have any personal relations – not with other brothers and not with correctional officers. I even lost contact with family on the outside. I was filled with hatred, anger, and a lot of sorrow. I was also filled with regret.

And so I refused to **drink from His cup**. I wanted my will, not His. All day I would just sit and think about wanting to take back the day that got me here. But I also wanted to get even with everyone I blamed for getting me here and keeping me here. Everyone except me. And so everyone was my enemy.

Then in my 16th year here, I found my Lord. And when I gave my life to Jesus, I let go and let God do His will in me. I started to **drink from His cup**. Now it was His will, not mine. And one day He told me to share His Word with others – including the correctional officers. So I had to continue to **drink from His cup** and allow Him to strengthen me to share His Word.

And because I let go and let God do His will in me, the blessings have been awesome.

Each day do you **drink from His cup**? At home? At church? How about in your workplace? I know sometimes you do not want to. Somedays you are angry. Hateful. Filled with so much sorrow, you don't know what to do. There are times when you are filled with anything but God's love. And you simply don't like where you are or what you do or who you are. And you don't want to take that drink.

As you go to work today, and throughout the weekend, let go and let God do His will in you. He will strengthen you so you can strengthen others.

Today at work, and this weekend, **drink from His cup**. And the blessings will be awesome!

Prayer

Father, in the name of Jesus, I pray. Thank You for strengthening me so I can carry out Your will. Amen.

Jimmy Davis, Jr.

Week 6, Day 1

idle talk about things

Reading

Proverbs 14:23 [NIV] All hard work brings a profit, but mere talk leads only to poverty.

Matthew 6:20-21 [NIV] But store up for yourselves treasures in heaven, where moths and vermin do not destroy, and where thieves do not break in and steal. For where your treasure is, there your heart will be also.

Reflection

Sometimes people at work boast about having things you only dream about. In the lunchroom, they highlight the details of the next cruise or the next skiing trip or the next fancy restaurant they want to try out. That new car or incredibly beautiful house on the corner lot – all of your dreams seem to be their reality.

And that leaves you feeling, well, disappointed in yourself. You begin to think you may not be working hard enough. Perhaps you'll end up as a failure steeped in poverty.

But remember what scripture says about this kind of **idle talk about things**. It is poverty. Bragging cheapens accomplishments and what they can buy. When earned for selfish reasons, the light of those accomplishments dims pretty quickly.

Remember hard work in this world will eventually bring profit – if accomplished in His glory – for this is God's promise. And He affirms, through a joyful heart, you will store up treasures in heaven.

So the next time you hear "big talk" in the lunchroom, just let it slide. It is just **idle talk about things**. Instead, praise God for His goodness and faithfulness in your own job and career.

Yes, today at work, don't be bothered by **idle talk about things**. Thieves of many kinds will break in and steal them from you. Focus only on hard work that glorifies Him. And remember the best treasures can't be destroyed for they are stored in heaven.

And heaven is a place your heart wants to be.

Prayer

Heavenly Father, thank You for providing me with an opportunity to work today. Through my hard work, I want to give You all the glory. I place all my treasures in Your hands. In Your Glorious Son's name, I pray. Amen.

Rachael Monnin

Week 6, Day 2

the furrow you cut in the field

Reading

Luke 9:61-62 [RSV] Another said, "I will follow you, Lord; but let me first say farewell to those at my home." Jesus said to him, "No one who puts his hand to the plow and looks back is fit for the kingdom of God."

Reflection

Each day the focus you and I take pretty much sets our course. And if we are unfocused, it's easy to ramble through that day. Sometimes it may be tempting to ramble – looking here and there – and not really accomplish much. But we should view our day as *plowing a field.* A good farmer picks one point in front by which to steer the plow and stays focused on that point. Yes, the temptation is great to look back on the turned soil, but to guide the plow based on what has been done in the past leads to mistakes – and sometimes disasters.

When Christ is your focal point throughout the day, the mark you make – **the furrow you cut in the field** – is straight. No rambling. All else falls into place.

As a *Christian public servant*, remember first to serve Christ. As you interact with coworkers and citizens, do so from a place of compassion and empathy – even if the answer you must give is "No, you can't do that." Whatever must be done, do it from a base of grace.

So at work today, make sure **the furrow you cut in the field** is done through a focus on Christ. Don't think of the past. Don't compare side by side. Don't lose sight of Jesus as the beacon showing the way forward.

Yes, **the furrow you cut in the field** of relationships and accomplishments will be fit for the kingdom of God. And the soil will be turned accordingly.

Prayer

Lord and Father, You have given me Your Son as a beacon to guide me. Help me stay focused on Christ as I meet the challenges of this day – not looking to the past, but with my eyes clearly set on the direction You have for me. For it is in Jesus' name I pray. Amen.

Keith Jordan

Week 6, Day 3

a gentle and quiet spirit

Reading

1 Peter 3:4 [NIV] Rather, it should be that of your inner self, the unfading beauty of **a gentle and quiet spirit**, which is of great worth in God's sight.

Reflection

Over the past couple years, I have come to depend upon His specific command to be **a gentle and quiet spirit**. It seems like such a simple command, but my efforts to follow fall short now and then. Because of the nature of my job, there is just a lot of stressful emergencies. But when emergencies occur and I feel my fight instinct start to kick in, I repeat over and over again "be **a gentle and quiet spirit**." I am then able to remain in calm control of the situation.

Is your workplace stressful? Are there times of anger, hurt, fear, and even chaos? Does your fight instinct kick in more than you want? Just repeat over and over again "be **a gentle and quiet spirit**" until those other feelings go away.

Today at work, remember to shield yourself with the words of God – for the word of God is the most powerful armor you have. And your calmness is of great worth in God's sight.

Prayer

God, in times of stress, when it is so easy to react in an ungodly way, fill me with **a gentle and quiet spirit**. In Your Son's name, I pray. Amen.

Jessica Kay

Week 6, Day 4

see the goodness

Reading

Psalm 27:13(b) [KJV] ... I had believed to **see the goodness** of the Lord in the land of the living.

Reflection

As a youth, I asked my dad why he always watched the news. He said he found it interesting. I didn't understand then, but now I've become my dad. I'm a news addict.

Being aware of what goes on in the world is great, but it has its drawbacks. The news tends to center on evil and nastiness. It squeezes all the juice from one tragedy and then goes on to the next. The wickedness and evil reported can easily drag you down to where you see only hopelessness. Too often, you and I do not take the time to **see the goodness** of what goes on in the world.

Yes, if you look, there is hope all around. Good Samaritans risking their lives to rescue people. Unsung heroes sacrificing their own organs to give life to others. Adoptive couples opening their homes and hearts to neglected and unwanted babies and children. Birth mothers choosing life over death. Medical groups uniting to find cures. Volunteers helping the homeless in your country, and others raising capital to feed the famished in other countries.

Just look around and **see the goodness** that exists.

So what about your workplace? Are you focusing only on the struggles to meet budget? Inter-department rivalries? Bickering with another coworker? Is the atmosphere tense?

While you need to focus on some not-too-pleasant things, take time to **see the goodness** that is also present. The positive change in the person you mentor. The compliments from those you serve. Coworkers actually working together.

And thank the Lord for providing you a job!

As this workweek begins, look around to **see the goodness** of the Lord – while you are still in the land of the living.

Prayer

Father, I praise You for blessing me and my world in so many ways. Open my eyes to **see the goodness** of Your creation, and open my heart to receive the goodness of Your love. In Your Son's name, I pray. Amen.

Bill Dudley

Week 6, Day 5

just wait silently for His advice

Reading

Exodus 6:9(b) [HCSB] but they did not listen to him because of their broken spirit and hard labor.

Job 29:21 [HCSB] Men listened to me with expectation, waiting silently for my advice.

Reflection

One day Jesus put me in a position to help someone on Life Row – but I had trouble looking past the pain. And there was a lot of pain.

And it was a correctional officer, not an inmate.

You see, a correctional officer was stabbed and later died. All the officers were shaken by his death. And I saw suffering on their faces. I saw broken spirits.

To a particular correctional officer, I wanted to say something to ease his pain. But I didn't know what to say. Words, even scripture, escaped me. All I could do was reach between the bars and touch his hand when he passed by my cell. The first time I did this, he tried to smile but moved on. The second time, he stopped.

I could not find the words, and he couldn't say anything either. So we prayed without words, hand in hand, between the bars of my cell. With tears in our eyes, we chose to **just wait silently for His advice** on what to say.

And through our silent prayer, I know my friend and brother was comforted. I was, too.

It's OK to have nothing to say – especially when a tragedy strikes. Sometimes that's the best you can do when someone is suffering.

I pray there will never be a murder committed in your workplace like there are sometimes in mine. But tragedy strikes everywhere, maybe in your workplace, and sometimes the worst means someone died. When that happens, don't force words not there.

No, **just wait silently for His advice**. He will lead you, and I promise, He will show you how to comfort. And He will also comfort you.

Prayer

Father, in the name of Jesus, I pray. Continue to work on and through me so I can comfort and be comforted – even when I have no words. Amen.

Jimmy Davis, Jr.

Week 7, Day 1

trust Him and live by faith

Reading

2 Corinthians 5:7 [NIV] For we live by faith, not by sight.

Reflection

Traveling for work presents its own set of challenges, but it is even more challenging when you leave your family behind to venture into unchartered territory. Recently, I took a month-long training course for my job. As I got onto the plane and left my wife, who was pregnant with our first child, I could not help but worry. While my wife and I were apart, we spoke often by phone, yet it was still hard not to agonize about her and our unborn child.

Have you experienced anything like this?

As *Christian public servants,* our Lord wants us to go into unchartered territories… It may be you have to leave your family to travel or to correct an employee who has broken some rules or – even worse – to have to confront your boss about a wrongdoing. It is times like these God wants us to **trust Him and live by faith**. God will take care of <u>you</u> if only you have <u>faith</u>.

Now, I had a hard time focusing on the training course while I was away – wondering how my family was doing at home. I missed coming home at the end of the day and had to go to an empty hotel room instead. Perhaps what you are facing makes you feel as if you are all alone too. Yet Paul reminds you and me to **trust Him and live by faith** especially when the outward appearance is you are all alone.

Today at work or at training, you can accomplish any task – even if it means leaving family behind. If you **trust Him and live by faith**, it will be a job well done before you know it – and you will be heading home once again!

Prayer

God, please watch over my family, especially when we are apart. Help me to continually live by faith and trust You in everything. Help me to complete all the tasks You send me to do and return safely home. I pray in Your Son, Jesus' name. Amen.

Chris Meconnahey

Week 7, Day 2

what makes organizations successful

Reading

Luke 18: 11(b) [NIV] God, I thank you that I am not like other people—robbers, evildoers, adulterers—or even like this tax collector.

1 Peter 3:8(b) [NIV] be like-minded, be sympathetic, love one another, be compassionate and humble.

Reflection

In nearly a quarter century of public service, I've worked alongside people with different backgrounds and dispositions. While it's rewarding to learn more about each individual, it's not an easy process. In fact, you can find yourself focusing on personal critique so much, by the end of the workday, you fall into the same judgmental trap as did that Pharisee in scripture – holier-than-thou.

You know when people make an effort to understand each other, especially in the workplace, many misunderstandings are avoided. And so I find joy in helping employees connect with each other because the interpersonal relationship is **what makes organizations successful**.

Today at work, when you start to judge the habits of others, stop and remember to be sympathetic, compassionate, and humble. Because you are not perfect, give some grace to the coworker who is just like you.

Yes, at work today, remember **what makes organizations successful**. Work to see things from a like-minded perspective. Get to know those around you a little bit better.

Don't be like that Pharisee in the temple. In your workplace, find ways to love one another. Truly it's **what makes organizations successful**.

Prayer

God, I thank You I am just like other people. Thank You for Your grace, for Your mercy, and for Your forgiveness when I fall short of expectations. Please give me humility when I see coworkers struggling just like I am. Keep me willing to share Your gift of grace, mercy, and forgiveness when someone else falls short of what is expected. In Jesus' name, I pray. Amen.

Wendy Standorf

Week 7, Day 3

save yourself from the corruption

Reading

Acts 2:40(b) [NIV] "Save yourselves from this corrupt generation."

Reflection

Peter pleaded these words to a crowd of Israelites during a period of great chaos and confusion. Not long before, Jesus was crucified and was risen again. The temple was destroyed. Now Jesus' followers were speaking in different languages. Some in the crowd before Peter were amazed, and others were perplexed. But Peter spoke with great discernment and clarity. He concluded by begging each person to **save yourself from the corruption**.

On electronic news feeds and TV, you see chaos and confusion. Different tongues of false reporting. Misinformation. Disinformation. Rumors. And as a *Christian public servant*, there is also chaos in your work-life. Each day you face confusion with public leaders, coworkers, subordinates, and citizens you serve.

When everything is falling apart, the temptation is to save yourself by adding to the corruption – accepting and spreading innuendo as fact. Blaming others or other institutions. Stepping over others. Hurting. Doing whatever it takes to justify your own interests, position, and reputation.

But Peter pleads just the opposite. Yes, you are not to add to the world's corruption but to **save yourself from the corruption** inside you. He begs you repent of your sins – your chaos and confusion – and look to God for your forgiveness.

This is a direct step away from the corruption of this world and a step toward the only thing that will save you – God. And a repentant attitude changes everything. It brings peace and wisdom into chaos and radically changes the situation surrounding you.

So at work and throughout your day, **save yourself from the corruption**. But don't blame or attack the other guy. Don't rationalize. Just repent. Look to God for forgiveness.

Only God will provide peace from chaos and confusion.

Prayer

Heavenly Father, keep me honest so I can bring peace and wisdom into my world. In Jesus' name, I pray. Amen.

David Shultz

Week 7, Day 4

prosper the mission and achieve success

Reading

Nehemiah 3:20 [NIV] The God of Heaven will make us prosper, and we will arise and build.

Colossians 3:23 [NIV] Whatever you do, work heartily, as for the Lord and not for men.

Reflection

Nehemiah was a senior civil servant working for the king of Persia. As the king's cupbearer, he had proven himself, and when the time came, he was appointed to lead a mission to rebuild his native city of Jerusalem.

Now, this was not an easy mission. Nehemiah faced a lot of challenges. Allegations of treachery. Physical intimidation. Even death threats. Yet he saw the mission as divinely ordained, and he kept focused on God's promises and plan.

While Nehemiah was grateful to the king for this opportunity, he knew he ultimately was accountable to God. Despite the many obstacles, he relied on God to **prosper the mission and achieve success**.

As a *Christian public servant*, you face hurdles every day over schedules, deadlines, personalities, and politics. Yet in your workplace, you are the difference in the outcome. In order to **prosper the mission and achieve success**, you must rely on the wisdom and spirit of God. Even when the boss is moody, coworkers are deceitful, or the tasking is overwhelming, provide His wisdom and generosity – and God will honor you for your faithfulness.

Today at work, remember to rely on God to **prosper the mission and achieve success**. Rely on His wisdom and spirit!

Prayer

God of Heaven, You have given me a position of responsibility with tasks to do. Please prosper my effort. Help me arise and build in my workplace today. I will strive and excel heartily, for I work for You. In Your Son's name, I pray. Amen.

Eric Patterson

Week 7, Day 5

a half-stick of gum

Reading

Hebrews 13:16 [MSG] Make sure you don't take things for granted and go slack in working for the common good; share what you have with others. God takes particular pleasure in acts of worship—a different kind of "sacrifice"—that take place in kitchen and workplace and on the streets.

Reflection

The other day a discouraged brother came to me. I tried to comfort him – reassure him – God is with him every step of his walk in this world and on Life Row.

As we talked, this brother offered me a stick of chewing gum. He only had one piece, so I insisted we split it. Not having any in a long time, **a half-stick of gum** was a special treat!

Before we departed, God showed us something we didn't realize. A little thing like **a half-stick of gum** could change our outlook – help us bond – help us not be so discouraged over the big worries in life. He used it for our common good. And it opened a different act of worship.

You see, chewing **a half-stick of gum** made us laugh a little over not having anything else to share. It made us realize a little more about how our Lord is with us – even here on Life Row. And because He is with us, we have no reason to be discouraged.

Big things are important, but it's too easy to worry about them – in life, with family, and at work. When that happens, you can miss the little things – things God offers to get His point across. Things God offers to help you get through the day. Things God offers to help You worship Him.

So at work today, do not take the little things for granted. Something you see from your window. A smile on someone's face. An invitation to chat. A small gesture of great kindness.

The little things are BIG – even if it's only **a half-stick of gum**.

Today, use the little things to help do His work for the common good.

<u>Prayer</u>

Father, in the name of Jesus, I pray. Keep my eyes and heart not just on the big things, but also on the little things You provide that mean so much in Your ministry. I don't want to take anything for granted in my life. I seek every act of worship that pleases You. Amen.

Jimmy Davis, Jr.

Week 8, Day 1

even the wicked!

Reading

Matthew 18:32(b)-33 [NKJV] You wicked servant! I forgave you all that debt because you begged me. Should you not also have had compassion on your fellow servant, just as I had pity on you?

Matthew 6:14-15 [NKJV] For if you forgive men their trespasses, your heavenly Father will also forgive you. But if you do not forgive men their trespasses, neither will your Father forgive your trespasses.

Reflection

True story – there once was a *wicked* senior executive. One day he locked himself in a small room with a young female worker against her will. In a fit of rage, he screamed and threatened her – terrifying this young lady beyond belief.

Now in the following days, with his job on the line and facing possible legal action, this wicked senior executive begged for forgiveness. And guess what? The woman and the grievance board graciously showed mercy and forgave him!

A few months later, a worker accidentally printed the wrong document for a weekly meeting. The same senior executive head fired him on the spot. When the employee begged for mercy, the wicked senior executive said, "Our standards are too high to permit mistakes no matter how small." While he was *forgiven much*, he was unwilling to *forgive little*.

Do you know anyone like that wicked senior executive? It's so hard to forgive that kind of person, yet God commands you to do so: *forgive much* – even those who do not forgive – **even the wicked!**

Forgiveness is not about others – it's about you! When you refuse to forgive unforgivable people, you are only hurting yourself by separating from the God who desires nothing more than to walk in fellowship with you. *Unforgiveness in your life, especially at work, is a cancer bringing death to your soul long before your body dies.*

Today at work, walk closely with your Father God. Emulate Him. He has forgiven much about you. Hasn't He? And your unforgiveness toward others will destroy your life, your work-life, your career, and most of all, your testimony.

Yes, today at work, give the same forgiveness He gives <u>you</u>. *Forgive much –* even those who do not forgive – **even the wicked!**

<u>Prayer</u>

Lord, remove all unforgiveness from my heart. I want to be more like You today. Let me show mercy so I may walk closer with You in my workplace. In Your name, I pray. Amen.

Kevin Cooney

Week 8, Day 2

that uncomfortable feeling

Reading

1 Corinthians 16:13 [ESV] Be watchful, stand firm in the faith, act like men, be strong.

Reflection

At college, I was elected to the student government. I was motivated to lead people through service, but this service came with many challenges. Some wanted me to go "right," and others demanded I go "left." Still a few wanted me to go "backward." No matter what I tried to do, it appeared someone was always upset with me – and this gave me **that uncomfortable feeling**.

As *Christian public servants*, you and I face much larger challenges than that college kid in student government. Many competing viewpoints from the people we serve <u>and</u> from those we work with. Sometimes, it's really difficult to say "no." Yet our Lord wants us to be strong and stand firm in faith so you and I do what is right.

Yes, competing views pulling in different directions still give me **that uncomfortable feeling**. Yet I know the Lord is always there asking me to trust Him and turn the battle over to Him.

As you face conflicts today at work, stand firm in the faith and be strong. Keep the Lord central to your thoughts and decisions.

Then, and only then, can you ease **that uncomfortable feeling**.

Prayer

Dear God, thank You for always being there for me, and thank You for letting me rely on Your strength. Please help me always realize when the wind begins to blow hard and I start to get **that uncomfortable feeling**, You will help me stand against it. I pray in Jesus' name! Amen.

Paul Bayer

Week 8, Day 3

find paths of integrity

Reading

Proverbs 10:9 [NIV] Whoever walks in integrity walks securely, but whoever takes crooked paths will be found out.

Reflection

If you've worked in local government for a while, you know one of the most challenging times is the transition between old and new elected leaders. It doesn't specifically matter if the incoming mayor was "your" candidate – the stress is there. And typically the stress comes from appointed department heads, insecure about their future, trying to accomplish self-selected glorious tasks in unreal amounts of time – driving their staff nuts – and frequently doing so without regard to local codes that establish legal guidelines for decision-making.

Yesterday two coworkers approached me for advice. Both are tasked by the current department head in ways that pushed them to the edge of integrity and ethical behavior. I advised each to document what they were asked to do and keep documenting their every step – providing a truthful paper trail should legal action be necessary in the future.

But I did not suggest blocking the director, which would be insubordination. Instead, I encouraged each to **find paths of integrity** that would provide light to the transition team, the future mayor, and the citizens as to what happened, why, and by whom.

It can appear hard to **find paths of integrity** in the modern workplace. And it is even harder to stay on that path once found. But today's issues are no more complex than those found in scripture. And like the Proverbs teach, if you keep your eye on integrity, you will avoid the crooked paths. Today at work, apply His way to the tasks ahead and **find paths of integrity**. You will walk securely!

Prayer

Lord, I am in the trenches of public service not because I expect great monetary reward or personal glory but to help create a better life for the people in my community. You have given me good workplace skills – guide me always to use them for Your Glory while serving those You have created. In Your name, I pray. Amen.

Patricia A. Maley

Week 8, Day 4

the hands and feet of Jesus

Reading

1 John 3:17 [NIV] If anyone has material possessions and sees a brother or sister in need but has no pity on them, how can the love of God be in that person?

Reflection

My dearest friend is a very successful businesswoman. One day she shared, for some time, she takes meals (tuna packets, crackers, cups of fruit, and water) in plastic zipper bags to homeless people on the street near where she works. She said God calls her to feed them and get to know them. So my friend knows each name and each story. And I am not sure who gets more out of the encounters – her or the people she feeds!

Last week, she was walking to her office from a parking garage and a colleague joined her. My friend was a little nervous because she hadn't yet given meals to her homeless friends, and this particular colleague was not the nicest of people. As they walked, one of her street friends waved and called out to her. My friend got the meal out of her bag and delivered it to her homeless friend. And they chatted briefly.

Well, her colleague was speechless – probably for the first time in his life. For the rest of the way to their office, they had minimal conversation. But her actions – of being **the hands and feet of Jesus** – had an obvious effect on this coworker.

Have you ever been hesitant to do something God was calling you to do – hesitant because you were afraid to have your actions witnessed by a coworker?

Next time, don't hesitate! Today as you go to and come from work – and while you are at work – be **the hands and feet of Jesus**. Don't be afraid. Be bold like my friend. Your actions will glorify God and show the love He places in your heart. Today, be **the hands and feet of Jesus**!

Prayer

Dear Heavenly Father, thank You for *boldness*. Give me courage to always make my actions represent what You are putting on my heart to do. And when there is doubt or fear, remind me You are in control and are protecting me! In Your amazing Son's name, I pray. Amen.

Wendy Standorf

Week 8, Day 5

seize the day for Christ

Reading

Luke 9:61-62 [MSG] Then another said, "I'm ready to follow you, Master, but first excuse me while I get things straightened out at home." Jesus said, "No procrastination. No backward looks. You can't put God's kingdom off till tomorrow. Seize the day."

Reflection

In my country, there is an athlete named Tim Tebow. He is an excellent football player. In college, he won the most prestigious award. In the professional league, he helped his team get to the playoffs for the first time in years. Yet throughout his football career, he was mocked and ridiculed. And when he was cut from the professional team and became a sports announcer, he was ridiculed even more.

And that's because he puts God's kingdom first.

Instead of drinking and taking drugs, Tim Tebow prays and ministers. He never makes excuses nor does he apologize for being a *practicing* Christian. And so he never speaks ill of those belittling him because he's too busy putting God's kingdom first. It must not have been easy, but Tim Tebow never looked back – even <u>after</u> being cut from the team – even <u>before</u> he ever played sports. No, sir! He decided long ago to **seize the day for Christ**, and that is what he focused on – and still does – and that is why he keeps following Him with joy and a smile on his face. And he continues to show the world how to **seize the day for Christ** in everything he does!

This is what Tim Tebow did – and does – in <u>his</u> workplace. What about you?

Are you willing to make no excuses? No compromises? No looking back?

Will <u>you</u> **seize the day for Christ**? Or will you say "I'm ready to follow you, Master, but first excuse me while I get things straightened out."? Do you think "If I just fit in a little longer, I will make more money and my job will go better and my career will go the way I want it to?"

Are you <u>not</u> ready to give up fitting in a little longer?

Choose wisely today, my friend. You don't know how many days you have left.

Today at work, **seize the day for Christ**! And don't worry about fitting in a little longer.

Today at work, make Christ the center of your game plan.

Prayer

Father, in the name of Jesus, I pray. Thank You for Your love and grace so I can no longer make excuses to put You and Your kingdom second. I don't want to fit in a little longer. In Your workplace, I simply want to **seize the day for Christ**! Amen.

Jimmy Davis, Jr.

Week 9, Day 1

to beat the truth

Reading

2 Timothy 2:24-25 [NKJV] And a servant of the Lord must not quarrel but be gentle to all, able to teach, patient, in humility correcting those who are in opposition, if God perhaps will grant them repentance, so that they may know the truth.

Reflection

The "win at all cost" mantra tends to affect many of us more than we would like to admit.

I used to think my job as a believer was **to beat the truth** into the victim of my biblical rant – hence my nickname "Bible thumper." My emotions quite often took control when someone was not getting my message. I thought my job was to make sure they got it…really got it. I spent more time quarreling over the things of God – so I would win the argument – than presenting the truths of God and letting God work in their hearts. The reality is, my winning the argument often resulted in me losing the opportunity to ever present the Gospel to that person again.

As servant leaders, our job is not **to beat the truth** into coworkers – but to teach and demonstrate a godly leadership. How will you react to objections to your leadership today? Will I react with emotion or gentleness? Are we out to prove our power or provide godly direction?

Today at work, do not quarrel and try **to beat the truth** into your coworkers. Be gentle to all so God will grant repentance and reveal the truth to those you encounter. Yes, today at work, teach God's leadership through an example of love rather than showing your power.

Prayer

Holy Spirit, give me the strength today to fight against the desires of my flesh. Fill me with Your Spirit, and use me to provide truth and wisdom to those You place before me. May the change You made in my life make a difference in the life of a coworker, and may You receive the glory for what is done. In Your Son's name, I pray. Amen.

Bill Dudley

Week 9, Day 2

not your home

Reading

Hebrews 13:14-15 [ESV] For here we have no lasting city, but seek the city that is to come. Through him then let us continually offer up a sacrifice of praise to God, that is, the fruit of lips that acknowledge his name. Do not neglect to do good and to share what you have, for such sacrifices are pleasing to God.

Reflection

It's easy to think job and career are central to our lives. Our salaries, after all, pay for a lot in life – mortgages, food, things for the kids, college, weddings, spoiling grandchildren, vacations, retirement.

The list just grows the longer you think about how important your job and career are to the betterment of yourself and loved ones.

As important as your job and career might seem, scripture reminds it is not lasting. And like all aspects of this life, it is **not your home**.

The fruit of your lips and what you share can demonstrate a workplace-world much different from the normal workplace values of this world – if your words and acts point to and acknowledge Jesus.

And yes, doing so will push against the tendency of workplace selfishness. But pointing to and acknowledging Jesus will be a sacrifice of praise – a desire to please – our Lord.

So at work today, know it's OK to do your best and make money so you maintain all those things God blesses you with each and every day. But remember this workplace is **not your home**. You are a visitor – one who visits to find ways to acknowledge Christ.

Today at work, use your visit to do good and share what He has given you. And seek His city that is to come. For this is **not your home**.

Prayer

Father, help me remember where I am, where I long to be, and why You have me visiting here. In Your Son's name, I pray. Amen.

Chris Summers

Week 9, Day 3

the Kingdom of God is within

Reading

Luke 17:20-21 [NLT] One day the Pharisees asked Jesus, "When will the Kingdom of God come?" Jesus replied, "The Kingdom of God can't be detected by visible signs. You won't be able to say, 'Here it is!' or 'It's over there!' For the Kingdom of God is already among you."

Reflection

There are mornings when I don't want to turn on the radio or television because the news is so bad. Another terrorist attack, a riot, more shootings, politicians attacking opponents rather than working for the good of the people they represent. It would be easy not to get out of bed.

Yes, we live in anxious times. We feel tension in every facet of life. Some even believe the end of days is approaching. *Newsflash – it is!* With every breath we draw, our end draws nearer. But it's not life that ends, it's the living in fear of never finding the peace that already exists. So stop getting sidetracked with unnecessary emotions like fear. The peace you seek is within you.

As a *Christian public servant*, go to work today and live out Christ's example of meeting fear head-on with faith. It may be natural to want to know what's ahead and to be in control of the outcome, but that's not faith. God is in control. Focus your eyes skyward and your thoughts inward and say to yourself, "**the Kingdom of God is within** me."

Today at work, be the disciple you are called to be and seize every opportunity to share the Gospel with coworkers deceived by fear. Let them see the light of Christ shine through you. Let them see **the Kingdom of God is within** them – as it is within you. Now *that's* news worth getting out of bed!

Prayer

Father, thank You for the opportunity to serve Your purposes. Help me emulate Your Son, Jesus, who taught **the Kingdom of God is within** me because I believe. Give me courage to share the Gospel today with a coworker who remains fearful. In the mighty name of Your Son, my Lord and Savior, Jesus Christ, I pray. Amen.

David Boisselle

Week 9, Day 4

the politics of His love

Reading

Titus 3:9 [ESV] But avoid foolish controversies, genealogies, dissensions, and quarrels about the law, for they are unprofitable and worthless.

Reflection

Elections were recently held in my country. As usual, campaign ads dominated the electronic media. But this election season seemed unusually captured by *fake news* – spewing false and negative ads about opposing candidates. More than any time before, the lying and misrepresentation in this election cycle certainly did not demonstrate **the politics of His love**.

But there are politics everywhere you look in most workplaces. Budget development and implementation bring perception, and sometimes perception is based on hidden agendas. In project development, some build alliances that leave others out. Still others gossip or spread rumors and false stories to cause controversy just to get their own way.

It doesn't have to be like this.

God placed us, His *Christian public servants,* in our particular jobs to be the example of His righteousness. He has a specific purpose for you and me. No matter the job, He wants us to serve in ways that make a difference. God wants you and me to spread **the politics of His love** throughout the workplace and the world.

Today, as you encounter politics in the workplace, remember controversies and quarrels are unprofitable and worthless. Furthermore, *workplace fake news* is as unjust to coworkers and citizens you serve as electoral fake news is to every voter in your country.

Today at work, bring about positive change. Be profitable and worthy.

Spread **the politics of His love**.

Prayer

Lord, thank You for watching over me throughout my career and helping me bring Your values and morality to my workplace. Your influence has kept my subordinates and me productive and efficient in times of stress. Please watch over me as I make my way through the politics and pressures to align with others. Remind me the best thing is to spread constantly the politics of Your love. In Jesus' name, I pray. Amen.

Meredith Pulsford

Week 9, Day 5

not going to be easy

Reading

John 8:11(b) [KJV] Neither do I condemn thee: go, and sin no more.

Reflection

When my best friend turned on me, I almost gave up. I was tempted when the brother in the next cell rejected me. I almost went back to my old ways when the brothers in the yard ridiculed me. The doubt of correctional officers made me think twice.

I felt <u>very</u> alone after giving my life to Christ. I felt <u>all</u> alone when I first tried to speak faith instead of filth. That's when I realized it was **not going to be easy** – to *go and sin no more.*

I bet <u>you</u> thought it would be easy, too. Accept Christ and *go and sin no more.* After all, He removes past sins. You thought you were as safe as a newborn in his mother's arms.

But then both of us had to leave the mountaintop and return to work – doing whatever we do most of the waking hours. We had to go back among those who only liked us as sinners. Those who cared nothing about the rebirth that took place. Those who wanted us the old way.

Today at work, remember the person you see may not be the same as yesterday. So be watchful for the newborn Christian. Satan wants you to ridicule and challenge – or say nothing when the wolves circle up. He wants that newborn to go and sin <u>some</u> more.

But you know better. You have been there. You know the only difference between death and Life may be the person our Lord places in your path.

So at work today, be His person in someone's path.

Yes, today be watchful for the newborn. For this workday is **not going to be easy**.

Prayer

Father, in the name of Jesus, I pray. You forgive even <u>my</u> sins, but then You ask me to do what seems the impossible – *go and sin no more.* Without You and the Body of Christ, I am always tempted. With You and those You send into my life, I am stronger. And so today let me help the next person, surrendering to You, who bears the world's temptations. Amen.

Jimmy Davis, Jr.

Week 10, Day 1

an office-party heart weighed down

Reading

Luke 21:34 [NIV] Be careful, or your hearts will be weighed down with carousing, drunkenness and the anxieties of life, and that day will close on you suddenly like a trap.

Matthew 5:14 [NIV] You are the light of the world. A town built on a hill cannot be hidden.

Reflection

I saw an old friend yesterday after church. No, we didn't run into each other shopping. Nor did we meet at a restaurant. The fact is he didn't see me at all, and I didn't see him in the flesh. I saw my old friend on Facebook – postings from his Saturday night office party.

I may be wrong, but he appeared carousing and drunk. And I suspect others seeing his postings also agree. He looked like he had **an office-party heart weighed down** – he was not being the Light of God. And this morning, I pray he realizes that "good time" closed on him all too suddenly – *like a trap*.

There are many opportunities to gather to celebrate in any season of the year. Remember to be the Light of God and follow His Words. Don't partake in carousing and drunkenness. Be careful not to acquire **an office-party heart weighed down**. Stay sober in mind and body, and show your coworkers good times do not have to accompany drunkenness. Especially be His Light as the designated driver for that coworker who has **an office-party heart weighed down**.

And don't post anything suggesting you are not acting like the Light of God on Facebook. As a *Christian public servant*, you are built on a hill that cannot be hidden. And remember the life and job you save may be your own!

Prayer

Father, when I celebrate coworkers, let me be Your shining light in the world of darkness. Give me strength to stay sober so I may watch over my coworkers as You watch over all of us. In Your Son's name, I pray. Amen.

John F. Long, Jr.

Week 10, Day 2

deeper than eyes can see

Reading

Psalm 1:3 [NIV] That person is like a tree planted by streams of water, which yields its fruit in season and whose leaf does not wither- whatever they do prospers.

Reflection

Have you ever looked closely at a healthy tree? With each season, it changes and adapts. In storms, the top branches whirl around in frantic movements of the unseen wind while the trunk bends gently to stabilize. In all seasons and storms, the healthy tree survives because its roots are grounded and strong – **deeper than eyes can see** – connected to external nourishment.

There's a lot to learn from healthy trees – especially in the workplace. Things never stay the same in any job. Change can be threatening. And storms threaten careers.

Regardless of the season and the storm, the roots of faith have to go deeper than the winds of humanity – **deeper than eyes can see**. So connect with the Holy Spirit through prayer and get your nourishment from the Word. At all times, remember your root must wrap around Jesus Christ.

Yes, at work today, don't let the water of fear or the soil of uncertainty fill your roots with waste. Let your branches whirl in the storm, but keep your roots stabilized through by Him.

Stay strong and grounded in each work season and in all work storms. For your faith is **deeper than eyes can see**.

Prayer

Father, thank You for this workday. Thank You for giving me access to a strong foundation and all Your nutrients. Give me courage and wisdom to stay true, stay grounded, and stay strong in my faith – despite the season and the storm. In Jesus' name, I pray. Amen.

Kathryn Saunders

Week 10, Day 3

the need of the moment

Reading

Ephesians 4:29 [NASB] Let no unwholesome word proceed from your mouth, but only such a word as is good for edification according to **the need of the moment**, so that it will give grace to those who hear.

Reflection

I was hot when I arrived at the office yesterday morning. My car wouldn't start. I was late. And I was already behind before I walked in the door. Staring at me on my desk was a project I had already looked over and knew wasn't very good, and the people who created it needed my feedback. Here was a great way to let out my anger; I'd tell these people their work was lousy!

Instead, I paused. I read a devotional. I prayed. And then I looked over the project. I didn't tell them it was perfect, nor did I say it was awful. I praised its strengths and told them how to improve it. I tried my best to match instruction to **the need of the moment**.

It's easy to act out in anger. But had I not paused and written my review the way I originally intended, no one would have been the better for it. They wouldn't have received any instruction for improvement, and I wouldn't have been honest with my feedback.

Just because we are Christians doesn't mean we don't get angry. But when we do and when we are tempted to lash out in anger, we should pause and make sure what we say does not bring undeserved pain but instead builds up those around us.

Today at work, make sure your instruction or advice matches **the need of the moment**. Throughout the workday, give grace to those who hear.

Prayer

Father, I ask for forgiveness. When I want to act out of hurt, may I pause and may my words only serve to glorify You. In the name of Christ, I pray. Amen.

Michael Bednarczuk

Week 10, Day 4

if the reckoning is right

Reading

Romans 13:4(b) [ASV] But if thou do that which is evil, be afraid; for he beareth not the sword in vain: for he is a minister of God, an avenger for wrath to him that doeth evil.

Matthew 5:7; 21-22(a) 5:44(b)[ASV] Ye have heard that it was said to them of old time, Thou shalt not kill; and whosoever shall kill shall be in danger of the judgment: but I say unto you, that every one who is angry with his brother shall be in danger of the judgment … Blessed are the merciful: for they shall obtain mercy … Love your enemies

Reflection

A man will die tonight. Not by accident. Not in war. Not by protecting his neighbors. He will die by the state. The man committed murder, and by law the judgment is execution. Tonight the state bears the sword and becomes a minister of God.

Yet it's really a handful of <u>individuals</u> who will put this man to death. Public servants – *Christian public servants*. Each knows the law and, more importantly, each knows scripture. A murderer has been judged, and the final step in that judgment comes at their hands. Each will personally bear the sword, and each will ultimately be a minister of God – an avenger for the evil done.

But these individuals also understand the complexity of scripture. Anger <u>is</u> murder. Mercy from Him comes from mercy toward others. And He commands each to love the enemy. So tonight these *Christian public servants* will reckon, with great difficulty, the balance between the sword and Him. And after killing, each will go home wondering **if the reckoning is right**.

Public service is the most difficult career. Many will leave work today wondering, in their own jobs, **if the reckoning is right**. And it gets no easier when you are a *Christian public servant*. Regardless of the task, did you do what is expected – by the agency <u>and</u> by Jesus?

Today at work, you may not be one who uses the sword, but you <u>will</u> struggle to do what is right. Please remember the handful of individuals who will be the sword tonight. For like you in your workplace, they also wonder in their workplace **if the reckoning is right**.

For a man will die tonight – and *following Jesus is not easy*.

Prayer

Father God, as I struggle doing what is expected in my own workplace, bless those who suffer the consequences of my acts. Give me strength to seek guidance from <u>all</u> Your Word – not just the morsels that make me feel comfortable or cling to my ways. Help me keep the reckoning right with Jesus. In His name, I pray. Amen.

James D. Slack

Week 10, Day 5

the best food

Reading

John 4:34(b) [NKJV] My food is to do the will of Him who sent Me, and to finish His work.

Reflection

I like good food. We don't get a lot of it, but sometimes we do.

When my friend visits me, he stops at the vending machines near the visitation yard and buys me hamburgers, spicy chicken wings, bar-b-que rib sandwiches, and my favorite – several slices of strawberry cheesecake. And for Thanksgiving last month, all the brothers were blessed with an awesome meal of turkey and dressing with onions and bell peppers. Then last Sunday, we were each blessed with half a chicken!

Yes, I like good food. And lately, I've been blessed with some really good food.

But **the best food** comes not from vending machines or the prison's kitchen. It comes from ministering to a brother who once called me a fake Christian. It comes when I minister to my family – especially after the murder of my cousin. Even more of **the best food** comes from ministering to correctional officers who have to work on weekends and holidays.

You see, **the best food** comes from doing His will. It comes from doing His work in your work.

Today before you go to work, you will probably eat breakfast. At lunchtime, you might go to a restaurant or eat in the break room. Remember the good food you eat will nourish your body, but you can use that meal to gain **the best food**. Talk to that loved one at your breakfast table. Strike up a conversation over the good food at lunch. Listen to the person next to you at the vending machines this afternoon.

For it is **the best food** that nourishes your soul and the souls around you.

So at work today, seek **the best food**. And you will never go hungry again!

Prayer

Father, in the name of Jesus, I pray. Thank You for all the good food You have blessed me with these past weeks. But thank You for **the best food** You bless me with each day – the kind of food that helps me carry out Your will. And my soul is forever satisfied. Amen.

Jimmy Davis, Jr.

Week 11, Day 1

like a candle in front of a fire hose

Reading

Mark 8:36 [NLT] And what do you benefit if you gain the whole world but lose your own soul?

I Corinthians 15:33-34 [NKJV] Do not be deceived: "Evil company corrupts good habits." Awake to righteousness, and do not sin; for some do not have the knowledge of God. I speak this to your shame.

Reflection

Over the years I have worked many jobs. In one I had two bosses who were exceptionally corrupt. Both men lied, cheated, and stole from their customers and employees without remorse. They encouraged a culture of corruption that was endemic throughout the business. They encouraged small compromises among their employees, at first, and once an employee was compromised, they rewarded further corruption.

The problem was the job had great potential for my future if I stuck with it for a season. I kept telling myself I could be a light for Christ in an evil place – until one day I realized I would not survive unless I became corrupt to the core like my bosses. My light for Christ was **like a candle in front of a fire hose**; it could not stay lit in that environment. I had to choose between a career opportunity and my soul. *I chose my soul.*

People thought I was crazy to resign, and they told me so. "Just keep your head down and look what you will gain if you stick with it!" I did have a lot to gain, but I had even more to lose. *I left knowing God wanted me to leave.*

Some people are specially called to be the light of Christ in certain dark places. Maybe your place of work is one of these dark places and you are letting your light shine. However, to be a light you need to be a lighthouse – built for the storms—not a candle. Letting your light shine can be tough, but God prepares and molds us to be that lighthouse in the storm when we need to go into the darkness so we won't be extinguished **like a candle in front of a firehose**. God never wants to see our light put out, so He is constantly building us stronger to withstand what comes at us.

If you are working in a dark place today, ask God to mold and build you into a lighthouse that can stand the storms and stay lit.

Prayer

Lord, help me to always be a light for You wherever I am. Help me to never compromise my commitment to You. Help me to know when it is time to stay and be Your light and when it is time to go. Mold me into a lighthouse that is strong for You. In Jesus' name, I pray. Amen.

Kevin Cooney

Week 11, Day 2

be still and seek God's presence

Reading

Psalm 46:10 [NIV] Be still, and know that I am God; I will be exalted among the nations, I will be exalted in the earth.

2 Thessalonians 3:16 [NIV] Now may the Lord of peace himself give you peace at all times and in every way. The Lord be with all of you.

Reflection

Where were you the last time you experienced complete silence? I bet <u>not</u> at work! There, we are constantly listening to people's voices, computer keys clicking, and perhaps the sound of cars passing outside. No, you and I don't often have the opportunity to step away from the sounds of office life.

Where were you the last time you experienced the peace of God? Sadly, I bet <u>not</u> at work! The hustle and stress – it seems the workplace is the last place to find His peace. Even before I get to work, my mind is racing into the day.

But when I take time to **be still and seek God's presence**, it is easy to focus my attention on Him and what He is doing in my world – even in my workplace.

You may not be able to find silence at work today, but if you try, you <u>can</u> experience the peace of God. Take time to **be still and seek God's presence** – a moment at your desk, a glance out the window, a quickly bowed head in the break room. As you walk to that meeting, listen for the voice of God above the noises around you.

Find a quiet place in your heart to enjoy a moment of peace while the rest of the workplace hurries on its way. And be a source of peace to those around you.

Yes, **be still and seek God's presence** today at work. Remember God <u>will</u> be exalted in this new workday. Find peace in this certainty.

Prayer

Lord, I confess I am easily distracted by the clamor of my job. Please surround me with Your peace in this new workday. Help me be confident in Your strength and power. You are faithful. In Your name, I pray. Amen.

Jonathan Lantz

Week 11, Day 3

taken captive by the world

Reading

Matthew 5:37 *[ESV]* Let what you say be simply 'Yes' or 'No'; anything more than this comes from evil.

Colossians 2:8 [ESV] See to it that no one takes you captive by philosophy and empty deceit, according to human tradition, according to the elemental spirits of the world, and not according to Christ.

Reflection

In today's world, anything can be offensive. Words, gestures, and idioms may be used innocently by one but perceived as a cultural affront by another. And so workplaces have gone to great ends not to offend. Certainly good comes out of this, but it can lead to confusion, frustration, and further misinterpretation. The fact is our desire not to offend is often **taken captive by the world.**

As *Christian public servants*, we have an additional dilemma. You and I do not want to offend someone who then turns away from Christ. Yet we must communicate Christ simply and concisely to those around us – not bending to the fear of offending others. This is a difficult task. The words of Jesus will offend some who have been **taken captive by the world** of elemental spirits, philosophy, and empty deceit. And even when we follow Christ in straightforward responses, others will be infuriated by the simplicity of His "yes" and His "no."

So yes, anyone can be offended. And no, showing Him to others is never easy.

You cannot change the character of someone **taken captive by the world**. That job lies with Jesus. But you can change their perception of Christ by modeling what it is like to live for Christ. In doing so, your workday will be simple and straightforward – *more according to Christ* – rather than philosophy, empty deceit, human tradition, and elemental spirits of the world.

Today, remember you work for Jesus. Don't try to offend, but make His "yes" mean "yes" and His "no" mean "no." Jesus will do the rest.

No, don't be **taken captive by the world**! Yes, remain captive to Christ!

<u>Prayer</u>

Jesus, thank You for freeing me from being a captive of the world. Thank You for allowing me to serve others as a *Christian public servant* and to use my service to model Your life to others. In Your name, I pray. Amen.

Greg Smith

Week 11, Day 4

like sparks flying upward

Reading

Job 5:6-7 [MSG] Don't blame fate when things go wrong— trouble doesn't come from nowhere.
It's human! Mortals are born and bred for trouble, as certainly as sparks fly upward.

1 Corinthians 1:9 [MSG] He will never give up on you. Never forget that.

Reflection

Are you prepared for life's difficulties? Some things, like sickness or a reduction-in-force, may be beyond your control. And some things, like losing your temper or losing your integrity, are your own fault. Regardless, trouble comes from mortals, not fate, and it comes into your life **like sparks flying upward** from a campfire.

So are you prepared? Have enough seniority? Saved up enough sick days? Vacation days? How are the savings? Investments? Are you networked in your career path? Do you eat well and exercise? And how are your relations with family and friends? Do you have a solid *love-group* to lend support when trouble hits? Everything OK? Great!

But how is your relationship with Christ? That's the best thing you can do to prepare for disaster – have a daily personal relationship with our Savior. Spend time in prayer, study before work, and apply His Word throughout your workday. Don't be thankful to Him just for the good days; remember what Job learned: He is there with <u>you</u> even during the worst days. He is faithful to <u>you</u> on the day of disaster – when trouble really hits **like sparks flying upward**.

So before work today, build your relationship with Him. And keep that relationship sincere through all work tasks. For it is only through His faithfulness that all other preparations, including your loved ones, are possible – when trouble hits **like sparks flying upward**. Never forget that.

Prayer

Dear Jesus, thank You for Your faithfulness on all days, including the bad days. Thank You for Your faithfulness on this workday. In Your name, I pray. Amen.

Ronald Wilson

Week 11, Day 5

this new plain power

Reading

1 Corinthians 2:4 [NLT] And my message and my preaching were very plain. Rather than using clever and persuasive speeches, I relied only on the power of the Holy Spirit.

Reflection

I once was a negative and sly person. I always tried to play a game and win something from others. My words showed this. They had power over people, but they cut everything and everybody so I could gain something that really did not belong to me.

But then I gave my life to Jesus. Not only did my words change but my life and circumstances changed. See, the new me had **this new plain power** because, when I surrendered to Him, I stopped being clever and persuasive. I no longer used fancy words but let the Holy Spirit use me through **this new plain power**. It became His Words, not mine. *And the words work*!

It is difficult to follow Him in your workplace. I know. I used to have a job in the free world – a busboy at a restaurant on the interstate. And I have a job here on Life Row – being His ambassador. And I know it's sometimes easy to be negative and sly – so you get what you want – something that may not really be intended for you.

But you are in a position each work day to show **this new plain power**. Through you, the Holy Spirit's words can flow to others so they see a change in you. Even unreasonable people – still negative and sly – will see something different in you. And you will be persuasive, but not in the old way. You will gain something much greater than what really does not belong to you.

Today at work, do not be afraid to show **this new plain power** from the Holy Spirit. -- His Words will work!

Prayer

Father, in the name of Jesus, I pray. Thank You for giving me the Spirit and power to demonstrate Your goodness and love to others. Amen.

Jimmy Davis, Jr.

Week 12, Day 1

that one most-awful workday

Reading

Matthew 5:16(b) [NIV] let your light shine before others, that they may see your good deeds and glorify your Father in heaven.

1 Peter 5:7 [NIV] Cast all your anxiety on him because he cares for you.

Reflection

There was a time when I really struggled with going to work each day. All the drama. The negativity. The stress. It all just weighed heavy on me. One day the struggle became so overwhelming, I had enough. Either I was going to quit or my burdens had to be lifted. -- I decided not to quit. Instead, I chose God.

And after **that one most-awful workday**, everything started to change – not overnight, but I felt things moving in the right direction – His direction.

By casting my burdens to God, it changed my attitude. I started to walk around my workplace without a dark cloud over my head. I learned not to take the bad work environment personally. I learned with God's help, I could still control the affect the negativity has on me. And most importantly, it allowed me to help others.

Oh, my coworkers noticed the change in me! God gave me many opportunities to discuss the power of prayer and its impact on my "work-heart." Yes, many could see His light shining through me. And they started to feel His light beaming upon them.

Today at work, you may experience **that one most-awful workday**. If you do, pray and cast your cares to Christ. You cannot shine His light until you surrender all burdens to Him. And He is waiting for you.

So today, don't let **that one most-awful workday** get in the way of glorifying your Father in heaven!

Prayer

God, thank You for helping me get the devil's hand away from me. I yearn to be Your light in the face of darkness – and to share Your light with others. In Jesus' name, I pray. Amen.

Logan Dickens

Week 12, Day 2

the rules of the road

Reading

Ecclesiastes 12:13-14 [NIV] Now all has been heard; here is the conclusion of the matter: Fear God and keep his commandments, for this is the duty of all mankind. For God will bring every deed into judgment, including every hidden thing, whether it is good or evil.

Reflection

As a *Christian public servant,* you see the fears of people in this day and age. Some fear the condition of the economy. Others fear political candidates who may or may not have won an election. And many fear for safety in public places.

In those ways fear is negative, but fear can also mean a healthy respect. I fear deep water and fire, but I need both to live my life – yet I have a healthy respect for both.

You and I have *a duty to fear God.* We should fear (have a healthy respect for) Him and keep His commandments. Fearing Him and His Commandments are not just suggestions. They are **the rules of the road** to keep us safe along life's highway. And living by the rules removes many of the fears of this day and age.

Think about it. The worst evil can do is take you from this life and send you to the next. The worst evil can do at work is get you fired and send you where He needs you most.

So at work today, heed the conclusion of the matter. You certainly have nothing to fear. And you should not be afraid to help others see they too will have nothing to dread if they live their lives this way.

Yes, today at work, abide by **the rules of the road** – and show others how to do the same!

Prayer

Dear God, if there is anyone to fear it is You who gave me life. Help me follow Your commandments and guide others to Your path. I know You will judge good and evil, and I pray for Your courage to face evil as You would have me. In Your Son's name, I pray. Amen.

Stan Best

Week 12, Day 3

a promise to preserve

Reading

Psalm 40:11 [NKJV] Do not withhold Your tender mercies from me, O Lord; Let Your lovingkindness and Your truth continually preserve me.

2 Thessalonians 3:3 [NKJV] But the Lord is faithful, who will establish you and guard *you* from the evil one.

Reflection

A lot can keep you awake when it comes to your job. Things way out of your control. A budget cutback. A furlough or layoff. Handling the daily workload stress. Catastrophic illness. And then there's the Evil One.

So you worry. About family. About loss of wages or work. About healthcare and its cost. You want to be in control, but you really have no control.

Yes, workplace realities and potentialities are more threatening than reassuring. And self-protection from what may happen is not possible. But as David expressed in this *Psalm*, God's protection comes in the form of His truth and lovingkindness. Scripture affirms what He affords through His tender mercies – **a promise to preserve**. And scripture affirms His faithfulness.

So it's up to you. Worry yourself sick. Or recognize, acknowledge, and accept the protection God affords. It's **a promise to preserve**, and it's there <u>continually</u> in every area of life – including your job.

Today at work, will you allow God to protect you His way? Or will you run from His protection by worrying and doing things <u>your</u> way?

Today at work, have faith in **a promise to preserve**. And know He is faithful to <u>you</u>.

Prayer

Father, my workplace can be worrisome on a good day and even dangerous on another. The Evil One is always trying to break in. Thank You for protecting me. Truly I have faith in You, for You are faithful to me. In Jesus' name, I pray. Amen.

Chris Summers

Week 12, Day 4

regardless of circumstance

Reading

Proverbs 3:5-6 [KJV] Trust in the LORD with all thine heart; and lean not unto thine own understanding. In all thy ways acknowledge him, and he shall direct thy paths.

Reflection

It's a struggle working odd shifts at various stores just to keep the monthly bills paid. It's also a struggle to go to graduate school in the evenings to further my education. To add to everything, I haven't seen my son in six months because his mother and I do not see eye-to-eye anymore. Going to work, I fear my son thinks it's his fault I'm not there. While at work, I'm always afraid my son thinks I do not love him.

Have you had a time in your life when you didn't know how things would turn out? Wondering if you were going in the direction God intended instead of the way of your own selfish ambition? When the battle goes from flat ground to uphill with everything seemingly against you?

Scripture reminds us to trust in Him. Lean not on our own understanding. Acknowledge Him, and He will direct our paths.

So as I travel to work this morning, I praise God for He will enable me to pass all challenges in job, education, and, most importantly, in the life of my son. I will try not to worry because to worry is to lean on my own understanding – or lack of understanding.

As you go to work today, lean on Him because your *circumstances do not define who you are*. Do not turn your back on problems, instead face them head-on. Someone is waiting for you to succeed – **regardless of circumstance**. In my case, it's my son. Who is it in your case?

Today at work, lean on Him. Know your *circumstances do not define who you are*. It's His reality and love that define you. Trust in Him to direct your path – **regardless of circumstance**.

Prayer

Heavenly Father, thank You for both the good and bad placed before me. Keep Your arms around me, Lord, as I fight the good fight on so many fronts. Guide my actions to speak loud and clear that I am on Your path – **regardless of circumstance**. In Your Son's name, I pray. Amen.

Calvin Reed, Jr.

Week 12, Day 5

a Jesus change

Reading

Acts 3:5-6 [NLT] The lame man looked at them eagerly, expecting some money. But Peter said, "I don't have any silver or gold for you. But I'll give you what I have. In the name of Jesus Christ the Nazarene, get up and walk!"

Reflection

A young brother used to be very angry all the time. He cussed at everything, and he even cussed at himself. Worse, he cussed at Jesus whenever something went wrong. And things always went wrong for him because he was on death row – not Life Row. And being on death row is a terrible situation.

I could have tried to help by giving him something I bought from the prison store. A candy bar. Instant soup. Some Spam®. Coffee. But that would have been a temporary fix. And like the lame man in scripture where Peter wanted to change the condition by offering Jesus, I wanted to do the same for this young brother. Like Peter, I wanted to help make **a Jesus change** in him.

And now this young brother is off death row. He lives fully on Life Row. And each time I see him, I have to smile because he is now *up and walking*!

So many times, we want to change someone's situation but not the conditions that cause the situation. And when we do, we try to change earthly conditions. But what will really change someone – from surviving a life on a death row to celebrating living on a Life Row – is **a Jesus change**.

Is there an angry brother or sister at work? A coworker? Someone you serve? Next time you see this person-in-need, don't focus on the situation. Focus on helping to change the condition – **a Jesus change**.

Today at work, help that person find **a Jesus change**. And soon you, too, will smile seeing that person *up and walking* on Life Row!

Prayer

Father, in the name of Jesus, I pray. Thank You for opening my eyes so I can see and move in compassion to help someone's condition. Give me Your wisdom to help someone get *up and walk*. Amen.

Jimmy Davis, Jr.

Week 13, Day 1

that other workplace document

Reading

Proverbs 14:23 [NIV] All hard work brings a profit, but mere talk leads only to poverty.

James 2:12-13 [NIV] Speak and act as those who are going to be judged by the law that gives freedom, because judgment without mercy will be shown to anyone who has not been merciful. Mercy triumphs over judgment.

Reflection

I got a phone call from a younger colleague. She now holds a management position, and for the first time, she is required to evaluate others. She knows this is part of the job, but she doesn't relish doing it. And I told her she shouldn't enjoy doing it!

Performance appraisal is important, yet it should be the least-favorite task of the manager. But because of the distaste, many managers try to get around doing it honestly. Some water-down weaknesses to not offend. Or balance strength for every weakness to make the worker feel good. Or rate all employees at the same level in an effort to treat everyone equally. Naturally, these strategies have awful consequences for employee and agency.

In addition to job descriptions and workflow charts, I recommended my young colleague consult **that other workplace document** – the Bible. There's a lot in it about job performance. God expects benefits for hard-workers, as well as consequences for others.

Now, some believe **that other workplace document** is filled with contradictions. But I told my friend to read carefully. Evaluation must be done without prejudice – but it must be done with mercy. For poor performance, penalize. For no performance, terminate. For exceptional performance, reward. Do not be afraid of what others will say, but find *merciful paths* in speaking and acting about the performance.

Nowhere in **that other workplace document** does it suggest you should have fun in the performance process. And following Jesus is never easy – including at work.

Today at work, you will be more in line with Him if you do not forget to use **that other workplace document**! There you will find *merciful paths* in rendering judgment.

<u>Prayer</u>

Father God, it is never easy in my workplace. If I must assess, give me wisdom to rely on Your word as I follow the job description and other reports. But let me find merciful paths in rendering judgment. In Your Son's name, I pray. Amen.

James D. Slack

Week 13, Day 2

leave the day with integrity intact

Reading

Psalm 41:12 [NASB] As for me, You uphold me in my integrity, And You set me in Your presence forever.

Proverbs 22:19 [NASB] So that your trust may be in the LORD, I have taught you today, even you.

Reflection

It was high time I addressed a significant conflict with a fellow housing commissioner. The day before, she changed some procedures in a major program of my section – and did so with neither discussion nor notification. What added to my frustration was the mayor just appointed her as the lead commissioner – in essence, she was kind of my boss. And it was not the first time this housing commissioner imposed her will on my staff and me – but it had to be the last. Changing these procedures was <u>that</u> serious.

Before our meeting, I read my two morning devotionals and a chapter in scripture – all sources taught me how God wanted things done. He expected me to respect her, but He also expected me to maintain my own integrity – the integrity He gave me. For scripture teaches me to trust in our Lord and He will uphold me in the integrity He gives.

Well, the meeting went badly. I stepped down as a housing commissioner and returned to my old post. But still, He permitted me to **leave the day with integrity intact** – *His integrity*.

You might not have done what I did – quit your job. You might not have the luxury of returning to a former position in your agency. But some conflicts may require you to do <u>something</u>.

When those times occur, seek guidance in God's word before you say or act. Trust in Him, and He will let you **leave the day with integrity intact** – *His integrity*.

Yes, today at work, follow God's teachings, and whatever happens, He will let you **leave the day with integrity intact** – *His integrity*. And He will set you in His presence forever!

<u>Prayer</u>

Lord Jesus, let me seek Your will in all I do at work. As I serve Your people, be they citizens or staff, may Your trust shine through my actions and words. Whatever happens, teach me what to do and permit me to **leave the day with integrity intact**. For integrity comes from You, not me. It is Your integrity I bear. In Your name, I pray. Amen.

Alan Cox

Week 13, Day 3

this really simple question

Reading

Philippians 3:10(a) [HCSB] My goal is to know Him and the power of His resurrection and the fellowship of His sufferings

Reflection

I have **this really simple question**. *What are your daily work goals in your relationship with Jesus?*

Work goals? In relationship with Jesus? That's right. *What are your daily work goals in your relationship with Jesus?*

You spend most of the waking day at work, planning for work, working on work, and going to and from work. So doesn't it make sense the one place you spend most of your time ought to be linked to your relationship with Him?

Or do you think your workplace is off limits to Christ? Kind of like a recess from the responsibilities of knowing Him. That the *power of His resurrection* and the *fellowship of His sufferings* are just phrases – requiring no action – something to reflect upon on Sunday but not something to worry about during the workweek.

Oh, come on! Certainly, you don't think this way, do you?

And so **this really simple question** still stands. And only you can answer it.

What are your daily work goals in your relationship with Jesus?

Won't you answer?

Before it's too late.

Prayer

Dear Lord, my life seems so complex, yet it remains so simple. Today at work, give me wisdom to link what I do with who You are. Give me strength to recognize Your resurrection each minute I am at work. Give me courage to see the fellowship of Your sufferings in each person I meet. In Your name, I pray. Amen.

Chris Summers

Week 13, Day 4

the urgency of hope

Reading

Psalm 42:5 [NIV] Why, my soul, are you downcast? Why so disturbed within me? Put your hope in God, for I will yet praise him, my Savior and my God.

Jeremiah 20:11 [NIV] "For I know the plans I have for you," declares the LORD, "plans to prosper you and not to harm you, plans to give you hope and a future."

Reflection

"Susan, we made an offer to another candidate, and he accepted. It was a difficult decision because we could see what you would bring to the table. It was a pleasure meeting you."

A Christian sister emailed me last night. Susan had applied for a position, and the job looked like it had her name all over it. The interview went so fantastic she awaited the phone call offering the position. But the phone never rang. Instead, she received an email with the words above. Devastated. Depressed. Shattered. Above all, angry. Susan was angry at herself and at that agency. But most of all, she was angry at God for letting her down.

It's difficult to console someone who is convinced something of value was taken away. That "something" could be a relationship gone bad. A son in prison. A daughter killed in a car wreck. The fact is the loss of many things clearly surpasses the loss of a career opportunity. But at the time, that particular loss still hurts. In fact, the pain is tremendous.

So we exchanged emails throughout the night. We focused on **the urgency of hope** in God. That now is the time to praise Him – for His wisdom in this matter – and for being Savior. I reminded her God truly does have a plan – one that includes a career opportunity He needs Susan to take. All the more reason, I argued, to focus on **the urgency of hope**. He is all Susan has.

Today you may be in the same boat as my Christian sister. That promotion slipped away. That job opportunity went south. And it will be difficult not to get angry at God. But do not be angry. Instead, praise Him for keeping you from something that was not yours in the first place. Praise Him for having a plan for you. And focus on **the urgency of hope** in Him for the future.

Yes, regardless of what you think is lost today, focus on **the urgency of hope**. He is all you have.

Prayer

Lord, throughout this workday, my hope is in You. My hope is in You alone. You are all I have. I praise you in bad times and in good times. And only in Your name, I pray. Amen.

James D. Slack

Week 13, Day 5

you really can feed them all

Reading

Luke 9:12-13 [NLT] Late in the afternoon the twelve disciples came to him and said, "Send the crowds away to the nearby villages and farms, so they can find food and lodging for the night. There is nothing to eat here in this remote place." But Jesus said, "You feed them."

Reflection

Do you ever get tired of helping people? It happens despite being a *Christian public servant*. It happens to me on Life Row. I know it happens to you.

We are put in a position to help people. But there are so many of them. We get to the point we want them gone. Lots of excuses. Too busy. Too Holy. Too self-righteous. Too selfish. Too tired.

Scripture describes what the *tired twelve* wanted to do: send the crowd away. But Jesus said not to send any away – it was their job to feed them even if they only had five loaves of bread, two fish, and no money.

The really sad thing is these tired disciples came to Jesus not to seek His help in feeding the crowd. They just wanted them gone. But in the end, Jesus refreshed the followers with His Devine compassion – His endless, tireless, limitless love. And He renewed a faith that a miracle will happen each time they refresh in His Devine compassion.

And here we sit – you and me – doing the same thing. When we grow tired of helping, we find a way to chase people away. But we both can refresh in His Devine compassion. And a miracle will happen. Yes, **you really can feed them all**. And so can I.

Today at work, remember you are a *Christian public servant*. You are tired, sure. But He is not tired. So refresh in His Devine compassion – get an *addictive fix* of His endless, tireless, limitless love. And I promise you, a miracle will happen today.

Yes, **you really can feed them all**.

Prayer

Father, in the name of Jesus, I pray. Thank You for refreshing me in Your Devine compassion. I look forward to a miracle today! Through You, and only through You, I know I can feed them all. Amen.

Jimmy Davis, Jr.

Week 14, Day 1

start over and push on

Reading

Lamentations 3:22-23 [ESV] The steadfast love of the LORD never ceases; his mercies never come to an end; they are new every morning; great is your faithfulness.

Reflection

On my walk at dawn this morning, I marveled at the beauty of the sunrise and thought how gracious God is to renew His mercy each morning. He gives you and me the opportunity for a new beginning each day. Wow! I get a do-over, a chance to correct mistakes of the past and move forward!

When I was a small child, my mother used to encourage me by saying "When you fall, get back up, **start over and push on.**" Isn't that what our Lord wants you and me to do when we fall short and sin? Yes, in His divine mercy, He wants us to ask forgiveness then **start over and push on**.

In the workplace, everyone experiences times when people miss the mark. A coworker may be having a bad day and speak crossly without cause. A team member may not produce the deliverables on the project in a timely manner. A boss may chastise you undeservedly. A visitor to your office may be rude to you.

As *Christian public servants,* you and I must not only recognize when we miss the mark but also we are called to show mercy to others when they do the same. Hold them accountable, yet give them the opportunity to **start over and push on**. Do not hold mistakes against them.

As this new workday begins, remember God's mercies are new each morning for you and for me. Shouldn't we do the same?

Prayer

Father God, I often miss the mark, yet You show me mercy each day. Let me show mercy to others as You show mercy. When I fall, please forgive me and give me the courage to **start over and push on**. In Jesus' name. I pray. Amen.

Stephen Pincus

Week 14, Day 2

in a bullying culture

Reading

Proverbs 22:24(a) [NKJV] Make no friendship with an angry man

Ephesians 6:13(b) [NKJV] take up the whole armor of God, that you may be able to withstand in the evil day, and having done all, to stand.

Psalm 37:9(a) [NKJV] For evildoers shall be cut off

Reflection

A friend works **in a bullying culture**. Shouting. Threats. Scheming. Lying. Ignoring agency rules. All scenes in her workplace. And my friend can't seem to land another job. So I try to give her advice when she calls.

There is no difference between domestic abuse and workplace abuse. Both are caused by bullies, and both result in victims. Scripture offers insight into survival **in a bullying culture**. Our Lord does not want you to be friends with the bully. After all, a bully seeks only lackeys, never friends. And loyalty is a one-way street going uphill when it comes to people like that.

Sadly, bullies never go away unless they are chased away. And so He wants you to put on His armor and be prepared to do battle through formal procedures. And ultimately, He reminds us evildoers get their just desert. For a bully in the workplace is also a bully in other places. God is aware of the actions of bullies.

I hope you don't work **in a bullying culture**. But if you do, take the advice I give to my friend: follow His Word, not your emotions. Rely on His strength, not your fear. Wear His full armor.

And have faith in your ability to withstand the evil workday. Yes, having done all, you <u>will</u> remain standing when the bully is gone. Our Lord promises this – and He keeps His promises!

Prayer

Father God, make all workplaces Your workplace – as You make all homes Your home. Give comfort to all victims of abuse – domestic and workplace. Give strength and wisdom, found only in Your word, to all who seek You and love You. In Your Son's name, I pray. Amen.

James D. Slack

Week 14, Day 3

walk out the calling

Reading

Ruth 1:20(a) [NIV] "Don't call me Naomi" she told them. "Call me Mara"

Reflection

Poor Ruth! She followed Naomi into a foreign land, and then Naomi became bitter – literally changing her name to Mara, meaning bitter. If I were Ruth, I don't know what I would do.

I mean, we've all been in a situation like this. Perhaps finding yourself assigned to a two-person project-team but the other coworker is embittered about something – so embittered, despite all the talk about teamwork, you end up doing 80 percent of the work. Or you transfer to a new department only to find the supervisor dysfunctional. Or you take a new job only to find that agency filled with miserable coworkers.

What do you do? Try to change the supervisor or other coworkers? Try to control the situation? Or do you choose to *stay consistent* with whom God made you to be?

Ruth chose to *stay consistent*. Despite Naomi's bitterness, Ruth remained faithful – devoted to Naomi and continued to **walk out the calling** she had in God.

Yes, sometimes the best thing to do is not to try to change someone. Just continue to **walk out the calling** you have in Christ. After all, your ability to love the difficult coworker is not measured by your ability to change that person.

So at work today, don't be a controller. Be consistent in faith like Ruth. God can change that person, and He may task your help, but give up on the idea you can do the job yourself.

Yes, today at work, be like Ruth. Do your job – even if it means doing 80 percent of the team's work. Let Him take care of the others. Just **walk out the calling** Christ has given you.

Stay consistent in faith so no one can call you Mara!

Prayer

Lord, today difficult coworkers will cross my path. Let me not be one myself. No, let me be consistent in faith with You and not be a controller of this world. In Your name, I pray. Amen.

Valerie Steele

Week 14, Day 4

live without fear

Reading

Matthew 10:28 [ESV] And do not fear those who kill the body but cannot kill the soul. Rather fear him who can destroy both soul and body in hell.

1 John 4:15-18 [ESV] Whoever confesses that Jesus is the Son of God, God abides in him, and he in God. So we have come to know and to believe the love that God has for us. God is love, and whoever abides in love abides in God, and God abides in him. By this is love perfected with us, so that we may have confidence for the day of judgment, because as he is so also are we in this world. There is no fear in love, but perfect love casts out fear. For fear has to do with punishment, and whoever fears has not been perfected in love.

Reflection

A diverse group of Christians meets weekly to study the Bible and encourage each other to live by faith in meaningful ways at work. Once we discussed what it meant to really obey the command to **live without fear**. And in that conversation, an odd thing happened. Some raised qualifications for particular situations and issues. Weren't there cases where a "healthy" fear of potential danger and consequences was understandable – even desirable?

Fear, like anger, is an emotion given by God. <u>Sinful fear</u> only captivates and paralyzes, yet the *fear of the Lord* instructs and encourages. Situations arise that rightfully evoke fear, but my group was attempting to justify "sinful fear" by making it seem practical and necessary – like the notion of a benevolent white lie or attributing fits of anger to a personality trait. But it finally came to all in the group that the antidote for fear is <u>not</u> working-up courage. No, the antidote is banishing fear with His perfect love.

Now, imagine having the power to face real dangers each workday when you **live without fear**! Not ignoring or avoiding risks but moving confidently with Jesus visibly by your side. His power is in you through the Holy Spirit – and that power is meant to be seen by others. It is what He expects – no compromises – and <u>no</u> qualifications.

So at work today, make sure the power to **live without fear** shows in you. Because His perfect love is with you and within you, cast out fears – in your career and in your life.

Prayer

Kind heavenly Father, we confess an abiding fear of people and things other than You, of trying to change Your standard for what it means to live in the power of Your Holy Spirit. Please forgive this sin and help us to walk in Your perfect love that casts aside fear and energizes confidence each day with the hope of future glory. In Your Son's name, we pray. Amen.

Jonathan Waugh
Linda Waugh

Week 14, Day 5

filled to the brim

Reading

1 Samuel 16:1(a) [NIV] The LORD said to Samuel, "How long will you mourn for Saul, since I have rejected him as king over Israel? Fill your horn with oil and be on your way; I am sending you to Jesse of Bethlehem…"

Reflection

Last year Jesus' goodness showered down on me in all areas of my life. Yet my last judicial appeal was denied. My nephew was murdered. The Life Row church was under attack. People walked out of my life. And Satan attacked me in all sorts of ways. But I did not do like Samuel. No, I did not mourn and feel sorry for my situation. I just got up every day and went to work for the Lord here on Life Row.

Yes, I move forward with a horn filled with oil – **filled to the brim** – because I never know how far He is taking me in His work. And sometimes the journey can be pretty long around here. But He expects me to do His work, and I expect to see the goodness of Jesus – even in my disappointments and sorrow. Even in my earthly dying – if that is His will.

I'm sure last year was the same for you. Many ups and some downs. And this was especially true where you work. Am I right?

This year at work, move forward with a horn filled with oil – **filled to the brim**. You won't know how long your journey will take, but it doesn't matter. Just don't mourn the disappointments of last year or last week or even last minute.

Yes, today at work, be prepared to do His work. So move forward with a horn filled with oil – **filled to the brim** – for the journey may be long. But know His work must be in your work wherever He sends you! There's no time to mourn.

Prayer

Father, in the name of Jesus, I pray. Thank You for all Your Goodness You give to me each minute of the day. It is You, and You alone, who keeps me moving forward – always prepared. Moving forward because you have so much more for me to do. Amen.

Jimmy Davis, Jr.

Week 15, Day 1

walking it out

Reading

Jeremiah 29:11 [NKJV] "For I know the thoughts that I think toward you," says the LORD, "thoughts of peace and not of evil; to give you a future and a hope."

Ephesians 2:10 [NKJV] For we are His workmanship, created in Christ Jesus for good works, which God prepared beforehand that we should walk in them.

Reflection

Several months ago, I resigned from a very fruitful but grueling job I was blessed to have. With a newly-minted doctoral degree, I stepped out in faith by asking the Lord for a new mission and a new season of life. I used this time of preparation not only to hone and practice my God-given talents and skills but also to grow *closer to Him* in my faith. I even called getting *closer to Him* "**walking it out**"– using my faith in my walk and sharing it with others. I began to feel God, too, was getting closer to me – and then I realized He always had faith in me. Even before I surrendered my life to Him, He was already **walking it out** with me – He was favoring me just as He promised. I now understand I wasn't *earning* this favor at all; rather, I am *fulfilling* the future He predestined for me. All I have to do is remain obedient to Him and continue **walking it out** in my faith daily, including in my workplace. And so I am starting today with a new mission and a new season of life!

Today at work, are you keeping your faith close to Him? Are you **walking it out** by sharing your journey with others? Do you understand God is keeping His promises to you? Are you showing His faith in you? That He is **walking it out** each step of the way with you?

Today remember you are His workmanship. And He has prepared you well beforehand. Whether you stay with your current job or go elsewhere, you are blessed. So keep your faith close to Him as He does with you. He gives you a future and a hope. And a new mission and season can begin today!

Prayer

Father, thank You for the opportunity to serve Your purposes. Help me keep my faith close to you, **walking it out** in all avenues in my life, including the workplace where I can bring much-needed light. In the mighty name of Your Son, my Lord and Savior, Jesus Christ, I pray. Amen.

David Bouisselle

Week 15, Day 2

as if it were home

Reading

John 14:2-3 [NIV] My Father's house has many rooms; if that were not so, would I have told you that I am going there to prepare a place for you? And if I go and prepare a place for you, I will come back and take you to be with me that you also may be where I am.

Reflection

Do you know a workaholic? A person who seems *at home* while at work? I don't mean someone who likes work but someone who views the job **as if it were home**. Maybe that workaholic is you?

It's difficult for anyone – including a *Christian public servant* – to balance time between work and life. But doing your best at work should never mean treating the job **as if it were home**.

Home is a very encouraging concept. The singer Bing Crosby's "White Christmas" is the bestselling single, not because of memories of Christmas but because of the memory of home during the best time of the year. And the bestselling book, our Bible, is where Jesus speaks of a Home awaiting the believer. And it is to that eternal Home we should focus our labors.

So as one who is not yet Home, remind others they, too, must work to live and not live to work. Remind all, on the death bed, no one laments of not spending another day at work. But many are comforted by the memory of a worldly home and the hope for an eternal Home.

Today at work, do your best. But don't be *at home* at work – don't treat your job **as if it were home**. Work for your worldly home, and live for your eternal Home.

Prayer

Dear Lord, I long to be Home with You; although, I know there is still much to do here. Bless my worldly home, and let me carry hope for my eternal Home in my heart – so both may help coworkers learn about You. Help me keep the proper balance between work-life and home-life until I can finally be Home with You. In Your name, I pray. Amen.

Stan Best

Week 15, Day 3

the only life preserver you need

Reading

Hebrews 13:5(b) [NKJV] I will never leave you nor forsake you.

Reflection

"God either does not exist or He doesn't care."

A good friend said this while escorting me around a children's cancer ward. He was trying to cope with the trauma and death found in his workplace each day. I didn't respond right away because I, too, was deeply troubled by what was happening in the lives of these precious babies.

So many people work in settings where risk is high to either themselves or the people they serve. Some are led to ask "Where is God?" How should a Christian respond – especially in a workplace that is potentially filled with death and dying?

Eventually, I responded by avoiding all pious platitudes. I also stayed clear of being a fixer – someone who has a concrete plan. After all, misery seems to draw fixers from every direction, and no fixer ever fixes questions about God and His whereabouts.

What I did was simply love. I gave His love to my friend in this workplace. I listened to his feelings as we toured this ward, joined him in the midst of his misery, and wept with him at the foot of the throne of God.

Regardless of where you work – whether or not death and dying are common elements – when a coworker feels he has lost sight of God, give His love – for it is the only life preserver you have to throw into the icy waters of life. And that's OK because His love is **the only life preserver you need**. Remember God promises <u>never</u> to leave or forsake those who are suffering. God understands suffering – He had his only beloved Son suffer and die so you and I can someday return to Him as His children.

"God either does not exist or He doesn't care."

If you hear that today at work, respond with His love. Proclaim God's promise that He will <u>never</u> leave or forsake His people. And declare He keeps His promises because of His love!

Yes, His love is **the only life preserver you need** to throw into the icy waters of life.

<u>Prayer</u>

Oh Father God, I am deeply moved by the misery in the lives around me. Let me be a vessel who brings Your love and light into their lives. In Your Son's name, I pray. Amen.

Ronald Wilson

Week 15, Day 4

where He begins

Reading

Luke 5:4(b)-6(a) [NIV] "Put out into deep water, and let down the nets for a catch." Simon answered, "Master, we've worked hard all night and haven't caught anything. But because you say so, I will let down the nets." When they had done so, they caught such a large number of fish

Reflection

Lately, God has really wanted to show out in my work-life – give me a year of acceleration in my faith. Like Simon, I initially hesitated. I was just tired – as if I had already been working all night. But like Simon, I really felt like I was not catching anything.

So like Simon, I followed Him in my work. And He really did put me out into deep water. Oh, He didn't have me dive over my head. (He knew I couldn't swim.) It all started small. But then He called me into some huge waves. And now *the shore is out of sight and no other boat seems close*. And, frankly, it's been a struggle filled with fear. But I've come to realize God does His best work in deep water, and *into the deep water* is where He wants me to be – at the end of me is **where He begins**.

Do you hear God in your work-life? In your career? Is He offering you acceleration? Or are you choosing a comfort zone over Him? Today at work, follow His instructions. The deep water is not so bad for He is there next to you. You will feel overwhelmed, but isn't that how you want to feel about God? Overwhelmed by His love for you but also overwhelmed by His need of you.

So at work today, don't be afraid if you can't swim. Don't fear your boat being too small. Just be like Simon and put out *into the deep water*. The blessings will be there. They will overflow your boat. For *into the deep water* is where He wants you to be – at the end of you is **where He begins**.

Prayer

Father, I am thankful for the passion and calling You place inside me. Let me fear not the size of my boat or the depth of the water or even the distance from shore. Wherever You take me, fill me with Your peace and Your promise. I want to be at the end of me. I want to be where You begin. In Jesus' name, I pray. Amen.

Kathryn Saunders

Week 15, Day 5

line up with God's word

Reading

Luke 1:38 [NKJV] Then Mary said, "Behold the maidservant of the Lord! Let it be to me according to your word." And the angel departed from her.

Reflection

For most, the workweek is almost over. But when I was in the free-world, I worked on Saturdays and Sundays. So maybe you work weekends, too. Or maybe you have them off.

Either way, what is your plan for the next couple of days? Is it God's plan? Does it **line up with God's word**?

When Mary got the plan for her life from the angel, she did not understand it, but she trusted His plan – because she was the Lord's maidservant. And she was grateful His plan was using her to fulfill the Word.

Today, listen for God's plan. Whether you work the weekend or have a couple days off, trust and obey God's plan – for your job and for your family. It may not be as big as the plan He had for Mary, and it may not make sense. But be grateful you are helping fulfill His Word.

Even if you don't understand it, today have the spirit of Mary and just **line up with God's word**.

And what glory you will see and help Him make!

Prayer

Father, in the name of Jesus, I pray. Thank You for revealing Your plan to me so I can carry out Your will – even when I don't understand. Amen.

Jimmy Davis, Jr.

Week 16, Day 1

a griper or a gleaner

Reading

Ruth 2:2(b) [ESV] "Let me go to the field and glean among the ears of grain after him in whose sight I shall find favor."

Reflection

Working in public service really is a <u>blessing</u> of service. But you can get bogged down in the many tests and challenges of the day – the quagmire of bureaucracy and the seemingly endless demand for doing more with less. Someone is always needing something. And budgets get cut, people leave the job, and you are stuck with added responsibilities. If you're not careful, it can seem *nothing changes and only bad things happen.* And there is always that one coworker near you – the one who complains – the one who does not find favor in doing good.

Are you that coworker? Are you **a griper or a gleaner**?

Ruth was a gleaner. *She could have become a griper and with good reason.* She lost her husband, lived in a foreign country, and oh yes, chose to stay with her mother-in-law! But Ruth hung in there and did not give way to despair. She was ready to follow God and honor His plan, no matter what circumstances He brought to her. In every way, Ruth was a gleaner.

Gripers, on the other hand, never pass the test of servanthood! In fact, they tear up the test before it is given. Unlike Ruth, a griper never stays true to what she is supposed to do. Unlike Ruth, a griper can't seem to figure out how to find God's blessings and favor.

God promotes gleaners, not gripers. He sees faith in gleaners. They are truly *Christian public servants*. They don't give in to despair. Gleaners look for their blessing right where they are, and they focus on the good being accomplished.

Well, are you **a griper or a gleaner**?

Your workday is full of tests and blessings. It is the struggle of the test that puts you in the place to receive the blessing. And so God is waiting to see if you are **a griper or a gleaner**.

Today in the field, find favor in His sight.

<u>Prayer</u>

Lord, today at work, situations will arise and need to be addressed. Let my focus be on gleaning. Let me be ready to look for the good and receive the blessing in Your plan. Let me be ready to pass the test and be a gleaner, not a griper. In Your Name, I pray. Amen.

Valerie Steele

Week 16, Day 2

do justice today and be content with enough

Reading

I *Timothy* 6:6-8 [NASB] But godliness *actually* is a means of great gain when accompanied by contentment. For we have brought nothing into the world, so we cannot take anything out of it either. If we have food and covering, with these we shall be content.

Proverbs 21:3 [NASB] To do righteousness and justice is desired by the LORD more than sacrifice.

Reflection

It's so natural to want so much. There's the mortgage, savings for the kids' college, tithing, career investments, retirement plans –and just making ends meet each month. All of these are very important, and yes, we need and deserve material rewards.

But as a *Christian public servant*, don't forget righteousness is much more important to Him than all the material things you so desire and could ever offer Him in return.

Knowing He will take care of you, **do justice today and be content with enough**.

Yes, in your workplace, **do justice today and be content with enough**.

Prayer

God, lend me the will and support to recognize the blessings You give me, to be thankful for them, and to be satisfied within them. Help me recognize richness is to be found in the practice of justice, not in the accumulation of things I desire. Help me, too, to recognize You provide all I need – today and each day of my life. In Jesus' name, I pray. Amen.

Ruth E. Kelly

Week 16, Day 3

facing mighty mountains today

Reading

Philippians 1:6 [NIV] being confident of this, that he who began a good work in you will carry it on to completion until the day of Christ Jesus.

Reflection

I recently went hiking with a group of friends through the Rocky Mountains in Colorado. It was bitter cold – like using an outside icy stair machine. Halfway up the trail, my heart was beating so hard I thought it would pop out of my chest. But we made it to the top. And from there, we enjoyed a truly remarkable view – we could see the cities of Boulder and Denver and well beyond. And I thought of people who did not make it up this trail – those we met turning around, those who didn't think the view would be worth it and never started up.

Of course, after a short time enjoying the view, we started back down. At one point, I rolled my ankle and slid down a way. But I was alright, and we just laughed. Our minds were stuck on what we accomplished by taking this trail – and the confidence it gave us.

You know it's the same at work and in career. You and I are **facing mighty mountains today**. It is a struggle to climb each one of them. Others doubt our ability, and so do we. I question the worth of the trail, and you wonder whether the view will be worth it in the end. And we also witness coworkers giving up and turning back. And some coworkers never start up the trail. And once at the top, we are challenged by yet another mountain and this forces us to come down and start again – and the doubt and fears resume.

Yes, my friend, you are **facing mighty mountains today**. Just keep climbing in your job and in your career. Oh, your Father knows what you are up against. Know He is faithful. So be confident He will finish the good work He has started in you. Today at work, be confident. Through Him you will make that climb! And the next climb, too!!

Prayer

Father, thank You for the mountains in my life. Thank You for the journey. I ask You give me strength and confidence to continue on this journey – for You still have good work to do in my life and in my work. In Jesus' name I pray. Amen.

Kathryn Saunders

Week 16, Day 4

as bad as the bully

Reading

Proverbs 14:29, 33 [NIV] Whoever is patient has great understanding, but one who is quick-tempered displays folly... Wisdom reposes in the heart of the discerning and even among fools she lets herself be known.

Reflection

A friend works in a dreadful environment. Her supervisor is a bully, and she is his current target. The stress. The fear. Constant tension. All that plays against her patience and wisdom.

Sadly, there are many workplaces captured by bullies. Oppression. Yelling. Ridiculing. Threatening. That kind of workplace culture requires tremendous patience because it's all too easy to allow fear to turn into outrage and stress to turn into retaliation. If you don't watch it, you can become **as bad as the bully**.

Like my friend, if you work in such an environment, you need a calm heart and a steady mind to demonstrate confidence in God's intervention. Character of confidence is a trust in God's immediate presence in your "now," moment by moment, from one tense situation to the next.

Do you not think Jesus sees the bully? Do you not think Jesus sees <u>you</u>? Have patience and wisdom in responding so He doesn't see you being **as bad as the bully**.

As I told my friend, Jesus does not want victims to be hurt – physically or emotionally. They need to take appropriate steps to stop the bullying. But they also need to keep trusting in Him to combat the temptation of displaying rage for rage and matching emotion for emotion.

Today at work, seek protection from the bully. And remember to be patient and wise. Know Jesus sees the bully, and He also sees <u>you</u>. Don't let Him see you being **as bad as the bully**. That kind of folly does not belong in your heart.

Prayer

Lord, give me strength to be like You in all situations at work today. In Your name, I pray. Amen.

Chris Summers

Week 16, Day 5

prey to your I-mode

Reading

2 Corinthians 4:5 [NLT] You see, we don't go around preaching about ourselves. We preach that Jesus Christ is Lord, and we ourselves are your servants for Jesus' sake.

Reflection

You may be "addicted" to your iPhone, but do you ever fall **prey to your I-mode**? You know what I am talking about. God gives you an assignment, and if you're not careful, you end up preaching about yourself – not God – forgetting you serve for Jesus' sake, not your sake.

It happens to me sometimes. Does it happen to you?

When you fall **prey to your I-mode**, the "we" is barely remembered. Worse, the "He" is quickly forgotten.

You sometimes see it everywhere – at work and even on TV when elected leaders give speeches. Bragging and taking credit for all that goes right – but blaming others for all that is wrong. And before long, the preaching starts – but it is not about God.

Today at work, don't be tempted to take credit and forget others. Don't forget the "He" in what you accomplish. Don't fall **prey to your I-mode**. Just put it to mute or turn it off completely. Better yet, just throw the whole thing away.

Today at work, remember you are a servant for Jesus' sake, not yours. Give God all the credit. Preach about Jesus, not you.

And only then will you see the fruit Jesus brings to your table.

Prayer

Father, in the name of Jesus, I pray. Thank You for reminding me Jesus Christ is Lord. Let me preach that, and nothing else, throughout my day. Amen.

Jimmy Davis, Jr.

Week 17, Day 1

guide, advise, and watch over

Reading

Psalm 32:8(b) [NLT] I will guide you along the best pathway for your life. I will advise you and watch over you.

Reflection

Public servants help others in many different capacities. Some are physical or mental health therapists, and others are substance abuse counselors. You might be a child welfare worker or a teacher or a nurse. You may serve others through working at a foundation or a charity. Or you may be a government employee. All these different pathways have one task in common – to **guide, advise, and watch over** others in some fashion.

I wanted to be a public servant so I, too, could perform that task. I chose social work as a major in college, and after graduating, I entered the profession. And as I reflect on my career and life pathway, I realize the Lord has a similar task: to **guide, advise, and watch** over me – even before I chose my major – *even before I came to know Him as Savior.*

Imagine that! And now, saved, I am a *Christian public servant*!

As I **guide, advise, and watch over** those I serve, I know He is doing the same for me. His Word leads me and protects me. And through His Word, He is doing the same for those I serve.

As you **guide, advise, and watch over** others, know He is doing the same for you and those you serve!

So as this workweek begins, remember every interaction with others is an opportunity to introduce them to your Lord and His Word. To let them know how He is involved in their path, as He is with your path.

Remind all His pathway is always the best pathway.

Prayer

Father, thank You for guiding me along the best pathway for my career and my life. I ask You to give me confidence to continue on this journey. I ask You to give me strength to seize each opportunity to introduce You and Your Word and Your pathway to those I serve. I am truly blessed You still have good work to do in my life and in my work. I pray these things in the name of your Son, Jesus Christ. Amen.

Greg R. Winge

Week 17, Day 2

just really bad company

Reading

1 Corinthians 15:33 [NIV] Do not be misled: "Bad company corrupts good character."

Reflection

While I've been truly blessed to work with many wonderful people, sometimes I wasn't so lucky. Once there was a coworker who stole my joy, my time, my passion, and even some of my money! She took things from me I never intended to give away. And the worst part, I didn't even notice what was happening to my own character. For I had no one to blame but myself for who I hung out with – and what the consequences would be.

It's true, you and I are surrounded by many types of coworkers. Some with whom you have to associate, and others with whom you choose to associate. Some bring joy to your time at work, and others bring nothing but regret. And a few are **just really bad company**.

Today at work, choose wisely. Associate with coworkers who encourage your career-journey, love and respect you for who you are, and are dependable in completing their end of every task. Half of your career-journey is about people – not processes or product.

So at work today, don't be misled. Stay away from those who are **just really bad company**.

Remember your own character is at stake.

Prayer

Father, thank You for creating coworkers and companions. Give me discernment with whom I associate – in my work-life and in my real life. Help me take a healthy evaluation of the roles I give to those around me. Help me be grateful for the amazing people who cross my path, but give me courage to set boundaries with the ones who want to take from me. I trust You, Father, to provide me with an encouraging, motivating, and reliable circle of companions. I pray these things in Your Son's name. Amen.

Kathryn Saunders

Week 17, Day 3

like spring rain and sunshine

Reading

Proverbs 16: 14-15 [MSG] An intemperate leader wreaks havoc in lives; you're smart to steer clear of someone like that. Good-tempered leaders invigorate lives; they're **like spring rain and sunshine**.

Reflection

Have you ever had a leader who was pushy, insensitive, or often downright angry?

This type of personality may be good in the short term to motivate others to "get the job done," but ultimately it can wreak havoc. Leaders like this tend to destroy unity and vision since their way is always "right" – and if you don't agree, well, "there's the door."

Then there's the leader who is good-tempered, even-keeled. He is a breath of fresh air and an anchor of stability to all those around. The office seems brighter because she encourages others to a higher standard and does all she can to help everyone succeed. The leader still holds you and me accountable, but he or she still invigorates through accountability. Yes, a good leader leads well.

Which type of leader do you have right now? Or if you are the leader, what type of leader are you each workday?

As a *Christian public servant* – whether workplace leader or workplace follower – a renewal of attitude is needed every day. Be good-tempered and, **like spring rain and sunshine**, help others grow in job and career.

Today, invigorate those with whom you work and serve. Lead or follow <u>well</u>. Be **like spring rain and sunshine**. Yes, invigorate!

Prayer

Lord Jesus, please help me reach the higher goal of serving others before serving self – just like You did! Just like You <u>do</u>! In Your Name, I pray. Amen.

Ronald Wilson

Week 17, Day 4

using only one ear rather than two

Reading

Proverbs 17:27 [NCV] The wise say very little, and those with understanding stay calm.

Reflection

My grandmother used to say "God gave you two ears with which to listen and one mouth from which to speak…*and you should use them in that proportion*." Growing up, I guess I talked a lot and didn't listen nearly enough. And at the time, I didn't realize she was planting a seed in me – to turn to God's instruction for guidance so I would not mess up so much – like **using only one ear rather than two**.

As *Christian public servants*, people contact us because they have problems. They want someone to listen in order to get accurate information or useful guidance. And most people we serve are very nice and easy to listen to.

But there are always a few individuals who are frustrated with misinformation given by someone else not taking the time to listen. And we should expect that. I mean, wouldn't it make you mad to be given the run-around by one or more staff members who just didn't take the time to hear the full story?

Yes, most people you serve just want to be listened to and understood. But if you interrupt before they finish or appear as if you have limited interest in hearing their problem, it is understandable their anger and frustration can escalate right before your eyes. And not listening to the full story means you are **using only one ear rather than two**. And issues never find a remedy in that manner.

Today at work, take my grandmother's advice. Use His Word for guidance. Don't respond **using only one ear rather than two**. Say little and understand more. And stay calm, knowing Jesus has your back in all situations surely coming your way today.

Issues never find remedy **using only one ear rather than two**.

Prayer

Dear Heavenly Father, thank You for all You do on my behalf each and every work day. I ask, Father, You please help me listen fully when someone comes to me with a problem so I can properly guide them. Father, help me remain calm so even the angriest of persons sees only You in my response. Yes, help me remain calm in You. In Jesus' name, I pray. Amen.

Wendy Standorf

Week 17, Day 5

walk away to find a way

Reading

Hebrews 11:31 [NIV] By faith the prostitute Rahab, because she welcomed the spies, was not killed with those who were disobedient.

Reflection

Have you ever been attacked? Verbally attacked? Where you work? What did you do?

One day a young brother approached me when we were both outside in the yard. He was new to Life Row, and he was in pain – a lot of pain. He was just realizing what he had done, why he was here, and what was going to happen to him. It happens to all of us, and each brother handles it differently. This brother lost control of his feelings. For no reason on my part, he got in my face and started attacking me verbally. What did I do?

Well, my response could either <u>build</u> his faith or <u>hinder</u> his faith. And it was important for our Lord to build his faith. And so I knew I had to receive this brother with peace despite how he chose to express his pain. I had to be more like Rahab – be obedient to God so I will not die.

You see, I had to **walk away to find a way** to respond to this brother in Jesus' love. I could not do so when he was so angry, and I couldn't trust myself to do so when I was angry from his verbal attack. So I waited. Shortly, I found a way to welcome him into our church. And soon enough, this young brother started to grow in his faith.

Today at work, you may run into someone so much in pain he takes it out on you. Someone so frustrated, she really gets in your face. When that happens, do not be disobedient. Just **walk away to find a way** to receive that coworker in peace. Yes, **walk away to find a way** to be obedient to God – just like Rahab. And just like Rahab, you will not die.

Prayer

Father, in the name of Jesus, I pray. Thank You for pouring Your love into me so I can pour it onto others – especially when pain overwhelms them. Amen.

Jimmy Davis, Jr.

Week 18, Day 1

culture of bullying

Reading

2 Corinthians 4:9 [NLT] We are hunted down, but never abandoned by God. We get knocked down, but we are not destroyed.

Micah 7:8(b) [NLT] For though I fall, I will rise again. Though I sit in darkness, the Lord will be my light.

Reflection

One of my online students lives in another country where human rights are valued, including disability rights and protection from workplace bullying. I know she is a victim of workplace bullying, and her physician prescribes an accommodation – a service animal – to help in the healing process. I also know the accommodation was rejected by the state agency where she works – just like previous accommodations offered by the physician. But this time she called to tell me she suffered the trauma and humiliation of being escorted out of her building by security officers – escorted out for following the instructions of her physician.

Her voice trembled with trepidation. How could an accommodation be rejected when it costs the agency "not one pfennig?" How could it happen in a nation so deeply subscribed to human rights – even in the workplace? Why did a good coworker suddenly look with blank stare – as if passing a stranger – when "the fuss started"? And "why is this happening to me?"

We both prayed – for comfort and for strength. That while this was a knock-down day, tomorrow is a rise-again day. That those who hunt or hurt cannot destroy. That God is right next to her throughout this terrible mess.

You may work in an agency steeped in the **culture of bullying**. Lord knows, I once did. And now, so does my student. And you may blame yourself for the bad things happening. I once did that, too. And now, so does my student.

But fault belongs elsewhere, my friend. It belongs to those who deny bullying exists and now hope you will just go away. To those who allow a bully to get away with it. To those who look the other way. To those unaware bullies seek potential victims to control – in the workplace and elsewhere – and, once found, they do not let up until the light of day.

Today at work, you <u>can</u> fight the **culture of bullying**. And you will <u>not</u> sit in darkness long. For the Lord truly is your light of day. He is your <u>only</u> light in a place with the **culture of bullying**.

<u>Prayer</u>

Lord, where bullying exists, use me as Your beam of light. In Your name, I pray. Amen.

James D. Slack

Week 18, Day 2

training as continual learning

Reading

Proverbs 1:7 [NIV] The fear of the Lord is the beginning of knowledge, but fools despise wisdom and instruction.

Colossians 3:23 [NIV] Whatever you do, work at it with all your heart, as working for the Lord, not for human masters,

Reflection

Being part of the 21st Century workforce, we all know we need to be constantly learning and improving our skills. A lot of money is spent by organizations to ensure its employees are up-to-date with the latest in skills and technologies. Some workers embrace these needs as part of **training as continual learning**, while others absolutely hate going to class.

As *Christian public servants*, you and I should be a part of the group that sees **training as continual learning**. Having a healthy respect and love (fear) for the Lord, we can be open to whatever needs to be learned for the job. And this will help us to be our best at work just as scriptures require.

So at work today, if a skill needs to be learned or refreshed, just see it as **training as continual learning**. And view it as a requirement for your other job – being a minister at work for the Lord.

The knowledge gained for your job will permit you to give Him even more glory!

Prayer

Dear Lord, I desire to know all You would have me know. I thank You for the knowledge You have given me and ask for Your help to continually learn more for my employer and for Your ministry in my workplace. May You keep me from being foolish and always open to Your word. In Your name, I pray. Amen.

Stan Best

Week 18, Day 3

anything less than sharpening

Reading

Proverbs 27:17 [NIV] As iron sharpens iron, so one person sharpens another.

Reflection

I heard this verse on the radio driving to work this morning – and it got me thinking. How many times do you hear someone at work saying anything but negative stuff? And how many times do you hear yourself doing that? Watercooler talk. Whispers before a meeting begins. Comments in the middle of an appointment. Or just body language. If not from you, from a coworker, supervisor, a citizen, or member of the media – and it could be about any of the above. Someone's always trying to draw you into listening to (and then saying) something negative about someone else. *So much negativity* is bursting the seams.

Dwelling on the negative – doing **anything less than sharpening** one of His creations – is a reminder of how far short we fall of God's expectations.

And we both know it can be difficult at work. Some days are really bad. But as a *Christian public servant*, don't be tempted to pull someone down. Yes, formal evaluations are part of the job, but even the "real stinker" at work deserves more than backwater negativity.

So at work today, find only good things to chat about. Stop doing **anything less than sharpening** that other person. God expects nothing less – even for those who fall way short. And thankfully, He wants others to sharpen you on days when you fall way short! Yes, today at work, remember His iron must sharpen His iron. And you are His iron. Stop doing **anything less than sharpening** His iron – that other person!

Prayer

Dear Heavenly Father, thank You for loving me and blessing me even when I don't live up to Your expectations. Please guide me to say and do things that lift others up and not tear them down. This world has enough negativity, and I need Your help to make that change in me. It has to start with me trusting You to move me in that direction and trusting You to make that change in me one day at a time. Father, I love You. In Jesus' name, I pray. Amen.

Wendy Standorf

Week 18, Day 4

doing the rules right not just rote

Reading

1 John 5:3 [NIV] In fact, this is love for God: to keep his commands. And his commands are not burdensome,

Reflection

Have you ever worked with someone who knows <u>all</u> the rules – so well, in fact, that application seems by rote. You know the type. The man seeking boundaries rather than substance. The woman more concerned with process than with remedy. The coworker always confusing standardization for fairness.

Oh, things like boundary and process and standardization are needed. Those kind of rules give guidance in any workplace, as they do throughout life. But shouldn't we be concerned about **doing the rules right not just rote**?

Scripture reminds us love – love for God – comes from <u>inside</u>. And so doing right for God also comes from inside. That employee handbook or that policy memorandum may give you insight into "how" – and may explain "where" the out-of-bounds begins. But only the love for God inside you determines the "right" thing to do.

So at work today, show the love you have for Christ by **doing the rules right not just rote**.

Yes, do <u>whatever</u> your Father asks, and know His command will not be burdensome.

Prayer

Dear Father, as this world gets increasingly complex so does my workplace. Help me maneuver around the rote so I can truly do what is right. So I may show my love of You to Your people who come to where I work today. In Jesus' name, I pray. Amen.

Chris Summers

Week 18, Day 5

stop blocking the Light

Reading

1 Samuel 23:16 [NLT] Jonathan went to find David and encouraged him to stay strong in his faith in God.

Proverbs 6:23(a) [NLT] For their command is a lamp and their instruction a light;

Reflection

I became a Christian here on Life Row. Like anyone receiving the Light, I wanted to share it with others. And so I carried that Light to one brother, but he wasn't interested. He remained angry and hateful, and so I kept badgering him with the Lamp – even telling him he was going to hell if he did not accept Jesus. But that didn't work. He stayed dark to our Lord his entire time on death row. And I learned a lesson.

I had to stop being the lamp and start carrying the Lamp. I had to **stop blocking the Light**.

Then there was another brother, a big-time drug dealer in the free-world who never let anything get in his way. He was trying to act like that in this awful place. So I carried the Lamp to him. This time, I carried the Light of love, not judgment, encouraging him to stay strong – to find his way to the Light – to find faith in God.

And guess what? This brother chose Life Row over death row! No more anger or hate, he became a new beam of light around here. Because I learned to **stop blocking the Light** and let God do His thing, this brother is now happily sentenced to live on Life Row for eternity!

Is there someone at work who is like these two brothers? Darkness. Angry. Hateful. Living and working on a death row?

Share the Light with that person, but be careful. Love, don't judge. Encourage, don't badger.

Today at work, **stop blocking the Light** and let God do His thing. Don't be the lamp. Carry the Lamp.

And a new beam of light will surely appear! Someone will join you on Life Row.

Prayer

Father, in the name of Jesus, I pray. Continue to use me – I am to carry Your Lamp and be Your Light. I am to encourage, not judge. Thank You for Life Row. Amen.

Jimmy Davis, Jr.

Week 19, Day 1

take a stand for righteousness

Reading

James 4:17 [ESV] So whoever knows the right thing to do and fails to do it, for him it is sin.

Isaiah 1:17(a) [NKJV] Learn to do good; Seek justice, Rebuke the oppressor;

Psalm 121:1-2 [NKJV] I will lift up my eyes to the hills—From whence comes my help? My help comes from the Lord, Who made heaven and earth.

Reflection

I spent two hours on the phone the other day with a non-Christian friend of many years. He was in a situation of *workplace retaliation*. His union abandoned him, workplace "friends" abandoned him, and he had lost his home to pay legal fees. In the end, he was completely cleared by the courts and ordered to be fully reinstated to his former rank with tenure intact. However, the emotional and psychological toll has been devastating. He cannot sue for compensation or recoup legal fees because he was never actually fired. Yet he says the hardest was the loss of people who he thought were his friends. They abandoned him in his time of need. My heart went out to him and his family.

Many years ago, I watched a colleague at my place of work in a similar situation. He was a friend, not close, but a friend. I was faced with a choice. Do I stand by and keep my head down or do I **take a stand for righteousness**? I was young in my career and maybe a bit naïve about the ways of the world, but I took a stand. I was amazed once I did others began to do the same. My employer was forced to clear my colleague of ridiculous charges. Six months later, however, I began to understand the cost of my choice to **take a stand for righteousness**. The retaliation against me was ruthless. This time there was no one willing to **take a stand for righteousness**, not even the friend I had stood up for! In the end, however, God was on my side, and I was delivered from the situation.

This is what I learned from these situations: People are weak; *our God is strong*. It is not about what others do, it is about what we do; the choices we make. Our God made the heavens and the earth; do you honestly think He cannot deliver you from your situation? When it comes time to **take a stand for righteousness**, are you willing to trust God has your back and is your true friend who will never let you down?

As a *Christian public servant*, you represent the righteousness of Christ in your workplace. It is your job today to trust in Him, and Him alone.

Can you trust your God?

<u>Prayer</u>

Lord, help me always remember to trust You for my deliverance. Help me **take a stand for righteousness** and be the light of Christ no matter the personal cost to me or my career. You are my friend in time of need. I will trust in You. In Jesus' name, I pray. Amen.

Kevin Cooney

Week 19, Day 2

the antidote

Reading

Psalm 37:1-4 [HCSB] Do not be agitated by evildoers; do not envy those who do wrong. For they wither quickly like grass and wilt like tender green plants. Trust in the Lord and do what is good; dwell in the land and live securely. Take delight in the Lord, and He will give you your heart's desires.

Reflection

You know the workplace can often seem like a battlefield. People with hidden agendas will smile in your face and then do or say something evil when you are not in their presence. A coworker may even undercut you to your boss so he can get the promotion. Some angry citizen may come into your office and spew downright lies or half-truths. At times, you may not even see an attack coming until harm is already done. Sound familiar?

Often times we allow the influence of evildoers to disrupt our peace of mind in Jesus. So much negativity can be overwhelming. It can even creep into our own practices and poison our work ethic if we are not careful.

Yet, as *Christian public servants,* you and I actually have **the antidote** – God's many promises. His promises help us to keep focused and combat evil, negativity, and lack of internal peace. Trust in the Lord and do what is good. By focusing on God's many promises, we can have peace even in the midst of the battles.

Memorize God's promises, and at work today, speak them out loud and share them with others as well. Remind everyone of **the antidote**. Share the way to combat the evil works that attempt to destroy your peace.

If you use **the antidote** daily, you will dwell in the land and live securely. You will also be able to truly delight in the Lord and keep His peace.

Prayer

Heavenly Father, You are the author of all things good. Help me remember Your promises – **the antidote** – especially during the battles of work and life. Let me always trust in You and lead others to You so we may share in Your peace. I ask this in Jesus' name. Amen.

Chris Summers

Week 19, Day 3

live well, live full, and live free

Reading

Proverbs 3: 5-7 [MSG] Trust GOD from the bottom of your heart; don't try to figure out everything on your own. Listen for GOD's voice in everything you do, everywhere you go; he's the one who will keep you on track. Don't assume that you know it all.

Reflection

A friend asked, "What is your favorite book of the Bible?" I told him I'm a big fan of *Proverbs*. While I like the entire Bible, *Proverbs* ranks at the top of the list – especially when I'm trying to figure out how to work with other people. It is the premier textbook on relationships and living – for both sinners and saints.

Proverbs calls us to **live well, live full, and live free**. The call is to choose the strong pillars of God's wisdom, discretion, integrity, discipline, honor, and judgment. It gives direction for our lives, offering both the blessing of a life well lived and the curse of a life lived selfishly.

Each day before you go to work, read a bit of *Proverbs*. His Word will speak to you in the moments you need them most. Whether you feel anger toward a supervisor, impatience toward a coworker, or disrespected by a citizen – *Proverbs* has an answer full of wisdom.

So today at work – **live well, live full, and live free**!

And look to the guiding treasures found in *Proverbs* as you serve Him in your workplace.

Prayer

Dear Father, please hear my prayer. Lend to me Your wisdom as I work in my life today – in total dependence on You. May this workday bring glory to You! In Jesus' name, I pray. Amen.

Ronald Wilson

Week 19, Day 4

value true wisdom

Reading

Proverbs 1:7 [AKJV] The fear of the Lord is the beginning of knowledge: but fools despise wisdom and instruction.

Proverbs 8:1-3 [AKJV] Doth not wisdom cry? and understanding put forth her voice? She standeth in the top of high places, by the way in the places of the paths. She crieth at the gates, at the entry of the city, at the coming in at the doors.

Reflection

We are currently in the "award" season for television and movies. There will be many star-studded events at which commentators will say "I wish I could look like that!" Or "I wish I could be like that person." There will be many stars proclaiming "you should do this or that." Or "here" is the way things should be.

The funny thing is for all their beauty, fame, and riches – these stars have the same problems (and sometimes worse!) you and I have. Many of their lives are really bad examples of how to live your life. Many do not **value true wisdom**. They have no *fear of the Lord*.

We need to remember all good things come from God and wisdom is one of His great gifts to us. The beginning of knowledge is *the fear of the Lord*. Knowing Who made the universe is the beginning of wisdom. As it says in *Proverbs*, wisdom cries out declaring to all the way of life. Wisdom isn't hidden; it's everywhere declaring the ways of God.

As you go throughout your work today, **value true wisdom**. Seek His wisdom around you. Sometimes you might be foolish and think one of the "stars" at work has all the wisdom. However, you need to be humble, fearing God and seeking His wisdom and instruction. Today at work, **value true wisdom**. His wisdom. It starts with having *fear of the Lord*.

Prayer

Lord, I seek only Your voice and word for wisdom and instruction. Help me find coworkers who fear You and can help me stay in Your way. Help me be an example of Your wisdom at work as I serve You. In Your name, I pray. Amen.

Noah M. Griffing

Week 19, Day 5

leave a legacy for Christ

Reading

Acts 26:28 [KJV] Then Agrippa said unto Paul, Almost thou persuadest me to be a Christian.

Reflection

We come across a lot of people who are just like King Agrippa. No matter what we say or share about Jesus, we cannot persuade them to be a Christian.

After all, only Jesus and the Holy Spirit can do that, right?

But we can **leave a legacy for Christ** in the hearts of others – even where you and I work. In fact, we have an obligation to plant that seed – just like Paul did – especially under the worst circumstances.

Regardless of where you work, today **leave a legacy for Christ** with someone else. Carry this seed in your heart and plant it graciously. Give someone Someone to think about over the weekend.

And who knows, over the weekend that seed may start to take root. And someday at work, you just may get a glimpse of another harvest for His Kingdom!

So before you go home tonight, please **leave a legacy for Christ** with someone's heart.

Prayer

Father, in the name of Jesus, I pray. Thank You for continuing to use my life to bring a legacy for Your Son. Let me not let You down. Amen.

Jimmy Davis, Jr.

Week 20, Day 1

make something that lasts

Reading

Jeremiah 10:11-12 [NASB] Thus you shall say to them, "The gods that did not make the heavens and the earth will perish from the earth and from under the heavens." *It is* He who made the earth by His power, Who established the world by His wisdom; And by His understanding He has stretched out the heavens.

Reflection

At work last week, did you **make something that lasts**?

From the boss to the intern, everyone contributes uniquely. And at times, any worker may stand out because of his or her creative powers. But too often, that energy is only temporary. The idea for efficiency-in-task may work in a particular area but fail the test in another application. That "big idea" for productivity may be the best this year, but it will certainly be replaced by better ideas next year. The unique plan for program assessment soon becomes "old hat" by better plans down the line.

At work as in life, the only lasting creativity comes through the hand of God – forged and fixed with our Father's divine wisdom and understanding. When your creativity comes with a God-centered focus, you will **make something that lasts** – by giving all glory to Him.

As a *Christian public servant*, use your gifts and talents at work today. Just remember Who gave them to you. So use them for God because they are from God. Don't use your gifts just to impress your supervisor. Don't tap your talents just to find a solution before someone else. Don't be creative just to get through the workday. No!

Wherever you are on the organizational ladder, find a way to use your God-given gifts and talents to excel at work in a manner that leads others to Him. Establish the presence of the kingdom of God in all you do.

So at work today, **make something that lasts** – beyond the workday. Yes, **make something that lasts** beyond your career. Make it last for eternity.

And when you do, just watch how the heavens stretch out!

Prayer

Father God, all things good come from You. I thank You for all of the talents and skills You bestow on me. Please never let me become complacent with Your Gifts. Show me the opportunities to use them to excel in my work but also to bring others to You. I ask this in Jesus' name. Amen.

Chris Summers

Week 20, Day 2

that kind of prosperity

Reading

2 Corinthians 9:8 [NKJV] And God *is* able to make all grace abound toward you, that you, always having all sufficiency in all *things,* may have an abundance for every good work.

2 Peter 3:18 [NKJV] but grow in the grace and knowledge of our Lord and Savior Jesus Christ.
To Him *be* the glory both now and forever. Amen.

Reflection

A colleague recently received a greeting card congratulating him on an accomplishment and wishing him much prosperity. As he shared the card with me, we started to wonder what "prosperity" the sender had in mind. Nowadays, the images conveyed about prosperity center on power, money, freedom, jewelry, luxurious vacations, or expensive cars. Some greeting cards may focus on good health, but material prosperity is commonly intended. And that's OK.

But what about s*piritual prosperity*? Rarely expressed is **that kind of prosperity** because it seems linked to having less freedom or a life of complacency. Who wants to live with so many "restrictions" and have to give up everything just to "prosper" spiritually?

My colleague and I agreed, in order to appreciate all the material things in life, prosperity needs to *come from within.* Turning to the Word of God changes our mindset and prepares our soul to embrace the multiple blessings God has in store for believers. His Word renews our spirit and helps us grow in grace. Feeding on the truths of the Word is like milk; it's good and solidifies the bones. And naturally, when something is good, you tend to share it! Yes, **that kind of prosperity** – spiritual prosperity – affects all other visible prosperities in life.

As a public servant, citizens imagine you as being prosperous because of what is visible: material things in your office, paintings hanging on the walls, diplomas, clothing, or even job security and titles might fill them with envy. Too often they don't see your spiritual prosperity. And sadly, many do not understand **that kind of prosperity**.

Today at work, remember you are a *Christian public servant*. Don't hesitate to spend time in prayer for your coworkers and the people you serve. Don't be ashamed to show **that kind of prosperity** – spiritual prosperity – along with the material blessings bestowed on you.

Today at work, seek God's guidance to find practical ways to promote spiritual prosperity around you! Seek His guidance through all of your blessings.

<u>Prayer</u>

Dear Father, thank You for the multiple blessings You bestow on me. I know You are not against material prosperity for me, Your child, but I know You need me to attain spiritual maturity in order to manage my worldly life. Help me gain a prosperous soul so I can inspire others to *change within* – their hearts, minds, and souls. In the name of Jesus, I pray. Amen.

Evelyne F. Altema

Week 20, Day 3

in His hand

Reading

Proverbs 16:9 [NASB] The mind of man plans his way, But the Lord directs his steps.

Reflection

Sometimes it's a struggle to think about the future. My plan and hope are to enter the public service. I am asking God to open that door, and I pray I will always be in His will. However, that's the future. In the here and now, I struggle with student issues: Should I step into this campus leadership role? Should I write about this or that topic? I know the choices I make today can affect my future. I want to be in God's will when it comes to whatever I do.

When worry starts getting the better of me, I always take great comfort that the Lord is the one who is directing my steps. Regardless of worry and struggle, deep down inside I know I am **in His hand**. What a great joy that the Lord of all creation takes a special interest in me, where I am going, and what I will do with my life! You know he takes the same interest in you. God loves us all equally enough to care about all of our futures.

As *Christian public servants*, there are many decisions you and I face about the future. There are also plenty of decisions we face in the here and now.

Take comfort in the Lord and rest in Him. Thank Him, in the quiet of your office or over mealtime or in the library, for holding your today and your future **in His hand**.

Yes, throughout this workday or study day, know deep down inside you are **in His Hand**.

Prayer

Lord, thank You for holding my future in Your hand and carrying the burden of what comes tomorrow. Please walk with me, always guide me, and be not far from me! Help me listen to Your will and to follow it. In Jesus' name, I pray. Amen.

Paul Bayer

Week 20, Day 4

faith, love, and hope

Reading

1 Thessalonians 1:3 [NIV] We remember before our God and Father your work produced by faith, your labor prompted by love, and your endurance inspired by hope in our Lord Jesus Christ.

Reflection

Usually, we remember to bring what we need to work. Keys and security ID. A laptop or briefcase. Mobile phone with a calendar filled with the day's itinerary. Maybe some tools or gadgets. And perhaps even a lunch. But it's easy <u>not</u> to remember to pack some other things –**faith, love, and hope**. And it's too easy to forget why these kinds of "tools" are most important at work.

You and I cannot see the future. We can't even see the end of the workday when it's only 9:00 a.m. You do not know if the budget will last, and I don't know if the completed task will be of value. In essence, our work is the product of things we cannot see – <u>faith</u>. It is the same faith that leads us to assume the sun will rise before work and permits us to assume our families are safe when we are at work. As *Christian public servants*, the faith we bring to work is the same faith we have in our Savior and Lord, Jesus Christ – and that faith sustains us throughout the workday.

It's also easy to forget our hard work is prompted by <u>love</u>. Yes, the salary may be sufficient and the perks good, but the work you and I do is really out of love. Love for family. Love for loved ones. Love for career. Love for those we serve. As *Christian public servants*, we know His love – and our love for Him – will protect and guide us throughout the workday.

You and I easily forget we return each workday because of <u>hope</u>. Hope for a better life. Hope for more opportunities for loved ones and those we serve. Hope for a better community. Hope for a better world. As *Christian public servants*, that worldly hope comes from our eternal hope. By following Christ in this life and in this workplace, you and I place our hope in Him and His Word.

Before you go to work today, make sure you take the most important tools. Remember to pack **faith, love, and hope**. They will remind you of <u>how</u> (by faith) to work and <u>why</u> (because of love) you work and give the <u>endurance</u> (hope) for returning to work tomorrow.

Today at work, remember to bring **faith, love, and hope**. As a *Christian public servant*, remember these tools before your God and Father.
Use them throughout the workday so others may gain **faith, love, and hope**.

<u>Prayer</u>

Father God, throughout this workday, let me show everyone my **faith, love, and hope**. Let me do so through my words, actions, and deeds. In Your Son's name, I pray. Amen.

Larry Hanson

Week 20, Day 5

in-Christ

Reading

Exodus 32:22 [NLT] "Don't get so upset, my lord," Aaron replied. "You yourself know how evil these people are.

Reflection

I am in a place where evil is all around me. It is a place where evil has come against me. But since I am a man **in-Christ**, I can't act like the evil ones. No, I can't respond like the evil ones.

It's easy to be overcome by evil. Aaron was overcome by the evil people. He allowed them to defile his character to the point he did not act like a man **in-Christ**.

The type of evil where you live and work may not be as bad as mine. Then again, it may just be different in the community you serve than it is where I serve. It doesn't matter if it is my place or your place. It doesn't matter if you are a man or a woman. As a *Christian public servant*, do not allow the evil ones to lead you to live, act, or thrive like you are not **in-Christ**.

Today at work, be aware of the evil around you. Be aware of the evil that comes against you.

That evil is there. It is real.

Remain **in-Christ**.

Prayer

Father, in the name of Jesus, I pray. Thank You for the new life You give me each day – the new life in Your Son, Jesus Christ. Amen.

Jimmy Davis, Jr.

Week 21, Day 1

just to replenish

Reading

1 Kings 19:7-8 [NLT] Then the angel of the LORD came again and touched him and said, "Get up and eat some more, or the journey ahead will be too much for you." So he got up and ate and drank, and the food gave him enough strength to travel forty days and forty nights to Mount Sinai, the mountain of God.

Reflection

Do you take time **just to replenish** yourself?

With the pressures and demands of work last week, I got exhausted. I barely found the mental energy to think about the physical energy it took to go to the grocery store later in the afternoon. My levels of stress and irritability were high, and my level of caring was minimal. I discovered I was depriving myself of all relationships – family, friends, and God. To be quite honest, I was doing just enough to get by.

As this workweek begins, I need **just to replenish** myself spiritually, mentally, and physically. This is vital to being a *Christian public servant.* God gives you and me tremendous talents and abilities, but without the energy to perform, we neglect His gifts. If we are not able to give our best, we are depriving ourselves, others, and God of our full potential.

Today, remember to find time **just to replenish** yourself. Take that quick moment to do so spiritually, mentally, and physically. I know you have to go above and beyond in your job do your best in all situations.

So at work today, find the time and opportunity **just to replenish** yourself. A break. A minute. Or even a second. Revitalize your mind and heart so God can fully use you to go the forty days and forty nights of this coming week!

Prayer

Heavenly Father, You know my heart and mind. You know when I am mentally and physically drained. Help me keep Your temple filled with energy and vitality derived from You so I may constantly be Your physical hands and feet. In Jesus' name, I pray. Amen.

Angela Arbitter

Week 21, Day 2

some kind of new

Reading

2 Corinthians 5:7 [NIV] For we live by faith, not by sight.

James 4:7(b)-8(a) [NIV] Resist the devil, and he will flee from you. Come near to God and he will come near to you.

Reflection

Are you navigating **some kind of new**? You might see the "new" bringing excitement and curiosity. Then again, you also might feel the "new" bringing discomfort and fear. It's true, "new" easily changes the comfort level, and that can be scary. Fear of the unknown can limit success and prompt second-guessing about happiness and security.

Right now, I'm walking through **some kind of new**. And I struggle. What if the door God opens doesn't look like the one I prayed for? What if God's plan doesn't look like my plan? What if I fail?

I struggle with these thoughts of fear even when a dear friend reminds me God never intends for anyone to be miserable. Yet I struggle. Though my faith says my God is a good God who always looks after me, my brain can doubt that very foundation.

Then it hit me. These doubtful thoughts are of the devil. I need to resist the devil, for he <u>will</u> flee. I need to turn my mourning into joy and my gloom into praise. The Lord – my Lord –requires me to live by faith. Does the Lord – your Lord – not require the same of you? And living by faith leaves no room for either living by sight or living by thought.

Today at work, don't be afraid of **some kind of new.** Just come nearer to God, and He will come nearer to you! And the fear from Satan will quickly flee.

Prayer

Father, thank You for the desires and dreams You give me. Thank You for opportunities to navigate the new. Give me wisdom to recognize the devil and his schemes of evil. Give me the ability to be joyful in hope, patient in affliction, and faithful in prayer. I pray all these things in Jesus' name. Amen.

Kathryn Saunders

Week 21, Day 3

the same question Jesus asked

Reading

Luke 9:20(b) [ESV] "But who do you say that I am?"

1 Peter 2:25 [ESV] For you were straying like sheep, but have now returned to the Shepherd and Overseer of your souls.

Reflection

"*Who do you say that I am?*" That's the question Jesus asked those closest to Him in His work. Jesus didn't need to ask this question to know who He was, but He wanted to know how His disciples perceived Him. You and I can grow closer to Him by asking Christians around us this same question about ourselves.

Especially in the workplace, it seems so easy to drift. After all, we are away from family and friends. Left alone, we're like sheep prone to wander – and there are many who prefer us that way. The temptation is great to do what we want rather than what God wants and what is best for coworkers. So accountability to others is one of the ways God holds us accountable to Him.

One way to grow in your Walk is to ask the Christians in your workgroup **the same question Jesus asked**: "*Who do you say that I am?*" Be prepared to learn more about yourself and how others perceive you. If your Christian coworkers are honest, some will approve of who you are. But honest brothers and sisters may also point out spiritual weaknesses. Remember both encouragement and critique are necessary for your growth in Christ to be more like Him.

At some point today at work – perhaps at a break or at lunch – pull aside one or more close Christian coworkers. Ask **the same question Jesus asked**. And have ears to listen so you can grow in Him and grow toward others.

Prayer

Heavenly Father, thank You for growing us through our brothers and sisters in Your workplace. Help us have teachable ears and a heart that speaks truth with love when we are asked to share our thoughts. May You be pleased and honored by our words. In Your Son's name, we pray. Amen.

Jonathan Waugh
Linda Waugh

Week 21, Day 4

look back with regret

Reading

Genesis 19:26 [NKJV] But his wife looked back behind him, and she became a pillar of salt.

Philippians 3:14 [NKJV] I press toward the goal for the prize of the upward call of God in Christ Jesus.

Reflection

In *Genesis*, Lot's wife looked back. We don't know why she looked back. We only know she was told not to.

It is easy to **look back with regret** at some of our decisions in life, especially career decisions. If I had continued my original course in college, which was to become a lawyer, I would have ended up in a totally different place than I am today. I would likely wake each morning and be looking into the eyes of a different wife and children. I might be richer or poorer. I would likely be living someplace else. My life would be different. However, no matter how different life would have been, my life's mission would have been the same: serving our Lord through the work of my mind, hands, and heart on a daily basis. I would still be pressing toward Him.

Somedays it is easy to look at the past and wonder about "the road not taken." It is easy to **look back with regret** when you are having a bad day at work. Like everyone, you have made both good and bad career decisions. Regardless, God can use you where you are, if you let Him. You must look to what you can do for God, not what you could have done. God wants to use you; just be willing to say "Yes Lord, use me."

I have no regrets about past career choices because I know God has blessed me in the here and now. I am blessed with food, shelter, and a loving family, so I look forward. I do my best to serve God through my work on a daily basis. You can too.

Today at work, strive to build His kingdom because you will one day be with Him there. Your job is your ministry. So do not **look back with regret** at what might have been, but look forward to what you can do today for God through your work.

Dedicate this workday and all that follow by serving God *without regret*. Press forward!

Prayer

Lord, help me never to regret where You have allowed me to serve You today. Keep me focused on serving You in the here and now so one day I can be with You with no regrets for my service for You. In Jesus' name, I pray. Amen.

Kevin Cooney

Week 21, Day 5

get out of God's way

Reading

1 Samuel 16:6-7 [NLT] When they arrived, Samuel took one look at Eliab and thought, "Surely this is the LORD's anointed!" But the LORD said to Samuel, "Don't judge by his appearance or height, for I have rejected him. The LORD doesn't see things the way you see them. People judge by outward appearance, but the LORD looks at the heart."

Reflection

A lot of times, we pick the people we want to love and show compassion – especially to share our testimonies and fresh revelations. We tend to choose comfortable people to do these things with because it makes us feel secure. And we convince ourselves they deserve our attention because they are Holy enough.

And this seems true in the workplace. It is in mine. How about yours?

But if you and I **get out of God's way**, we will find God's choice is better than ours. We find this in scripture where Eliab looked the part, but David was God's choice.

Today at work, **get out of God's way** and try to look upon others – everyone – with God's eyes. And let Him choose, not you.

You won't be as comfortable as you'd like, but being comfortable is never part of His deal!

Prayer

Father, in the name of Jesus, I pray. Thank You for continuing each day to not only change my heart but to remove everything out of my eye-gate so I can pick who You are leading me to. Amen.

Jimmy Davis, Jr.

Week 22, Day 1

lunch food that really matters

Reading

Amos 8:11 [MEV] The time is coming, says the Lord God, when I will send a famine on the land, not a famine of bread, nor a thirst for water, but of hearing the words of the Lord.

Jean 6:26(b)-27 [MEV] Most assuredly, I say to you, you seek Me, not because you saw the signs, but because you ate of the loaves and were filled. Do not labor for the food which perishes, but for the food which endures to everlasting life, which the Son of Man will give you, because God the Father has set His seal on Him.

Reflection

Around the table at my lunch room, coworkers share all sorts of foods and recipes: gourmet, organic, desserts! The scents are, every day, quite delightful. For many of us, how we eat is deeply connected to our social lives, and certain dishes connect us emotionally to some memories. For my part, sweets and pastries bring me an important level of comfort and joy! And the amazing thing is good food usually brings coworkers closer to the table.

But in too many workplaces, junk food abounds. Despite health claims, marketing still disguises junk food as being more attractive with the *magic words* of "LOW FAT, LESS SALT, alternate sugars" to give them legitimacy. But junk food only satisfies for a limited time. Science is right. Wholesome food, especially at breakfast, makes a difference in how you fuel your body for the rest of the workday.

The same applies spiritually. Workplace "munchies" – like listening to one gospel song or a quick "microwave" prayer or mumbling a few words before eating or even reading a verse on the run – provides *spiritual junk food* that gives only limited satisfaction to the soul. And when a real crisis comes, you have no energy. You have no fuel for the fight.

Choosing **lunch food that really matters** – spiritual food and earthly food – is a lifestyle, not a quick fix. So at work today, enjoy a good lunch that truly fills your body with health. Remember your Savior was born in Bethlehem, the city called *the house of bread*. Feed on that bread, too. Let it bring others closer to the table so they may share its multiple recipes for God's glory!

Yes, take time at lunch to really connect with God. Reading His Word, spending time in prayer, and singing praises sound like a blessed *three-course meal*! Food from His field and loaves from His Word. Today, pick **lunch food that really matters**.

Bon appétit!

Prayer

Dear Father, thank You for providing me with daily bread. Help me thirst for Your presence and feed on Your Word so I can stand stronger in my workplace and in this world and share my bread with those who are seeking You. In Your Son's name, I pray. Amen.

Evelyne F. Altema

Week 22, Day 2

the spiritual lens He gives

Reading

Proverbs 27:3 [ESV] Let another praise you, and not your own mouth; a stranger, and not your own lips.

1 Peter 3:10(b)-11 [ESV] let him keep his tongue from evil and his lips from speaking deceit; let him turn away from evil and do good; let him speak peace and pursue it.

Reflection

The workplace brings on competitive behaviors, but one behavior is rather dangerous: *unbridled self-promotion.* You know what happens. This kind of self-promotion undermines coworkers, oversteps boundaries, operates from a place of dishonesty, and manipulates others in order to get something or someplace. But what becomes even more dangerous is how Christians react to unbridled self-promotion. It's easy to be quick to remove our spiritual glasses – to respond in our natural shades – in ways that may also be just as deceitful. It's easy to forget **the spiritual lens He gives** us renders perfect vision. It is this lens that keeps our sight firm in our witness to others in the workplace as we respond to the egos surrounding us.

As a *Christian public servant,* give pause when someone brags – even when bragging begins to undermine and overstep. Don't respond in your natural shades – even when self-promotion becomes dishonest and manipulative. Instead ask who you will allow your response to reflect? And what lens you will choose to use – your own shades or **the spiritual lens He gives** you? Then keep your tongue civil – away from evil – and find a way to do good in your response. Find a way to do good for the self-promoter and for others. Do good for Him.

Today at work, carry the light of Christ so you know where you are walking. Wear **the spiritual lens He gives** so you can see what you are looking at. Let your response to self-promotion not add to deceit. Rather, let it show the character of the One who gives you that light of grace, favor, and strength. Your response will bring others – even that one who self-promotes constantly – onto the path of righteousness, goodness, and peace.

And, oh, what a better workday this will be!

Prayer

Lord, I ask You to clean my spiritual lens today so I can see what You want me to see. So I may not add to deceit and may respond to others the way You want – not by my shades, but by Your lens. In Your Name, I pray. Amen.

LaShonda Garnes

Week 22. Day 3

the scariest verse in the Bible

Reading

Matthew 13:58 [ESV] And he did not do many mighty works there, because of their unbelief.

Reflection

This is **the scariest verse in the Bible**. Jesus was ready to do many miraculous things, but because of their lack of belief, He passed them by. *Passed them by*!

I think sometimes we challenge God by saying "If You do this mighty work, I will believe in you!" Or "If You do *this* in my life, then my faith will be strong and I will do *that* for You." I suspect, all the while, God is saying "I conquered death! If you would just believe."

When I read this passage, I think about me. About the lost people around me – and what God may be calling me to do. The coworker I don't believe could ever come to know Christ. The person I serve I don't even pray for. And, of course, the times when He wants me to step out on faith and tell my coworker about Christ, trusting in the work only God can do within her.

And what about when I am too afraid to dream BIG because I don't think it could ever come true? Oh, me of little faith! Perhaps those very dreams are from God, and He is calling me to strongly believe in the only God who can accomplish ALL things.

And you? Are you missing out by not believing as strongly as you should? Do you remember when God did mighty works in your life because you did believe strongly?

Today at work, believe strongly. Don't let Jesus pass you by. He has plans to do mighty works in your life. Let Him. And then praise Him!

Remember **the scariest verse in the Bible**. And then, don't let Him pass you by! Not today.

Prayer

Oh God, forgive me of my unbelief! I believe nothing is impossible for You. I believe You can melt the stone heart of one coworker and open the eyes of another. I believe You will do immeasurably more than I could ever ask or imagine. So please Lord, do it. I believe. I strongly believe. In Your Son's name, I pray. Amen.

Brooke Neale

Week 22, Day 4

riches in your heart

Reading

Luke 6:45 [ESV] Good comes from a good man because of the riches he has in his heart. Sin comes from a sinful man because of the sin he has in his heart. The mouth speaks of what the heart is full of.

Reflection

Have you ever lived with a bad roommate?

A good friend called complaining about the myriad of offenses her roommate commits. The dishes are never cleaned but remain stacked throughout the apartment. A stench comes from the refrigerator because of the weeks-old food conveniently pushed to the back. Furthermore, the roommate brought an immense amount of items from her previous residence that extensively brought clutter and chaos. In short, my friend is having trouble showing love and patience to a roommate who clearly doesn't think of those around her.

As a Christian, this wasn't the first time I've been asked about how one loves a seemingly "unlovable" person. I struggle, and I'm sure you've also struggled with this issue. The way we respond is a reflection of Christ. Hence, we must remember, at its base, love is a matter of the heart. Are there **riches in your heart**, or is your heart simply full of sin? To love an unlovable person, our hearts must be uncorrupted by the hatefulness of the world – uncorrupted even by the antics of a roommate.

So many people go to work from an apartment shared with roommates. Do you? As a *Christian public servant*, be aware of the potential damage the world can cause to your heart. Replace destructive worldly influences with supportive righteous influences from Christ. It's not easy, I know. But if you allow yourself to love the unlovable roommate, it might be easier to love the unlovable coworker!

Before you go to work today and before you return home, don't have sin in your heart. Instead, make sure there is nothing but **riches in your heart**. Your mouth will speak with the love found within. Every time.

Prayer

Lord Jesus, I want a heart filled with Your love and compassion. Help me in my daily struggle to live and work with those who may not necessarily recognize

Your righteousness. Help me show them Your love. In Your Name, I pray. Amen.

Kathryn Saunders

Week 22, Day 5

help keep the advantage

Reading

Exodus 17:11 [NLT] As long as Moses held up the staff in his hand, the Israelites had the advantage. But whenever he dropped his hand, the Amalekites gained the advantage.

Reflection

Brothers here on Life Row are from different parts of Alabama. They come from different kinds of families, and they are in different stages of appeals. Some went far in school, and some did not. Some are new to Life Row, and some have been here for many years. Everyone is different.

When everyone is different, there is a chance people do not help each other. But here we **help keep the advantage** for each other – even when the advantage is hard to find. A death of your mother – and knowing you cannot go to the funeral. The loss of a court appeal – knowing you are one step closer to the end. Just waking up and knowing you are not where you thought you would be in your life. And the loss of sleep from lying awake and thinking about it all.

Sometimes God plants us around people to **help keep the advantage**. Helping to hold someone strong like others did for Moses. Holding up hope for someone who needs it. Holding up someone's faith in God. *And this needs to be done where you live but also where you work.*

Today at work, **help keep the advantage** for someone. It may be a coworker or it may be someone you serve. It may be someone you see every day on the street going to work. Whoever it is, know that person will be in front of you today. Don't overlook that person.

On this workday, don't let the Amalekites gain the advantage.

Prayer

Father, in the name of Jesus, I pray. Thank You for planting people in my life to help me win. Let me **help keep the advantage** for someone else today. Amen.

Jimmy Davis, Jr.

Week 23, Day 1

just a fleeting memory

Reading

Matthew 3:1-3 [NIV] John the Baptist appeared preaching in the desert of Judea and saying, "Repent for the kingdom of heaven is at hand!" It was of him that the prophet Isaiah had spoken when he said: *A voice of one crying out in the desert, Prepare the way of the Lord, make straight his paths.*

Reflection

When the Christmas season drew near, everyone seemed to be in a hurry. A rush to get the house decorated, the tree adorned, Christmas cards, shopping, etc. Wow, there was a lot to prepare for! But, in all that rush, did the true meaning of Christmas get lost?

January is now **just a fleeting memory**. Like a whirlwind, February passed by too. And so has the season of Lent. We celebrated His resurrection. Did you make any changes? Or was Easter like Christmas, now **just a fleeting memory?**

You know at work it's easy to become engrossed in the "present moment." At times I was tasked with preparing months ahead for a big event. First, I began by making checklists, then setting up planning meetings, revising plans, calling other agencies for assistance, and laying out how the event was supposed to come off. As the event approached, tension seemed to increase – requiring more focus so nothing was overlooked. However, sometimes I would lose focus of the bigger picture – the event, itself.

You know it's easy to lose focus of the bigger heavenly picture once you are caught up in the moment. Just like in the days of old, *Christian public servants* have that same charge from Isaiah, "Prepare the way of the Lord, make straight his paths for the kingdom of heaven is at hand." You and I need to "prepare the way" for Jesus' return – even in the workplace – simply by setting the example: kindness to coworkers, citizens, and visitors; forgiveness for those who do us wrong; performing work duties with a positive attitude; and most importantly – demonstrating God's love for each person.

Don't let our Savior's gift become **just a fleeting memory**! Not even at work. Not even today.

Today at work, *make straight His path.*

Prayer

Heavenly Father, let me never take for granted You gave <u>me</u> the best gift to the world, Your dearly beloved Son. Help me prepare Your way in my workplace by giving me strength to be an example that leads others to You. Through my every action today, help me share the memory of what Your Son did for <u>me</u>. I ask this in Jesus' name. Amen.

Stephen Pincus

Week 23, Day 2

specks in coworkers' eyes

Reading

Luke 6:42(b) [NASB] You hypocrite, first take the log out of your own eye, and then you will see clearly to take out the speck that is in your brother's eye.

Reflection

A close friend recently said his most frustrating workplace interactions come with fellow Christians. He hears or reads things from them and thinks, "What are they thinking!? Are they acting Christ-like?" He said he knows what he is doing is truly God-inspired and cannot figure out how a Christian could think or act otherwise.

Oh, my!

I told my friend while his Christian coworkers may do wrong, he needs to be more Christ-like in his own behavior. He cannot assume only the worst from others and only the best from himself. He reflected on my advice and later told me his frustration with coworkers is largely about himself and not them.

My friend is not alone. Too often, you and I not only see the flaws in others but we are angry at them for having those flaws – especially when they are brothers- and sisters-in-Christ. Before speaking of their flaws, we must never forget we are all sinners and, therefore, perpetually flawed. Those **specks in coworkers' eyes** are in our own eyes and are usually larger than we think!

At work today, remember this: while your coworkers are flawed, so are you! Before pointing out their specks, try first to work through your own problems. You may find a better understanding of yourself leads to a more gracious understanding of those around you.

Today at work, remember those **specks in coworkers' eyes** aren't anything like the log in yours.

Prayer

Lord, I ask for forgiveness, for I am a sinner. May I be cognizant of the specks in my own sight when I look upon Your world. In Your name, I pray. Amen.

Michael Bednarczuk

Week 23, Day 3

God has blessed you

Reading

II Kings 7:9 [MSG] Finally they said to one another, "We shouldn't be doing this! This is a day of good news and we're making it into a private party! If we wait around until morning we'll get caught and punished. Come on! Let's go tell the news to the king's palace!"

Proverbs 11:25 [MSG] The one who blesses others is abundantly blessed; those who help others are helped.

II Corinthians 9:6 [NKJV] But this I say: He who sows sparingly will also reap sparingly, and he who sows bountifully will also reap bountifully.

Reflection

Think back on some way God blessed you at work. Do you ever have one of those epiphanies where you can see Him really teaching you something about His love for you in the workplace? Has God ever blessed you unexpectedly in the workplace because you were being an example for Christ or following what was right when others would choose the wrong path?

God has blessed you! When God blesses you, shouldn't you share it with others? In today's scripture, the lepers were blessed when they found food but recognized they needed to share with the people who were starving in the city. God blessed them with the goal of them sharing the blessing with others!

I have a challenge for YOU today. Write a short one paragraph story of how God has blessed you or taught you something in the workplace. Change the names, make it generic or third person if necessary. Then write a short paragraph of what the story taught you and/or how you applied it to your life. Next, write a third and final short paragraph that challenges others to apply the lessons or blessings **God has blessed you** with. End with a short, simple prayer of commitment to practice the lesson or thankfulness for God's blessing and a promise to remember what God has done for you. Find a relevant scripture or two (Google is great at this!) Finally, email what you have written to Jim Slack at jslack0229@live.com. Bless others with a *Christian Public Servant* devotional that can inspire.

God has blessed us all in the here and now. Isn't it our responsibility to share our blessings with others? God blessed you for a purpose. He teaches you for a purpose. That purpose is to advance His kingdom. What better way to recognize and show gratefulness for God's blessing on our lives than to be a blessing to others? We are blessed to be a blessing! And finally, guess what? If you do this and bless others because **God has blessed you**, God will bless you right back because you cannot out bless God!

Accept my challenge. Send us a devotional. **God has blessed you**. He loves you so much, and He wants you to love each other with His blessings.

Prayer

Lord, help me remember the blessings and lessons You have bestowed on my life. Help me bless others with Your blessings. Help me to do it TODAY, not tomorrow or the next, but TODAY. I can do all things through Christ Who strengthens ME. In Jesus' name, I pray. Amen.

Kevin Cooney

Week 23, Day 4

let it go

Reading

Colossians 3:12-13[NLT] Since God chose you to be the holy people he loves, you must clothe yourselves with tenderhearted mercy, kindness, humility, gentleness, and patience. Make allowance for each other's faults, and forgive anyone who offends you. Remember the Lord forgave you, so you must forgive others.

Reflection

The Greek translation of *forgiveness* is to **let it go**. If you're like me, how many times do you find yourself so angry or offended you cannot **let it go**? Does this ever happen at work?

It happens to me at work. Sometimes it seems I just can't forgive a coworker or supervisor. But when I don't **let it go**, God is convicting me because He has already set me apart and shown me the character He desires me to exhibit. My faith leads me to repent, and when I do, God forgives me! Yes, He will **let it go** only when I **let it go**!

I am not talking about workplace harassment or bullying or violence. If that happens to you, please take action because God does not want you to be harmed.

But if someone offends you in routine ways – still important ways – forgive that person. After all, He has chosen you to be one of the holy persons He loves – *even in your workplace*. So today, wear the clothes of tenderhearted mercy, kindness, humility, gentleness, and patience.

Yes, today at work, **let it go**.

Prayer

Lord, teach me to not hold on to those things that distort or jeopardize my witness. Let me remember who You are in times of chaos. Teach me Your art of forgiveness, and let me never forget to Whom I belong. Let me not fall into the traps of the world's standards. Rather, transform me and guide me. In Your name, I pray. Amen.

LaShonda Garnes

Week 23, Day 5

the door to one of the vending machines

Reading

Ephesians 4:27 [KJV] Neither give place to the devil.

Reflection

I had an awesome visit with my Christian brother a few weeks ago, and something happened that reminded me of today's verse. As we sat at a table in the visitation yard enjoying a talk, **the door to one of the vending machines** suddenly opened. And no correctional officer saw what had happened. I looked at my brother and said, "The devil is funny."

You see, too many times we don't act, love, respond, or forgive like a child of God. We give place to the enemy, which leads to pain – not only in our life but in the lives of others.

I could have given place to the devil when **the door to one of the vending machines** opened. I could have stolen a candy bar or ten candy bars, and it would not have been the end of the world. I mean, given I am on death row, there are other crimes just a little more serious – don't you think? But taking something for free – stealing something that does not belong to me – would have invited the devil to take place in my life. And it would have meant having my brother also give place to the evil one.

You may not be tempted to steal something when **the door to one of the vending machines** opens in your break room. Then again, you just might be tempted – especially if no one else is watching. Or your "vending machine" might be office supplies or something left on the counter.

Today at work, live like a child of the God who created you in His image. Don't give place to the devil – even when **the door to one of the vending machines** suddenly opens! The devil *is* funny.

Prayer

Father, in the name of Jesus, I pray. Thank You for creating me to be Your child so I will never give place to the devil. Amen.

Jimmy Davis, Jr.

Week 24, Day 1

all kinds of nasty weather

Reading

Galatians 6:9 [NIV] Let us not become weary in doing good, for at the proper time we will reap a harvest if we do not give up.

Reflection

Wouldn't it be great if every workday was that perfect "blue sky" spring morning! However, the real public sector workplace tests our minds, bodies, and spirits with **all kinds of nasty weather** from irate citizens, irritating coworkers, and intimidating bosses. Whatever the workplace climate, *Christian public servants* have eternal assurance, if we resist the impulse to "fight or flight," the Holy Spirit will guide, teach, and comfort us as we endure the inclement weather.

During this workweek, count on dealing with **all kinds of nasty weather** from many situations. No matter the storm, take time to pray and ask Jesus and the Holy Spirit to be the *umbrella for your soul*. Then count on the peace of God to return quickly.

So don't become weary in doing good in your workplace. Believe in the harvest that is surely coming! God's umbrella <u>will</u> give protection from **all kinds of nasty weather** you face this week and all the weeks that follow.

Prayer

Dear Lord, help me keep my eye on You during the wind and waves of my stormy workday. I know Your peace will return because You will never leave or forsake me. In Your name, I pray. Amen.

Gary E. Roberts

Week 24, Day 2

something that shows His love

Reading

1 John 4:10 [NLT] This is real love—not that we loved God, but that he loved us and sent his Son as a sacrifice to take away our sins.

Reflection

My desk is covered with all sorts of symbols of love – cards and notes from my wife, pictures of my kids, and even an hourglass, a gift from my wife, with the inscription *I love you every second of the day*. That hourglass is something that gets the attention of many coworkers.

All these things on my desk are wonderful because they show how much my <u>family</u> loves me. However, something recently dawned on me. I didn't have anything that shows how much <u>God</u> loves me. Oh, I know He loves me. So last night I added **something that shows His love** for me, and I gave it a place of honor on my desk.

Today when coworkers stop by, I know their eyes will be drawn to the spot on my desk where there is **something that shows His love** for me – as much as they are drawn to the hourglass. And who knows what conversations will take place!

Today at work, let me encourage you to do the same. It's great to have all those symbols of love from your family sitting on your desk. It's even greater to have **something that shows His love** for you sitting on your desk.

Hint: You don't have to look far for **something that shows His love** for <u>you</u>. God already gave you His Son! And <u>that</u> proves He loves you *every second of your life*!

Prayer

God, thank You for all the love You give me. Let me show others at work the love You freely give through Your Son, my Savior, Jesus Christ. It is in His name I pray. Amen.

Graham Somerset

Week 24, Day 3

one seat open

Reading

Luke 11:37 When Jesus had finished speaking, a Pharisee invited him to eat with him; so he went in and reclined at the table.

Reflection

I recently visited a dear Christian brother on death row. As we talked in the visitation yard, I noticed something that reminded me of today's verse. Each death row inmate must sit away from the other inmates – at an individual four-seat table. While a few inmates were fortunate to have three visitors, hence filling all seats at the table, most were not. My friend and I were the only ones at his table – and this is true each time I visit him.

I told my friend about a tradition in many Emmaus communities – of deliberately leaving **one seat open** at every table during each meal. That seat is for Jesus. The meal's blessing is sung, and the words invite Him to come sit at the table. Agape gifts are left at His seat, as they are for everyone, and an actual meal is served to the seat reserved for Jesus. Now, nobody expects Jesus to appear in the flesh at each table, but the effort symbolically reminds everyone He (through the Holy Spirit) is always near and should be present at each table and in each heart.

And so my friend and I talked about leaving **one seat open** for Jesus at our table in the visitation yard. And how sad it is too many times we don't invite Him to sit in an empty seat – let alone leaving **one seat open** specifically for Him. How different would the world be if everyone invited Him to sit for each meal? How changed would the workplace become if Jesus was invited to sit at each lunch table? We concluded our lives are enhanced each time Jesus sits at our table, and we took joy in knowing He is never too busy to enter our hearts.

Today at work, who will you invite to sit at your table? Will you leave **one seat open** for Jesus? Will you invite Him into your heart? If He accepted the invitation of a Pharisee – if He accepts the invitation from my friend on death row and me – certainly He will accept your invitation. He will gladly recline at your table. He will gladly recline in your heart.

Will you invite Jesus to sit at your table? Will you leave **one seat open**? Jesus will share much more than a meal. He will transform your heart, your workplace, and your life!

<u>Prayer</u>

Father God, I thank You for the gift and blessing of invitation. Let me always leave **one seat open** for Your Son – at my table and in my heart. It is in His name I pray. Amen.

James D. Slack

Week 24, Day 4

His encourager of hope

Reading

Psalm 105:1 (NLT) Give thanks to the LORD and proclaim his greatness. Let the whole world know what he has done.

Reflection

I once interned at a local government agency – I was the youngest by a solid 15 years. The full-time coworkers were well-established but highly stressed-out. Each felt the pressure of tremendous public scrutiny. At one point, the agency experienced drastic internal changes that left many employees even more emotionally and physically drained.

For some reason, several coworkers felt safe in talking with me about their stress. At first, I wondered why. After all, who wants anything to do with a 24-year-old intern? Yet they wanted to talk about their day. I did not mind. In fact, I cracked jokes and found things about which each could be thankful. I pointed out how the Lord was blessing them in so many ways – just as He was blessing me. As time went on, I began to view myself as **His encourager of hope**.

As *Christian public servants*, you and I are called to *let the whole world know what He has done*. The Good News He gives us must be shared with others. Yes, each one of us must be **His encourager of hope**.

So today, let the whole workplace know what He has done for you! Share it especially with those under the gun – those lost in anxiety; those victimized by fear. Share His Good News and proclaim His greatness.

Today at work, be **His encourager of hope**.

Prayer

Father, You have blessed me in so many ways. Let me fix my eyes on You, remember Your goodness, count my blessings, and share what You have done with those around me. Let me shower Your hope throughout this workday. In Jesus' name, I pray. Amen.

Angela Arbitter

Week 24, Day 5

with hearts in unity of cause

Reading

Nehemiah 2:18 [KJV] Then I told them of the hand of my God which was good upon me; as also the king's words that he had spoken unto me. And they said, let us rise up and build. So they strengthened their hands for this good work.

Reflection

How many times have you tried to rebuild a relationship? Maybe in your family. Or at church. Perhaps where you work. I have tried countless times, and it is impossible if you are the only one trying to repair what is broken.

Nehemiah had a heart to rebuild the wall of his people. Yet he could not do it alone. He started the process, but others said, "*Let us rise up and build.*" Let US rise up. Not just Nehemiah. They knew the wall could not be built without the help of others – **with hearts in unity of cause**.

Like Nehemiah, you and I need to have the heart to rebuild what we have taken for granted. What we have unvalued. What we have misused or even abused. But *nothing can be rebuilt without the help of one or more others* –all **with hearts in unity of cause**.

As you start work today, know it takes more than one to rebuild anything. As you rise up, know it takes more than just your heart. It is not easy, but think about the damage that can be repaired if you take the first step and find a way to encourage the other person or persons to join in.

When others strengthen their hands for good work, amazing things can be accomplished – even in your workplace.

Prayer

Father, in the name of Jesus, I pray. Thank You for renewing my heart so my heart may join others in building, rebuilding, and repairing. Amen.

Jimmy Davis, Jr.

Week 25, Day 1

your forgiveness quotient

Reading

Matthew 18:21-22 [NIV] Then Peter came to Jesus and asked, "Lord, how many times shall I forgive my brother or sister who sins against me? Up to seven times?" Jesus answered, "I tell you, not seven times, but seventy-seven times."

Reflection

How is **your forgiveness quotient**?

In every workplace, there is no shortage of people who can do things or say things that hurt us on so many levels. You and I cannot control the bad behavior of others, but God gives us a choice on how to respond: our own way of getting even, Peter's way of forgiving just a little, or Jesus' way of forgiving as many times as it takes.

So, as you drink your morning coffee, don't fantasize on how to take revenge and repay the suffering. <u>Remember</u> what Jesus said to Peter. <u>Realize</u> when you fail to forgive you become a prisoner in a jail of your own making – reliving the pain every time you see or think about that coworker or boss. <u>Know</u> the first step to reconciliation is to give the hurt to the Lord and ask for God's strength to forgive.

At the beginning of this workweek, reflect on your choice. How are you going to treat that *extra-grace-required* person? Are you "willing to be willing" to forgive countless times as it takes more than once to heal from the negative emotions? What path will you take? Your own? Peter's? Or the path of your Lord? As you go to work today, how is **your forgiveness quotient**? You and Peter are standing on the same mark. As with Peter, Jesus is standing right next to you. And He, too, is asking "how is **your forgiveness quotient**?" Is it high enough for Him?

Prayer

Heavenly Father, please grant me the strength to forgive those who hurt me. Help me be the good and faithful servant who recognizes Jesus forgave my sins and calls upon me to do the same with others. In Your Son's name, I pray. Amen.

Gary E. Roberts

Week 25, Day 2

like the watchmen in the Bible

Reading

Habakkuk 2:1(a) [NKJV] I will stand my watch And set myself on the rampart,

Ezekiel 3:17 [NKJV] Son of man, I have made you a watchman for the house of Israel; therefore hear a word from My mouth, and give them warning from Me.

Reflection

Where I live, "Old Man Winter" does not usually go quietly. One morning, I woke up knowing there was a heavy snowfall expected overnight. I was not looking forward to the morning commute or just getting out of my alley and my street to the main road. However, in the quiet of the morning, I heard a familiar sound of scraping going by my house. I looked out my windows to see not only the streets fully plowed but the alley as well. Public servants had been up all night preparing the city for the morning. I was so thankful for their planning, sacrifice, and desire to make things better for all of us. They were **like the watchmen in the Bible**.

You know all public servants are **like the watchmen in the Bible**. Some serve in the dark of the night and others during the light of day. Snowplow drivers. Street cleaners. Budget specialists. Correctional officers. Policy analysts. Police and firefighters. Librarians. Garbage pick-up crews. Custodians. Military. Information Technology specialists – just to name a few. All are *snowplow drivers* doing the jobs necessary for others to go about their daily routines with the fewest interruptions.

No one will thank you today for making their lives dependable. No one will notice you until you are not around to do the "plowing" for them. But as a *Christian public servant*, know Who has called you to guard the house. Truly you are **like the watchmen in the Bible**. May you have a blessed day with thanks, for you truly are **like the watchmen in the Bible**.

Prayer

Lord, help me remember the people who serve without being noticed. Thank You for them and their service. Bless them today for their faithfulness and remind them You notice what they do. In Jesus' name, I pray. Amen.

Kevin Cooney -- *A special thank you to the public servants of Snoqualmie, Washington USA who plowed my street and inspired this devotional.*

Week 25, Day 3

move mountains through faith

Reading

Mark 11:22-24 [NLT] Then Jesus said to the disciples, "Have faith in God. I tell you the truth, you can say to this mountain, 'May you be lifted up and thrown into the sea,' and it will happen. But you must really believe it will happen and have no doubt in your heart. I tell you, you can pray for anything, and if you believe that you've received it, it will be yours."

Reflection

How's life? Things good right now? Just so-so? Or are you searching for answers to no avail?

Every day we face trials in the workplace. Some are deadlines, others are meeting goals and making difficult decisions. Still other challenges center on difficult coworkers, managers, and citizens you serve. Sometimes the challenge is the loss of a job. What if the lost job belonged to you? I am guessing that would not make this a good day. You might be asking "why me"? You might be at the end of your rope.

This happened to a friend of mine, and the very next day after he was fired, God spoke through this reading. My friend had to trust God with his circumstances, career, and finances – trust in Him more than ever before. He had to believe he could **move mountains through faith** in Him – a God who has already gone before and worked everything out.

What challenge is in your way at work today? Whatever it is, know you can **move mountains through faith** in Him. Lay your heart out to God and believe He has already taken care of "it" but in His time. Today is not going to be easy, but trust in Him. If you believe you've received it, it will be yours!

Yes, you can **move mountains through faith** in Him – no matter how your life is going today.

Prayer

Dear God, help me trust You completely and know You will lead and guide me. You already know the outcome. Please remove any doubt in my heart because I know all things work for the good to those who love You. In Your Son's name, I pray. Amen.

Chris Whitaker

Week 25, Day 4

where the real treasure is found

Reading

Proverbs 3:5 [NASB] Trust in the LORD with all your heart And do not lean on your own understanding.

Matthew 6:21 [NASB] for where your treasure is, there your heart will be also.

Reflection

Well, it's 7:00 a.m., and I haven't yet received *The Christian Public Servant* devotional in my inbox. I always read this treasure as I get ready for work. But, I guess, not today. What am I going to do? Ahhh, here it comes. Thank You, Lord!

And then it dawned on me. I've become dependent on another earthly thing. That's OK, I guess, especially since it is a devotional – something directing me to God. (I mean, it could be something bad that attracts me.) But do I depend as much <u>directly</u> on our loving God? If I ranked every thing and item I treasure in my life, where would He be on that list? At the top? Or someplace else?

So am I really dependent on an email devotional to get me through the workday? Or am I dependent on my Lord?

I think you know my answer. But if I don't explicitly focus on Him, my heart can get lost. I start taking God for granted. I forget **where the real treasure is found**. Devotionals help, sure, but even that is not what I need. I need to lean less on things of this world and focus more on the Lord – Himself – directly. I need to trust Him with all my heart – regardless if an email devotional arrives early or late.

So where does God rank in your priorities this morning? With apologies to all the devotionals out there, do not forget **where the real treasure is found**. As you get ready for work, as you travel to work, and as you work at work – trust in God with all your heart because only with Him will you find your heart.

Yes, today at work, do not forget **where the real treasure is found**. And then have a tremendously <u>treasured</u> day!

Prayer

Lord, may I strive to keep You first and foremost in my daily work life. May I honor You generously through the many blessings I receive from You. In Your name, I pray. Amen.

Alan Cox

Week 25, Day 5

balance in the storm

Reading

Mark 4:39 [KJV] And he arose, and rebuked the wind, and said unto the sea, Peace, be still. And the wind ceased, and there was a great calm.

Reflection

Two weeks ago, I got out of balance. Everything got to me – my ministry with the brothers and my ministry with some of the correctional officers. And my ministry with my family. It seems like everyone wanted or needed something from me. I was also anxious about something I would face in the upcoming days. There were so many storms at that point, and I knew I was out of balance.

Jesus faced a storm, and He did two things we all need to do. He got up, faced the problem, and kept His **balance in the storm**. See, Jesus did not allow the problem to speak to Him. Instead, He spoke to the problem. He kept his balance so He could gain victory.

You may face a lot today. A storm at home. A storm of memory and regret. A storm of present words. And that storm may follow you to work. It may start at work and follow you home.

I know how you feel, for I have storms all around.

As you get ready to do His work today, use Jesus as your example. Speak to your problem rather than letting the problem speak to you. Get up in the boat and keep **balance in the storm**.

The wind <u>will</u> cease, and there <u>will</u> be a great calm.

Prayer

Father, in the name of Jesus, I pray. Thank You for keeping me focused on You in the life of my storms. Thank You for Your balance. Amen.

Jimmy Davis, Jr.

Week 26, Day 1

even more is required

Reading

Genesis 50:19-21 [NIV] But Joseph said to them, "Don't be afraid. Am I in the place of God? You intended to harm me, but God intended it for good to accomplish what is now being done, the saving of many lives. So then, don't be afraid. I will provide for you and your children." And he reassured them and spoke kindly to them.

Reflection

I'm sure you've witnessed it. You may have even been a part of it. It's not unusual for one to see grudges held even over the slightest error. As a *Christian public servant*, you know forgiveness is necessary – but at times **even more is required**.

Each year much of the world celebrates St. Patrick's Day. You know, the day many wear green and too many go out and drink green concoctions. It is a shame so few know the powerful truth about St. Patrick. Do you?

Patrick was an English farm boy who was kidnapped and enslaved in Ireland. Once free, he prepared to return and share Christ with his very captors. Thankfully, he was successful because Ireland became the repository of many manuscripts from antiquity we have today as a devotion to God.

Like Patrick, Joseph knew, although the intent was to harm him, God used that opportunity to show more than forgiveness – he provided for them and their children.

You don't have to remember St. Patrick just on the day we honor him. What he did is as important as what Joseph did. And what both did should be what you and I do today.

As this workweek begins, forgive those who are harming you. But know **even more is required**. Take care of that coworker in some special way. After all, as a *Christian public servant*, you are in the place of God – just like Joseph. Right?

Forgive, but know **even more is required** because you are in the place of God!

Prayer

Dear Lord, how can I hold a grudge when I know what price You paid so I may be forgiven? Help me look for opportunities to forgive and even more. When I put that into practice, I may find I give others the benefit of the doubt. I may find I am offended far less often. Like St. Patrick, I will truly chase snakes out of my workplace! In Your Name, I pray. Amen.

Stan Best

Week 26, Day 2

enough for Who

Reading

Ephesians 6:7 [NLT] Work with enthusiasm, as though you were working for the Lord rather than for people.

Colossians 3:23-24 [NLT] Whatever you do, work at it with all your heart, as working for the Lord, not for human masters, since you know that you will receive an inheritance from the Lord as a reward. It is the Lord Christ you are serving.

Reflection

Recently I helped a citizen who had a lot on her plate, and it was obvious she was having trouble focusing. After a while, she murmured she didn't believe God loved her anymore because all that was happening in her life. My heart sank, and I began to encourage her and offer my prayers. I started to assist her *above and beyond* my role in this department. I even reached out to colleagues in other units to help find her resources.

Yet afterward, I learned she called my director and complained about me. You see, she is white and I am black, and no matter how much I went *above and beyond* for her, she was upset someone like her had to depend on someone like me.

Thankfully, I served her with the attitude of Christ. Even after the report, I continued to work behind the scenes to find the resources she needed. And my director thanked me for serving unto Christ and not the racist person who stood before me.

Have you ever experienced a citizen inflicted with racism or sexism or nationalism or faithism? Was it difficult going *above and beyond* the call of duty because you knew it just wasn't going to be enough? But did you ask yourself "**enough for Who**?" As a *Christian public servant*, see beyond what you see in people and continue to serve unto Christ.

Yes, today at work, don't allow the misbehaviors and bigotries of the world to change Who and how you serve. Go *above and beyond* at each opportunity. Do more than enough at each turn. Just remember **enough for Who**?

And then continue to serve Him!

<u>Prayer</u>

Father God, thank You for allowing me to serve You. Continue to guide me and provide me wisdom to do Your will and not man's. In Jesus' Name, I pray. Amen.

LaShonda Garnes

Week 26, Day 3

a list for you

Reading

Ephesians 2:9-10 [NIV] not by works, so that no one can boast. For we are God's handiwork, created in Christ Jesus to do good works, which God prepared in advance for us to do.

Reflection

Do you supervisor or lead? How often do you prepare tasks for those who work for you? Sometimes they are tasks you don't want to do. Sometimes they are tasks you don't have time to do. Sometimes they are tasks you don't have the skills to do. But always you expect the delegated tasks to make you and your unit look good. Right?

Did you know God has prepared **a list for you**? A list of good works just for you! Not because He needs you. Not because He can't do it on His own. No. He has prepared **a list for you** because He loves to grow you, to build you, to stretch you, to involve you in His detailed plan.

Once you accept Christ, you must also accept the fact nothing you do is for your own glory. Not anymore. Not even in your workplace. You are now working for a greater purpose than your own. You are saved by grace, and you work from a place of grace.

So you may delegate out of need, and you used to delegate out of selfishness. But God delegates out of love and grace. And you need to do the same.

Today at work, God has prepared **a list for you**. A list of good works just for you. But nothing will be done for your glory, only His. And that will affect how you delegate to others.

And what a different workplace it will be!

Prayer

Father, thank You for involving me in the smallest details of Your biggest plan! Thank You for the intimate vision You have for my life. I ask You to help me lead like You lead. Help me change my motives on this work day. Help me grow those You have entrusted me to lead. Help me be the light. I pray these things in Your Son's name. Amen.

Kathryn Saunders

Week 26, Day 4

fail with grace

Reading

Romans 8:1 [ESV] There is therefore now no condemnation for those who are in Christ Jesus.

Reflection

I have a confession. As a *Christian public servant*, I hate to make mistakes and fail. I beat myself up and take out the internal whip of punishment. As an educator and practitioner in government, I know making mistakes and failing is essential to individual and collective learning and development. However, when it comes to "my performance," I would rather never test that principle.

But lately, I am learning an important concept: to *forgive myself* when I make a mistake and reject self-condemnation and shame. As a recovering perfectionist, I reject the fantasy and prideful delusion I can ever be perfect. I am learning to **fail with grace**, and this enables me to step out of the safe harbor and comfort zones.

If you're like me and have to resist the temptation of beating yourself up, rest in the freedom of knowing God does not demand perfection of performance. He only demands an attitude of forgiveness and a desire to learn from your mistakes.

Today at work, you will make mistakes. You may even mess up big time. And when you do, may you **fail with grace** knowing you are in Jesus Christ!

Prayer

Dear Jesus, I pray for the strength to forgive myself when I make a mistake. Only You are perfect. Help me recognize the only true failure is to quit. In Your name, I pray. Amen.

Gary E. Roberts

Week 26, Day 5

hold onto peace

Reading

Exodus 14:13-14 [KJV] And Moses said unto the people, Fear ye not, stand still, and see the salvation of the LORD, which he will shew to you to day: for the Egyptians whom ye have seen to day, ye shall see them again no more for ever. The LORD shall fight for you, and ye shall hold your peace.

Reflection

Each day from 3:00 a.m. to 6:00 a.m., I work as a runner on my hall. I get things for brothers locked in their cells: hot water, ice, maybe heat something up in the microwave, or just be someone they can talk to at that time of day. (Most are awake since breakfast comes before 3:00 a.m.) I am around over 50 different mindsets – correctional officers and brothers. Some are saved and some are not. It is not uncommon to run into "battles." A brother wants to take out his anxieties and aggression on you. Shouting. Sometimes throwing. Not being thankful for your efforts.

It is tempting to jump in and try to battle back and defend yourself against a brother at 3:00 a.m. Or it is easy to just walk away and be of no service to that brother. But every time I try to fight my own battle or show the brother I cannot be pushed around, I lose my own peace.

So I try to **hold onto peace**. It is all I have in life. If something arises at my "workplace," I try my best to allow God to fight the battle for me. It is not easy, but I have no choice if I want to **hold onto peace**.

Today at work, try not to fight your own battles. He is fighting for you, so you don't need to defend yourself. If you choose to fight, I am afraid you will miss God. You will lose your peace, and like me, peace is all you have in life.

As difficult as it is, try to **hold onto peace**. The Lord shall fight for you.

He is fighting for you right now.

Prayer

Father, in the name of Jesus, I pray. Thank You for fighting all my battles so I not only **hold onto peace** but can carry out Your will. Amen.

Jimmy Davis, Jr.

Week 27, Day 1

with road rage

Reading

Psalm 121:8 [ASB] The Lord will keep your going out and your coming in from this time forth and forevermore.

Genesis 28:15 [NIV] I am with you and will watch over you wherever you go

Reflection

Driving to work, I encountered a driver **with road rage**. He apparently expected me to move out of his way simply because he pulled in behind me and flashed his headlights. It wasn't safe for me to change lanes at that moment, so I maintained my position and speed. Apparently, that driver didn't appreciate my decision and indicated his displeasure (and immaturity) by flashing a hand gesture when he finally passed.

I said a silent prayer and asked God to bless him.

The commute to and from the job is a necessary part of the workday. You are probably prepared to model Christ at work, but are you prepared to model His love en route to work?

In your commute today, know the Lord is with you and watching over you. He wants you to be courteous but not unsafe. So say a prayer for the tailgater, the texter, the email checker, the phoner, the speeder, and the one **with road rage**. Ask God to watch over them, too.

And who knows. You might just get the opportunity to minister to one of them at work!

Prayer

Dear God, thank You for being with me each day during my passage to and from work. When I move through the rush-hour traffic congestion, keep me safe, as well as the drivers around me. In Jesus' name, I pray. Amen.

Samuel Henry

Week 27, Day 2

live by HIS standard

Reading

Matthew 20:1-12 [NLT] The Kingdom of Heaven is like the landowner who went out early one morning to hire workers for his vineyard. He agreed to pay the normal daily wages and sent them out to work…at nine o'clock…at noon…at three o'clock… at five o'clock...the landowner told them, "Then go out and join the others in my vineyard"… When those hired at five o'clock were paid, each received a full day's wage. When those hired first came to get their pay, they assumed they would receive more. But they, too, were paid a day's wage. When they received their pay, they protested to the owner, those people worked only one hour, and yet you've paid them just as much as you paid us who worked all day in the scorching heat.

Reflection

Often I read this story and feel much like the first workers of the day. I feel like I should receive more for the work I am doing. I live right, don't steal, haven't murdered anyone, pay my taxes, and try my best to do right by the people in my life – even the ones I don't like. I try to **live by HIS standard**, but in the end, I see others winning. They lie for promotions, engage in sexual sin, and do whatever the boss wants – even when unethical – just to get ahead. How frustrated I would get. I was doing my best to **live by HIS standard** as everyone else got ahead. I felt left out and stuck.

Then one day I realized I should be thankful for the work. It is *in the work* I find passion. It is *in the work* I reach and connect with people. It is *in the work* I see God move in people's lives. When I moaned and groaned about what I wasn't getting, I was missee all I was getting. I missed the opportunity to pray for a coworker. I missed the opportunity to plant a seed with my boss. I missed the opportunity to show compassion to the citizens I serve.

Yes, I learned when I **live by HIS standard**, He can work through me and bless me. In addition, I realized my rewards are eternal. I have peace, HIS providing love, and the hope of an eternal home. I don't live in fear and worry. Instead, I **live by HIS standard** and I am confident He is right beside me along the way.

So, on those days when you are frustrated by everyone else winning, rest assured you have already won.

As you **live by HIS standard**, the Savior is faithful to bless the work you are doing.

Prayer

Father, thank You for the daily work. Thank You for finding me and saving me long before I ever knew I needed a Savior. Thank You for working through me. Give me strength to work through the hot days, the long days, the holidays. Father, give me a peace in my purpose. Give me reassurance You still see me and You haven't forgotten me. Thank You for my Savior, Jesus Christ. It is in His name I pray. Amen.

Kathryn Saunders

Week 27, Day 3

capture the beauty

Reading

Romans 1:20 [ESV] For his invisible attributes, namely, his eternal power and divine nature, have been clearly perceived, ever since the creation of the world, in the things that have been made. So they are without excuse.

Reflection

When was the last time you took a stroll with a friend who loves photography? It may sound like a strange question, perhaps a little obscure, but really think about it – when was the last time? I ask this because I have a friend who, despite being an incredibly accomplished *Christian public servant*, is also a photographer who can **capture the beauty** in just about anything. He is never without his camera. He knows how to **capture the beauty** and share it.

My friend can pick out unique items most people just miss and walk past. He *makes art out of the unusual*, seeing God's creation a little differently than the typical person. My friend "sees" the details around him rather than just "looking" straight ahead.

This is what all Christians ought to be doing every day. We can "see" how God works around us while non-believers just "look" around without seeing the beauty as a created work by a loving God.

As a *Christian public servant*, use your ability to see Christ in order to project Him outward in your daily life. Non-believers will then be able to see Christ in you by just looking.

God has created you to radiate His eternal power and divine nature to the people you meet each day in the workplace. When you go to work today, "see" those who might need God – His grace, His love, and His hope. Like my friend, **capture the beauty** of what you see. Be a shining beacon of Christ to all you meet.

Prayer

Lord, let me see You and Your workings in my life today. Let me be a light that enables others around me to see You and the beauty You bring to their lives. Bless me at work so I may be a blessing to those around me. In Jesus' name, I pray. Amen.

Chip Harrell

Week 27, Day 4

things simply not known

Reading

Deuteronomy 29:29 [ESV] The secret things belong to the Lord our God, but the things that are revealed belong to us and to our children forever, that we may do all the words of this law.

Reflection

Since you and I spend the largest chunk of time at work, it's not surprising our faith is often tested there. Usually, the test is not a direct challenge <u>to</u> our faith. No, it comes from a question <u>about</u> our faith. Why does the Bible say this or that? How does this parable reconcile with that parable? Or maybe the question is about implementation? How can a loving God permit children to die from starvation, disease, or a chemical gas attack by an evil dictator?

The TV or newspaper in the break room often brings up many questions about faith, and you may not have the "right" answer – or any answer that seems "good enough." After all, the Holy Bible is our owner's manual, sure enough, but it is a manual with many complex sections. And the world acts almost random with too many evil people.

When things come up at work about your faith and you don't know the answer, keep in mind what scripture says. Those things biblically revealed and relationally known through Jesus belong to you. But there will be **things simply not known** – the secret things belonging to Him – and those things require faith in His wisdom and love.

So at work today, there <u>will</u> be **things simply not known** by you or the world. Just have courage to stand in faithful love and walk in the power of His might. Trust in what He reveals to you. Have faith in what is known by Him.

Prayer

Father, there is so much I do not know about You, and there is even more I do not understand about this world You create each day. Give me faith in knowing You know and strength of trust to know what You want me to know. In Your Son's name, I pray. Amen.

Chris Summers

Week 27, Day 5

through eyes of grace

Reading

Ruth 2:10 [KJV] Then she fell on her face, and bowed herself to the ground, and said unto him, Why have I found grace in thine eyes, that thou shouldest take knowledge of me, seeing I am a stranger?

Reflection

A few weeks ago, someone made my heart smile. Not only is he praying for me to someday be off death row, he is praying for my release from prison. He said he has plans for me every Sunday. He wants me to go to his church with his family, and then join them for Sunday dinner. He said I was part of his family – not a stranger – and this is what his family does. My friend was not just going through the motions. He was viewing me **through eyes of grace**.

I am encouraged by many sisters- and brothers-in-Christ who have come into my life, even though I am at first a "stranger" to them. Most by prayer, some by letter, and a few by prison ministry visits. I know there are those who know me only as a stranger and are just going through the motions, trying to say the "right" thing. But <u>real</u> encouragement brings a smile to my heart because it is given freely to <u>this</u> stranger **through eyes of grace**.

Is there a stranger needing your encouragement? At work? It need not be someone released from prison. (But you'd be surprised at the people around you who were once in prison.) Is there a stranger where you work or where you eat lunch or where you buy a newspaper or coffee? Is this stranger "there" on the way to work, as you walk into your building, or on the way home from work?

Remember Boaz did more than take knowledge of Ruth; he gave her grace. And grace, my friend, is the *mercy and love of God – of Jesus Christ*. Grace is giving that mercy and love to everyone – especially to that stranger.

Today find that stranger and give encouragement **through eyes of grace**.

Prayer

Father in the name of Jesus, I pray to thank You for continuing to mold my eyes to be the eyes of mercy and love – to be used to show strangers Your grace. Amen.

Jimmy Davis, Jr.

Week 28, Day 1

overcome evil with good

Reading

Romans 12:21 [NIV] Be not overcome of evil, but **overcome evil with good**.

Reflection

I had a coworker who was very difficult to work with. She was not a team player and often tried to avoid completing her portion of team projects. (Although, she often had time to read personal email and novels!)

Once as I was leaving to go home, I noticed she was still working to meet a deadline. Oh! How easy it would be to leave and let her fail.

But as I walked to my car, I was convicted to **overcome evil with good**. This was an opportunity to be like Christ and show her love. I dropped my bag in the car and walked back inside. We worked together for a couple hours, and she met the deadline.

Do you have a difficult coworker? Or is it a citizen you serve routinely? Do not be **overcome by evil** and seek revenge when you find them struggling.

Today at work, show the love of Christ and **overcome evil with good**.

Prayer

Heavenly Father, thank You for Your guiding Word. Help me **overcome evil with good** so others may see You working in my life. Thank You for Your example. In Jesus' name, I pray. Amen.

TaQuesha Brandon

Week 28, Day 2

pray for your supervisor

Reading

Titus 3:1-2 [ESV] Remind them to be submissive to rulers and authorities, to be obedient, to be ready for every good work, to speak evil of no one, to avoid quarreling, to be gentle, and to show perfect courtesy toward all people.

1 Timothy 2:1-2 [ESV] First of all, then, I urge that supplications, prayers, intercessions, and thanksgivings be made for all people, for kings and all who are in high positions, that we may lead a peaceful and quiet life, godly and dignified in every way.

Reflection

I once served in student government at college. I worked with many, but one person was in control of the entire organization. He and I joined together on a lot of projects, but we did not always agree on the boundaries of each other's roles. This, of course, led to disagreements. Sometimes knock-down-drag-out arguments. And while ultimately I was submissive in my role, looking back, I really dropped the ball when it came to praying for his vision and success.

As a *Christian public servant*, you work under the authority of others. You may not always agree with the direction, decisions, or values of your supervisor, but you should continue to be submissive to her. And you must always remember Christ commands you to **pray for your supervisor**.

So at work today, do just that. It doesn't matter whether you agree or disagree. You need to **pray for your supervisor** because he has appointed authority.

And when you **pray for your supervisor**, you will please God.

And He will bless both you and your supervisor!

Prayer

Dear Lord, thank You for the standards You set for me. As a believer, I want to follow Your appointed authorities. Remind me to pray for my supervisor and her supervisor. At work, let me be in submission. Plant patience in my heart to wait for all the good things to come! In Your name, I pray. Amen.

Paul Bayer

Week 28, Day 3

focus on God

Reading

Psalm 145:16 [HCSB] You open Your hand and satisfy the desire of every living thing.

Reflection

Great news! I received a considerable raise at my job! I worked so hard, and the past few months were very stressful. Despite the hard work and long hours, I kept my **focus on God**. Because my prayers centered on Him, not me, I felt His constant guidance and presence throughout this anxious time.

Upon learning about the raise, I quickly prayed a silent prayer of gratitude to God. However, as soon as I finished my prayer, I lost my **focus on God**. My mind automatically began wandering toward the things I could buy with my increased income. I started to imagine how my life would be better with access to luxuries and how I would be protected from the vagaries of everyday life. I started thinking about what *I* had accomplished and how *I* deserved this raise. Yes, *I* deserved these nice things.

In the middle of this revelry, I felt the Spirit of God speak to my spirit, "Where am I in all of this?" OOPS! I had lost my **focus on God** Who provides for everything *I* have.

When you are on top of the mountain, in moments of great self-satisfaction, and when everything is going your way, it is in those times *you* need God the most. Do not forget in the moment nothing accomplished is possible without God. Your complete reliance on Him in times of hardship is easy because there is nowhere else to turn. As soon as things start looking up, though, don't begin to look only to yourself as the source of your own success.

Whether this will be a good day or a bad day, remember all blessings flow from God and His eternal love for you. Resolve today to have the same attitude of thanksgiving to God no matter life's circumstances. Don't focus on yourself; **focus on God**.

Prayer

Dear Lord, I thank You for every blessing You provide me. Help me never to replace You with my own pride. For it is only through You I am anything. Help me to remember, in both good times and bad, You are the source of everything in my life. In Jesus' name, I pray. Amen.

Joshua Nierle

Week 28, Day 4

spice things up

Reading

Leviticus 2:13 [ESV] You shall season all your grain offerings with salt. You shall not let the salt of the covenant with your God be missing from your grain offering; with all your offerings you shall offer salt.

Matthew 5:13 [ESV] You are the salt of the earth, but if salt has lost its taste, how shall its saltiness be restored? It is no longer good for anything except to be thrown out and trampled under people's feet.

Reflection

Have you ever come out of a meeting at work feeling a sour aftertaste? Whether it was the subject discussed or the negative comments participants made, it left you with a bad impression. I have had my share. But after a few cynical and negative meetings left me heavy, I asked myself what I could do to **spice things up**? You know what I mean: lighten things a bit to bring out the best of what is offered and make everyone's time worthwhile.

Salt is probably the best-known spice. It is a flavoring agent and a food preservative. It balances sweetness and helps suppress other flavors, such as bitterness. It contains the sodium element, an essential nutrient our bodies need in small amounts. And where I live, salt is also essential to thawing ice on the roads during winter.

Jesus says <u>we</u> are the salt of the earth. You and I are to serve as a <u>preservative</u> (to stop the moral decay of our sin-infected world) and to **spice things up** (to show the excitement of living a life in Christ). As *Christian public servants*, you are I are blessed to have the opportunity to bring out the best in others, to soften even the hardened hearts of non-believers. We are to pray for our entourage and spread God's love in their lives to thaw the ice on their life roads that lead their way to God!

Salt is so important Jesus warns us not to lose our saltiness by becoming disobedient and indifferent.

Today at work, don't lose your saltiness. Don't give in to badmouthing. Don't sink to bitterness. Resist rumors. Don't let negativity taint your day. Instead, sprinkle discussions with love and laughter. Give your interlocutors food for thought. Pray before you throw out a comment.

Today at work, **spice things up**! Don't let the salt of the covenant with your God be missing!

Prayer

Dear Father, thank You for Your living word, especially Your warnings. Provide me with patience and courage to be of good heart with everyone I meet today at work – even those who may mock me for being so positive and supportive. I am Your public servant, and I pray You restore me to Your purpose of flavoring the world. In the name of Jesus, I pray. Amen.

Evelyne F. Altema

Week 28, Day 5

the road followed

Reading

Acts 15:19 [NLT] And so my judgment is that we should not make it difficult for the Gentiles who are turning to God.

Reflection

When I was a youngster, I started to imitate my uncles. They were big and strong, and I wanted to be just like them. They had good qualities – like taking care of family, being kind to me, and even letting me tag along with them. But they also had some bad qualities. Robbing. Gangs. Fights. Drugs. Things like that. And I imitated them in both the good ways and some of the bad ways. But overall, the bad won out, and **the road followed** did not turn me to God. I won't blame them for where I am today, but that road ended at the gate to death row. And I arrived here not knowing Christ.

A lot of times, as Christians, you and I are not aware others are watching. And because we are *Christian public servants*, the number of people watching is much larger than we think. Many want to imitate you and me, but we don't know which behaviors are shaping them.

We think we are always on the righteous path. Right? But think again. Bad attitude today? Selfishness yesterday? Judgmental every day? Or perhaps we are just filled with too many Christian rules that turn off would-be believers. A lot of times we make it difficult for others to take **the road followed** to Christ.

Is there someone at work who is watching you? Wanting to know what it means to be a believer? Wanting to imitate you because you claim to know **the road followed** to Christ?

Unlike my uncles, don't assume that person sees only your best qualities.

Today at work, make sure that person knows **the road followed** does not turn away from God.

Prayer

Father, in the name of Jesus, I pray. Keep me *street-wise* so my behavior points others down the road that leads to You. Amen.

Jimmy Davis, Jr.

Week 29, Day 1

a name really matters

Reading

Genesis 3:20 [NIV] Adam named his wife Eve, because she would become the mother of all the living.

Proverbs 31:10 [NIV] A wife of noble character who can find? She is worth far more than rubies.

Reflection

It's very discouraging to hear coworkers speak ill of their spouses. It may only be a joke, but the *Christian public servant* should not participate in such jokes. There is nothing funny about hearing a spouse called "the old ball and chain" or "a lazy bum" or even worse. Yes, my friend, **a name really matters**. What we call people affects how we and others see them.

Adam named his wife Eve. He knew she would be the mother of all humanity. It is not important that he named her but when he named her. Adam named Eve after the fall of mankind and the curse from God on all creation. We might forgive Adam if, at that moment, he could not see his wife as some great woman. But he calls her the "mother of all living," and it makes a difference in who she becomes.

If you are blessed with a marriage, then cherish this gift from God. Of course, your spouse will do something to let you down now and then, but that does not define that person. If you let it be known every day how your spouse is worth "far more than rubies," then your spouse will become more precious than gems. --- esspecially to you! So each day, say encouraging words about your spouse. Say them so your coworkers will hear. Do this so you can be a role model for your coworkers. Tell them **a name really matters**. It not only affects the way others see your spouse, it affects the way they see you.

Prayer

Dear Lord, I love my wife. Other than Jesus she is the greatest blessing You have bestowed on me. May the way I refer to her give voice to her value and show others the way to call their spouses. Help me encourage coworkers to see their spouses as You see them. In this way, there might be a little more of heaven here on earth. In Jesus' name, I pray. Amen.

Stan Best

Week 29, Day 2

fix both eyes on what is unseen

Reading

2 Corinthians 4:16-18 [NLV] Therefore we do not lose heart. Though outwardly we are wasting away, yet inwardly we are being renewed day by day. For our light and momentary troubles are achieving for us an eternal glory that far outweighs them all. So we fix our eyes not on what is seen, but on what is unseen. For what is seen is temporary, but what is unseen is eternal."

Romans 8:28 [NIV] And we know that in all things God works for the good of those who love him, who have been called according to his purpose.

Reflection

Several years ago, I went on a crazy self-discovery search. I had gone through a lot and wanted to discover more about who I was at the core of my heart. I stripped away all my safeguards to focus on God and discern His will for my life. Well, His will led me to travel 800 miles away from every safety net and support system I once heavily relied on.

I've discovered much along my journey. Most importantly, I found I struggle with the *fear of failing*. Whether in school, work, or relationships, the *fear of failing* mentally exhausted me and, worse, hindered my ability to trust God.

Does <u>fear</u> ever interfere with your relationship with God? As *Christian public servants*, God wants you and me to **fix both eyes on what is unseen** – put all faith and trust in Him.

Yes, failure sometimes seems inevitable. One small error can lead to major negative consequences. Failures in the workplace can get you fired. While labor laws tend to give some job security, this *fear of failing* remains haunting.

The awesome thing about God is He will <u>never</u> fire you. He will never kick <u>you</u> off His team. He will use each failure to transform you into something greater. Something stronger. Something of unlimited value. He will take your "lump of coal" and turn it into a beautiful diamond.

Today at work, trust God and **fix both eyes on what is unseen**. Do not let the fear of failure burden you. God <u>is</u> transforming you into something greater!

Prayer

Father, I am Your precious diamond. You see no failure in me. Let my heart and mind not be burdened by the fear of failure today as I recognize You as my ultimate boss. Take my work today, Father, and make it for Your glory. In Your Son's name, I pray. Amen.

Angela Arbitter

Week 29, Day 3

trust the Artist of that canvas

Reading

Galatians 3:3 [NIV] Are you so foolish? After beginning by means of the Spirit, are you now trying to finish by means of the flesh?

Reflection

This week marks the 3rd anniversary at my job. While the amount of time may not sound like much, it truly has been a journey. I never expected it to be easy, but it has definitely been worth it. If broken down into the particulars of single days, this time may look very ordinary. However, if examined at a much higher level, these three years have been extraordinary. The time here at this job, like my time here on earth, gives testimony to me being a work-in-progress – like *an unfinished portrait*. And what I've learned in my job is I am not the artist; I am just the bare canvas. And to be successful, I must **trust the Artist of that canvas**.

Every day we have a choice to make: turn over our dreams and progress to God or pick up the load and try to go it alone. Paul asked members of the Galatian church to examine their hearts. As believers, you and I must do that, too. I know it's hard to *remain in faith*. But God has started a work in you, and it's your responsibility to trust in what He promised to bring to completion.

Before you go to work today, examine your heart and your actions. Are you relying on God? Or are you relying only on your own strength? Do you intend to try to paint your own future today? Or will you confess you are simply the canvas – His canvas – and then **trust the Artist of that canvas**? Today, **trust the Artist of that canvas** and not yourself. The choice belongs to you, but I pray you will choose wisely. Do not let this day finish by just the means of flesh. ---- Do not be so foolish.

Prayer

Father, I thank You for being intimately involved in my life. Help me be honest with me. Let personal deceit not live within me. Give me strength, wisdom, knowledge, and peace to have *remaining faith* in You. *Crazy faith* that believes the vision and purpose You have set before me. Father, help me lay it all down at Your feet. What I started in faith, let me finish in faith. I pray these things in Jesus' name. Amen.

Kathryn Saunders

Week 29, Day 4

work problems beyond your control

Reading

2 Chronicles 20:15 [NIV] He said: "Listen, King Jehoshaphat and all who live in Judah and Jerusalem! This is what the LORD says to you: 'Do not be afraid or discouraged because of this vast army. For the battle is not yours, but God's.

Reflection

One of the loneliest situations in the workplace is to have the boss accuse you of incompetence when the situation was not your fault.

As a research analyst working on a major project with high visibility, I faced a dilemma when new information surfaced that dramatically changed my findings. I had a choice: bury the new information and stick with my initial conclusions, or tell the truth and risk embarrassment. I decided to change my report to accommodate the new information but at the cost of the wrath of my supervisor who had already sent the preliminary report forward. As a result, my boss reprimanded me for unprofessional conduct.

No "good deed" goes unpunished! However, I had the solace of a clear conscience and was able to move forward with the Lord's help. Thank God this situation never happened again, but I hope if faced with the same circumstances, I would repeat my decision to err on the side of the truth.

May the Lord give you the strength to trust God for protection against **work problems beyond your control**! After all, the battle is His, not yours.

Prayer

Lord, please help me to trust You for protection and vindication and to choose the path of integrity no matter the cost. I know You will never leave nor forsake me. In Your name, I pray. Amen.

Gary E. Roberts

Week 29, Day 5

cut the ropes

Reading

Acts 27:31-32 [KJV] Paul said to the centurion and to the soldiers, Except these abide in the ship, ye cannot be saved. Then the soldiers cut off the ropes of the boat, and let her fall off.

Reflection

Sometimes God's plan for me has nothing to do with my plans for me. I assure you, I did not plan as a child to spend most of my adult life on death row. And once here, my plan did not include following Him. And once following Him, my plan did not center on being an active member of the Death Row Church. And once being involved in my church, my plan did not include preaching on Sundays and ministering to others – here on death row, to my family, and to you through this devotional.

Time and time again, God commands me to **cut the ropes** to my plans, and then He takes me to amazing places through His plan. He places people in my life I would never have invited through my own plan. He will do the same for you whether you are at work or at home.

God's plan is <u>always</u> in your best interest. Is His plan changing your plans, too? I pray so!

Just like the soldiers in scripture who **cut the ropes** and followed a plan not their own, until you get rid of your plan and accept His – you will never walk in the fullness of God.

Today as you go to work, when you are working, as you come home tonight, and as you start your weekend – *trust God*. When He commands you to **cut the ropes** of your plan, follow through. His plan is better, and you will be blessed!

Prayer

Father, in the Name of Jesus, I pray. Thank You for revealing Your plan for me each day so I can carry out Your will in the places You plant me. Amen.

Jimmy Davis, Jr.

Week 30, Day 1

paths straight

Reading

Proverbs 3:5-6 [NIV] Trust in the Lord with all your heart and lean not on your own understanding; in all your ways submit to him, and he will make your **paths straight**.

Reflection

As this work-week begins, do you feel like you're walking on a tightrope or near a precipice? Not sure which way to turn. All the work that wasn't completed last week. That unfinished grant proposal. The scheduled meetings this week. That deadline just around the corner.

Good Lord! There's a *lot* to be anxious about, isn't there?

You know trust is a rare commodity in today's society – given the breakdown of values and principles, we shouldn't be surprised. It's the same in the public service regardless of where you work in this world. Trust is particularly taxing when so much may be at stake.

Trusting is the most difficult act, especially when we serve an *unseen* God. The awesome news, however, is He wants us to *focus on Him* in the difficult times as well as in the good times and trust Him unconditionally in all our paths.

As a *Christian public servant*, all you need to do is submit <u>to</u> Him and trust <u>in</u> Him.

Today at work, He *will* make your **paths straight**.

Prayer

Thank You, Lord, for making my **paths straight** in every facet of our lives, including work this week. Give me strength and courage to submit to You. I trust and love You with all my heart and soul. In Your name, I pray. Amen.

Lyse Lacourse

Week 30, Day 2

God's intended results

Reading

Genesis 50:14 [NIV] You intended to harm me, but God intended it all for good. He brought me to this position so I could save the lives of many people.

Reflection

You hold a public service position for one reason: *to bring good* to your neighborhood, community, country, humanity. This is true whether you hold an elected or appointed position in government or the nonprofits. It remains true if you are a governor or a custodian. Whatever position you hold, you do so to help your agency protect and improve the lives of many people.

Today at work, remember why God put you in the position. Then, stop questioning why things are not working so perfectly. Stop waddling in the mire and be bold in your faith, remembering only God can bring good out of a bad situation. We just need to be comfortable with God's will.

So, instead of getting angry, frustrated, or confused – be patient and allow **God's intended results** to prevail!

You don't know the full plan, but you know you *are* a player! You are His player!!

So wait for **God's intended results**!

Prayer

Lord, I pray we will fully have faith in You as we serve You and Your people today! I pray we will be bold enough to stand on Your Word regardless of confusion, uncertainty, or anguish! Lord, let us focus on the capacity You gave us as *Christian public servants*. Let us not get distracted from Your power. In Jesus' name, Amen.

LaShonda Garnes

Week 30, Day 3

why do I work

Reading

1 Timothy 4:10 [NIV] That is why we labor and strive, because we have put our hope in the living God, who is the Savior of all people, and especially of those who believe.

Reflection

It's another "hump day," and if you're like me, you might be asking **"why do I work?"** There are many important secular answers to this question. Yes, you have to eat and pay bills. Yes, you have dreams for our children. Yes, you have to save for retirement. But if you and I only have secular reasons, then we would not be able to continue for very long – at least not in a *hopeful way*.

Scripture reminds us work is a foretaste of communion and cooperation with God. Work is a participation in what God does: constantly creating and making new that which is broken. That's often the task of the public servant, is it not? We're charged with fixing things that are broken.

As a *Christian public servant*, realize every job you perform has a role in redemption. Not that works redeem you or me, but work can be a participation in the transformation of temporal things. Public servants are managers of relationships: relationships between and within institutions and relationships with the people we serve. If you labor and strive with a hope in the living God, these relationships can become transforming experiences that draw people closer to what God created them to be. If your job is executed without hope, however, despair characterizes the relationships you forge and an opportunity is lost to reflect the goodness of God. *Nothing done well is done without hope.*

So, if you are asking today, **why do I work?** God powerfully uses you to serve Him well, particularly in bringing hope to others.

Prayer

Dear God, hope is a virtue that comes only from a relationship with You. Help move me from the hopelessness of the temporal order into the hope of eternity. May the work I do this Wednesday echo the sounds of heaven. In Your Son's name, I pray. Amen.

Dominick D. Hankle

Week 30, Day 4

chaplains do not carry rifles

Reading

Leviticus 19:11[KJV] Ye shall not steal, neither deal falsely, neither lie one to another.

Reflection

A wise old minister once advised me, "Remember when you visit a hospital following the birth of a newborn baby, there is no such thing as an ugly baby, or at least you should never say so. And if you ever come across that nonexistent ugly baby, just say: 'Now *that's* a baby!'"

While life sometimes requires a bit of tact, civil society begins to deteriorate when it can no longer differentiate between dishonesty and veracity. Too often today, the norm of our discourse centers on small but growing untruths. The media may call it "spin," but why shouldn't we call it *deceit*?

It's not just people in the news that "spin," it's also public servants in their workplaces. For a while, my workplace was Afghanistan. One day my roommate was caught without his rifle. When a Marine corrected him on this carelessness, my roommate (a *physician's assistant*) said, "**Chaplains do not carry rifles.**" The Marine, now under the impression my physician's assistant friend was a chaplain, quickly apologized.

It's true, **chaplains do not carry rifles.** But by fooling the susceptible Marine, my friend was doing nothing to develop his own character. He forgot *lying erodes our communion* with God and our fellowship with one another.

So yes, sometimes you should be tactful so not to offend a mother and her ugly baby. But as a *Christian public servant*, what are you saying today that reflects your own character? What are you saying that confirms your communion with God and your fellowship with coworkers and those you serve?

Do your words differentiate dishonesty from veracity?

Are you really in a position to make that claim "**chaplains do not carry rifles?**"

Prayer

Father, may my words always be true. Today at work, help me to speak truth to power and trust in Your grace that my communication might lead to building rather than demolishing. May truth always be my guide, and may I be willing to hear the truth as a sound source of encouragement. In Jesus' name, I pray. Amen

Loren Crone

Week 30, Day 5

gain the more

Reading

1 *Corinthians* 9:19 [NLT] For though I be free from all men, yet have I made myself servant unto all, that I might **gain the more**.

Reflection

Each week, many free-world volunteers – truly *Christian public servants* – come to share Jesus with us. When they come here, they sacrifice much: time away from family, gas money, oil and tires, and meals on the road. Sometimes they get turned away because the prison may be on lock-down or because they may have violated the dress code in some small way.

Given all this, these men make that trip with joy and peace – just to be a servant to us on Life Row. They come to **gain the more**.

Have you ever had something so precious and powerful you want to keep it to yourself? Yet something compels you to release it so someone else can be blessed, too.

Before you get out of your car to start your workday, set it in your heart to be a servant to all that you might **gain the more** for Jesus.

Prayer

Father, in the name of Jesus, I pray. Give me the confidence to be a servant unto all to gain more sisters and brothers into the Family of our Savior, Jesus Christ. Amen.

Jimmy Davis, Jr.

Week 31, Day 1

fear may be conquered

Reading

Psalm 27:1 [NIV] The Lord is my light and my salvation – whom shall I fear? The Lord is the stronghold of my life – of whom shall I be afraid?

Reflection

As a Christian, you know God rules your life and is with you day and night. You know He loves you and has a plan for your life. Human instincts, however, sometime cause you to *fear a situation or even a person* who may have entered your life.

As a public servant, there are often times I dread a particular meeting concerning a controversial issue. To make matters worse, there are often people at those meeting who are known to create an atmosphere of discontent.

As a *Christian public servant*, it's during these periods I must stop and remind myself God is watching over me and *no situation or person is too big for Him.*

Today at work, remember **fear may be conquered** – but only through Him.

Prayer

Father, I know as a Christian I'm not immune to human frailties and emotions. I know at times both people and situations will enter my life and cause me great concern. I thank You, Father, for giving me the peace in my heart to know through You **fear may be conquered** – even in my work today. In Your Son's name, I pray. Amen.

John Greene

Week 31, Day 2

open to recognize Him

Reading

Luke 24:28-31 [RSV] So they drew near to the village to which they were going. He appeared to be going further, but they constrained him, saying, "Stay with us, for it is toward evening and the day is now far spent." So he went in to stay with them. When he was at table with them, he took bread and blessed, and broke it, and gave it to them. And their eyes were opened and they recognized him; and he vanished out of their sight.

Reflection

Before work one day, I was in a grocery store checkout line with my only purchase being an intact case of bananas weighing 40 pounds. The case was not marked with a weight because the lid was missing as the produce had been staged to be placed on a display in the store. The checkout attendant instructed me to wait as she checked out other customers while an assistant verified the weight with the department manager.

When the assistant returned, the attendant asked the next man in line if it was OK with him for her to check me out since I had been through the line already. He moaned, "No, it's not OK with me, but go ahead. You're going to do what you want to do anyway!"

Well, I was shocked. I did not want to cause this hostility, but the attendant proceeded to check out my bananas. That angry man then asked me what I was going to do with all 40 pounds of them. "They are for a downtown soup kitchen my church serves tomorrow," I answered. That man then asked where the soup kitchen was, and I gave him the street name. His facial expression and tone changed immediately. In a consolatory voice, he asked the attendant, to whom he had just snapped at so rudely, for her pardon. Then he instructed her to put all the bananas on his bill.

Christ's presence was surely in the midst of this fleeting moment in the grocery checkout before work. You see, that once-angry man's eyes were now **open to recognize Him**. And guess what, my eyes were also now **open to recognize Him**!

How often is Christ in your midst? Can your eyes **open to recognize Him**? As a *Christian public servant*, do you look for places to find Christ in your daily interactions with those you serve and others in your community? Christ is there, you know. You should be keen to see Him.

Today, look for opportunities to see Christ in the interactions with people in your path. A coworker. A citizen. Even that person in the check-out line. And don't forget the attendant.

Have your eyes **open to recognize Him**. And know the Kingdom is ever-present.

Prayer

Dear Lord, help me to see You in the midst of this workday. Open my eyes to Your presence that I may recognize You and serve You faithfully. For it is in Your name, I pray. Amen.

Keith Jordan

Week 31, Day 3

change as a bad thing

Reading

Hebrews 13:8 [ESV] Jesus Christ is the same yesterday and today and forever.

Joshua 1:9 [ESV] Have I not commanded you? Be strong and courageous. Do not be frightened, and do not be dismayed, for the Lord your God is with you wherever you go.

Reflection

Change. Most people usually look at **change as a bad thing**. This is especially true in the workplace – given the economy and the chance of a down-size. Reductions-in-force. Relocation. Budget cutbacks. Tampering with the pension. People are afraid of change. With change, things can go from bad to worse before the workday is over.

However, there is good news for *Christian public servants* like you and me. We know despite all the changes going on around us God will never change. He – and He alone – is constant, and in being constant, He is our Comfort and our Shield. He is our Refuge when the changes at work make us anxious.

So at work today, you may still view **change as a bad thing**. And just maybe that change is a bad thing. But don't be frightened. God is standing right there with you and for you.

Be strong and courageous. He is never going to change.

Prayer

Dear Lord, please help me remember You are constant. Whatever changes take place today, I know you will never change. I will not grow weary but have strength in You. In Your Holy name, I pray. Amen.

Samantha Pineiro Graham

Week 31, Day 4

begin afresh each morning

Reading

Lamentations 3:21-23 [NLT] Yet I still dare to hope when I remember this: The faithful love of the LORD never ends! His mercies never cease. Great is his faithfulness; his mercies **begin afresh each morning**.

Reflection

I was almost killed one morning before work as I drove to deliver some items to my church's homeless mission. The interstate was under repair, and I was on the cloverleaf building up speed toward the entrance lane. I suddenly discovered the repairs temporarily negated the entrance lane. I had no place to go but into the first lane of traffic. From the corner of my eye, I noticed an 18-wheel semi-truck bulleting down that lane without the possibility of breaking or pulling into another crowded lane. To make matters worse, the entrance to the freeway opened at the start of a bridge. I had nowhere to escape the wrath of that truck.

I veered as close as possible to the edge of the bridge and hoped the truck would not push me over onto the street below. As I felt the rumble, I prayed and quickly thought about my family. Then I heard the scraping of the side of my van, and the rear-view mirror exploded.

Everything happened in just a couple of seconds, and when all was over, I was OK. The van was totaled, but I was alive and unharmed and remained on top of the bridge.

This was not the first time I have been close to death, and with heart-disease, it probably will not be the last time. But I felt the Lord with me as the truck scraped everything but me. I knew He was with me when I did not fall over the side of the bridge.

He <u>will</u> take me Home someday, but I know His mercies will never cease. And so far, He permits me to **begin afresh each morning** – just like His power and His love.

On this work morning, do not take anything for granted. As you go to work, know His mercies will never cease. He <u>will</u> take you Home someday, perhaps today. But until then, **begin afresh each morning**. He has work for you to do, and His faithfulness is great, His love never ending.

Prayer

Father God, Your mercies will never cease – even when You decide to take me Home. Yet I rejoice in another day because I know You have work for me. Let me begin this day afresh, just like Your mercies begin afresh, knowing Your faithfulness is great. In Jesus' name, I pray. Amen.

James D. Slack

Week 31, Day 5

it's the how that counts

Reading

Colossians 3:10 [MSG] You're done with that old life. It's like a filthy set of ill-fitting clothes you've stripped off and put in the fire. Now you're dressed in a new wardrobe. Every item of your new way of life is custom-made by the Creator, with his label on it.

Reflection

How do you dress? Notice, I asked how you dress – not what you wear.

Where I am, brothers wear nothing but white clothes. So the what does not matter; **it's the how that counts**. Some brothers wear their whites almost as rags. They cut the legs off to make shorts when it's hot. They don't tuck their shirts in and cut off the sleeve's when it gets really hot. They do not bother to press their clothes, laying them under their mattresses, and they wear the same filthy pants and shirt for way too long.

Other brothers press their clothes. They change them each day. They glorify God in how they wear their whites. And other brothers notice, too.

I am not perfect. There are days when I don't care how I look. Something going on in my mind lets me dress like me and not like the Christ in me. So I am glad I surround myself with brothers who do glorify God in every way – including how they dress. And they let me know when I am wearing rags.

A lot of times, you might not care how you dress. Oh, you have the right work clothes on, but **it's the how that counts**. It shows either respect or disrespect for God.

Even though you work in the free-word and this is probably "casual Friday," remember the Lord has given you a new wardrobe. Custom made by Him. With His label on it!

It really does not matter what you wear today. But dress to show Jesus your old nature has died. Dress to show others you are living your new nature in Christ. Remember, brothers and sisters, **it's the how that counts**. Whatever you wear, wear it to glorify God!

Prayer

Father, in the name of Jesus, I pray. Thank You for dressing me every day. Thank You for having faith in me even when I lose focus and forget my new wardrobe. Amen.

Jimmy Davis, Jr.

Week 32, Day 1

foot slipping away

Reading

Psalms 94:18 [NAB] When I say, "My foot is slipping," your mercy, LORD, holds me up.

Ephesians 4:31 [NAB] All bitterness, fury, anger, shouting, and reviling must be removed from you, along with all malice.

Reflection

Yesterday a coworker confided a story about an argument she had with her brother. As we whispered alone in a corner of the breakroom, she told me how furious she was with him. It was obvious she was looking for me to acknowledge she was right.

Well, was she right? That's not the point.

God called me to respond with grace and understanding, but I felt my **foot slipping away** because I was tempted just to say the things she wanted to hear. She was asking me to support how she shouted at her brother, but I needed to support her faith. This was a distressing task. She may never confide in me again, but my Christian task was to bring her closer to God for remedy. And just as I felt my **foot slipping away**, the Lord started to hold me up!

Today at work, someone may confide in you. A family problem. A situation involving a coworker. A workplace incident. That coworker may be very angry and want the comfort of your support. You, too, may feel your **foot slipping away** from God because it's easier to say what someone wants to hear than to speak about what Jesus wants done. When you feel your **foot slipping away**, have the courage to speak on what scripture says about bitterness and anger. Be a reminder of how God might want the situation remedied. Doing so may be tough, I know, but you are in that situation to represent Him, not you.

Today at work, have the courage to speak from His perspective. Listen and be patient, but when you feel your **foot slipping away**, remember His words and not who was right.

Prayer

Lord, keep my feet firm. Allow me to come to You for acknowledgment of my actions. Take my anger from me and release me, hold me up with Your love.

Give me the courage to listen to others and show them Your way. In Your name, I pray. Amen.

Joanna Knight

Week 32, Day 2

far more precious than jewels

Reading

Proverbs 31:10, 31 [ESV] An excellent wife who can find? She is **far more precious than jewels** ... Give her of the fruit of her hands, and let her works praise her in the gates.

Reflection

I recently had the unfortunate privilege of attending my cousin's funeral. And this scripture in its entirety was read and reflected upon, shining light on my cousin's glowing personality and the abilities she displayed as a godly woman.

It set my mind to thinking about what will be said about me when my time comes. My grown daughter was with me for the ceremony, and afterward, we discussed the attributes found between verses 10 and verse 31. Both she and I agreed neither of us came anywhere near the example described of the woman in the scripture – not for lack of trying but because life's circumstances have not allotted either of us the privilege of a loving, kind husband.

I found myself explaining to my daughter the scripture we heard was an example of what a woman could be, given the right circumstances. However, not having a godly partner did not mean we cannot aspire to be the best we can be on our own. Not having idle hands, and working to help others. Staying busy and being kind.

The maze of life is not simple. You must find your own way out of bed today. It may be a struggle each morning because of depression or loneliness or trauma from a past experience. These things can take a deep hold on you.

But if you measure yourself using ONLY the yardstick God provides, you will not be as frustrated as you become when the measure is the one others line up to use on you.

Regardless of what you are going through, in His eyes you are **far more precious than jewels**. As you ready for work today, remember in His eyes, you are **far more precious than jewels**!

Prayer

Father, thank You – in the name of Jesus – for helping me see myself through Your eyes of love and kindness. Let me never forget condemnation for my past failures does NOT come from You – and negative thoughts are meant to rob me of the blessings You have for me when I give of myself to others as You would do. Amen.

Gigi Baker

Week 32, Day 3

suffer grief in all kinds of trials

Reading

1 Peter 1:6-7 [NIV] In all this you greatly rejoice, though now for a little while you may have had to **suffer grief in all kinds of trials**. These have come so that the proven genuineness of your faith – of greater worth than gold, which perishes even though refined by fire – may result in praise, glory and honor when Jesus Chris is revealed.

Isaiah 64:8(b) [NIV] We are the clay, you are the potter; we are all the work of your hand.

Reflection

Do you ever wonder why you may have to **suffer grief in all kinds of trials**? I have, and it seems sometimes to be overwhelming. I mean, I think I am a good, godly *Christian public servant* (most of the time), and I truly try my best to be conscious and prayerful with the decisions I make – especially when I know how much weight my advice carries when trying to make sure a supervisor is fair to an employee and an employee is fair – all the while ensuring we are fair to the citizens who have entrusted us to care for the people within our organization and within the community…. Whew!

I am learning God is still molding me. When I **suffer grief in all kinds of trials** at work, He is refining me by making me more like Him in those situations. When I feel like I have it covered and am getting pretty good at it, He continues to give me trials so my immediate response is to love like Jesus loves in any given situation and regardless of whether I am having a bad day or don't feel like dealing with a certain person. He gives me that trial because He knows my patience needs work, and the person I'm dealing with needs to see Jesus and not my irritation.

God knows just how to continue to work in me, to mold me to be more like Him. I am His clay … his masterpiece-to-be … a work-in-progress until the day I go Home to Him.

Today at work, you may **suffer grief in all kinds of trials**. Or if not today, certainly tomorrow. When the trials begin, remember He is working on you. He is allowing trials in your work life or trials you bring to work so someday your faith – which is *of greater worth than gold, which perishes even though refined by fire* – may result in praise, glory, and honor when Jesus Christ is revealed.

Prayer

Dear Heavenly Father, thank You for Your amazing grace. You care enough about me to continue molding me into the person You want me to be. Thank You for not giving up on me. I have peace in knowing You understand I am still Your priceless work-in-progress. In Jesus' name, I pray. Amen.

Wendy Standorf

Week 32, Day 4

a slow suicide

Reading

Proverbs 8:36 [NIV] But those who fail to find me harm themselves; all who hate me love death.

1 Corinthians 3:16-17 [NIV] Don't you know that you yourselves are God's temple and that God's Spirit dwells in your midst? If anyone destroys God's temple, God will destroy that person; for God's temple is sacred, and you together are that temple.

Reflection

My fishing buddy passed away yesterday. He was a good man with a kind heart and quick wit. He just couldn't quit those cigarettes. No matter how many times he tried to give them up — no matter how many times he was hospitalized – he kept picking up that pack. Buying that carton. He was committing **a slow suicide**, and he knew it.

You know there are many ways to commit **a slow suicide**. Food is one way. That machine in the break room contains a lot of pastries and candy. And I am tempted. Drink is another way. Do I select that soda with all the sugar from the machine, or do I choose the bottle of water?

And then, of course, there is **a slow suicide** that comes from not finding and loving God. Do I do my job but not in a way that glorifies Him? Do I answer every phone call as if Jesus is on the line? Do I help a coworker as if I were helping Christ? And what about that citizen needing help?

And do I find time before work to be alone with God? Do I find moments at work to pray?

Yes, there are lots of ways for me to commit **a slow suicide**. My body is His temple, and I so often abuse His temple. My spirit belongs to Him, and so often I get lost from Him.

How about you? Are you any different?

Before you go to work today, get rid of whatever is causing you to commit **a slow suicide**. Physical wrong-doings. Spiritual mistakes. Bitterness. Wrath. Malice. Lust for things not good.

Stop committing **a slow suicide**. Don't live a dead life!

Prayer

Dear Jesus, without You I am nothing. Without You I am dead. I want to live – <u>really</u> live for You. Help me, please. In Your name, I pray. Amen.

Ronald Wilson

Week 32, Day 5

the right attitude

Reading

Psalm 100:2 [KJV] Serve the LORD with gladness: come before his presence with singing.

Reflection

For some time, I have "worked the hall" in here. If a brother wants some ice, I go get it for him. If he wants something warmed up in the microwave, I do that for him. If he wants to talk with a correctional officer, I let the officer know. If the brother wants to send a message down the hall to another brother, I am the mailman. When it is time to eat, I help take the tray to the brother's cell. And when he wants to complain or yell, I stand there and take it.

This job gets me out of my cell for several hours each day. But I got to the point where I almost quit. So many brothers were selfish, greedy, prideful. So many complained about everything. I just wanted to be back in my cell where I did not have to listen to anyone.

Then God led me to this verse, and the light went on! You see, I was working with a wrong attitude. At times, I was doing it for me – getting me out of my cell. Occasionally I was doing it for a few of my friends in their cells – doing things that made them happy. But I didn't have **the right attitude**. I was not serving God. I was taking a blessing from God, but I was not serving Him in return. I was not *serving in His presence with singing.*

So I started to serve our Lord with *gladness*! And then my heart re-opened to the pain each brother feels. My ears started to hear again their hopelessness. I started to feel again their discouragement. And I re-understood why I am working the hall. By serving with **the right attitude**, God reminded me of His need in them. And then I was truly blessed!

How is your job going? Are you doing things for your sake? What you can gain? Or are you serving with **the right attitude** – so God can show you the "what" and the "why" of His needs in others? Are you working in ways that please Him?

Today at work, serve with **the right attitude**. Show others you are serving the Lord with gladness as you see His need in others. Sing in His presence! Sing!!

Prayer

Father, in the name of Jesus, I pray. Continue to show me how to serve You with gladness everywhere You send me and every job You give me. Amen.

Jimmy Davis, Jr.

Week 33, Day 1

the beauty life still holds

Reading

2 Corinthians 1:3-4 [NASB] Blessed be the God and Father of our Lord Jesus Christ, the Father of mercies and God of all comfort, who comforts us in all our affliction so that we will be able to comfort those who are in any affliction with the comfort with which we ourselves are comforted by God.

Reflection

It has been one of those weeks, in fact, one of those months. It seems everything that could possibly go wrong has. If ever there was a good time to be glum, this was it.

But while performing some work at a patient's bedside, I noticed a few other patients standing at the window. From the 9th floor of the hospital, one could see the entire city – a breathtaking view! Together they were pointing out areas of interest, reminiscing on memories made on the streets below. These patients had worries. They had challenges certainly far greater than mine. Then it hit me. Even during their difficulties, they managed to appreciate **the beauty life still holds**.

As children of God there is so much to be grateful for, but too often we fall into the accepted role of victim to our worldly troubles. Gratitude is attractive, and it can be a blessing to others who forget **the beauty life still holds**.

Are you facing challenges at work today? Are troubles surrounding you?

As you work, don't let the day's troubles make you glum. Today, appreciate the gift God has given you. See **the beauty life still holds**, and encourage others to see it too.

And He promises, the view will be breathtaking!

Prayer

Lord, You are a gracious God. You provide for my every need. Help me appreciate all You do for me even in the difficult times. Help me inspire others through Your blessings. In Your Son's name, I pray. Amen.

Stephanie Van Straten

Week 33, Day 2

excited for the vision

Reading

Luke 23:34 [NIV] Jesus said, "Father, forgive them, for they do not know what they are doing." And they divided up his clothes by casting lots.

Psalm 73:26(a) [NIV] My flesh and my heart may fail, but God is the strength of my heart

Reflection

Have you ever been surrounded by people but still felt utterly alone? Does it happen at work?

Sometimes you start a project and are surrounded by everyone **excited for the vision** – gung-ho for the agency's mission – eager to engage in the new program. But expectation leads to stress, and stress can decrease the morale and support of the team. Oh, there are people still around you, but the number of true team members has diminished.

It's easy to invest so much time, energy, and emotion into the people on your team. But it's easy to become vulnerable by such an investment. And so often you find yourself as the only one still **excited for the vision.** Then you feel betrayed. Overlooked. Frustrated. Angry.

You know Christ had many followers, yet only 12 disciples, and only one disciple was found at the site of His crucifixion. There were numerous bystanders and torturers but few friends and members of His team.

Today you may feel isolated by coworkers. Maybe your supervisor is not fully behind your investment. You may feel like the citizens you serve do not appreciate the effort you put in.

Whatever the circumstance, remain faithful to God and learn to forgive those who don't know your sacrifice or do not recognize your worth. Remember God is faithful and has promised not to leave you alone. He will reward you for your faithfulness.

So at work today, forgive and remain **excited for the vision** God has placed in your heart.

And that's something you can really be excited about!

Prayer

Father, thank You for forgiving me before I even knew I was a sinner. Thank You for allowing Your Son to show me what it means to forgive. I am never alone for You are there always. You are the source of strength in my heart. You are what excites me! I pray these things in Jesus' name. Amen.

Kathryn Saunders

Week 33, Day 3

need to give pause

Reading

2 Timothy 2:25 [NLT] Gently instruct those who oppose the truth. Perhaps God will change those people's hearts, and they will learn the truth.

Reflection

During a coaching session, one participant expressed dismay with conversations from her work unit. She described how these were pejorative in nature, personally attacking her character, and mocking her abilities to teach and mentor other coworkers. She was upset the people attacking her were ones she had spent a lot of time teaching, supporting, and encouraging through ups and downs of their careers.

Throughout our coaching session, she revealed disbelief, anger, and frustration over the situation. These emotions are human; however, when I asked why she serves ... she felt a **need to give pause**.

We all **need to give pause** before we react. To remind ourselves while others may be the ones who judge and denigrate, you and I still must serve purposefully – as God wants. Today may be the day at work when you really **need to give pause**. Do so and remember He has placed you here – in this workplace, now – for a reason. Also, remember He had to instruct and love those who assassinated His character, lied on Him, and questioned who He was. Keep in mind, He expects you to instruct and love no less.

Today at work, don't stop mentoring others. Whatever they do to you or say about you, just continue teaching, loving, supporting, and encouraging. Most importantly, pray they will learn the truth. So if you **need to give pause**, do so. And then look to God to change hearts.

Prayer

Lord, thank You for Your conviction! Please continue to convict my heart to stay focused on purposefully serving You in my workplace. Show me the light, and give me the ability to stand boldly even in times of adversity. Soften my heart, anoint me with Your wisdom throughout this work day, and move on my behalf. In Your name, I pray. Amen.

LaShonda Garnes

Week 33, Day 4

in someone else's shoes

Reading

Romans 12:2(a) [NLT] Don't copy the behavior and customs of this world, but let God transform you into a new person by changing the way you think.

Reflection

It's not yet Friday, but I sure need the weekend. I've had several assignments due for class, and those are on top of my work duties. Then there's my kid's softball awards ceremony. Not to mention they are still playing games that were rained-out from earlier in the season.

As I pull into the parking lot, I notice several of my clients standing outside the building. I run group therapy sessions, and I notice this isn't the typical time for a break. As I proceed to go inside, I speak to everyone and ask, "Why hasn't 'group' started?" The answer was simple: "We're waiting on you."

With so much on my plate, I had forgotten. Still, my coworker was perfectly capable of starting the group due to my absence. There are lesson plans in my office, and she knows it. And I have covered for her in the past when she's been absent.

I was getting angry, but then I looked at things differently. As a *Christian public servant*, should I make a big deal? The answer was "no." After all, I talk about stressing less and becoming the bigger person during my group sessions. I figure I should practice what I preach.

Taking time to put yourself **in someone else's shoes** can really change the way you think! Regardless of what is going on at work today – despite commitments to school and to family – don't let your busy schedule take control over your judgment. Have sympathy and compassion for others. Yes, today at work, change the way you think. Put yourself **in someone else's shoes**, and God <u>will</u> transform you into a new person!

Prayer

Father, guide me and give me a humble spirit to have compassion for others. Let Your light shine through me. I want to be pleasing in Your sight. In Jesus' name, I pray. Amen.

Erica Carr

Week 33, Day 5

the Truth itself stand up

Reading

3 John 1:129(a) [MSG] Everyone has a good word for Demetrius—the Truth itself stands up for Demetrius!

Reflection

The lives of two of my spiritual mentors speak to me in so many ways. Every minute of the day, both seem to have something I crave: a deep peace in this place. I get that peace at times on most days but not like those two brothers.

So I asked them how their lives are so peaceful. They affirmed what I already knew. Their deep peace comes from His Truth – and they let **the Truth itself stand up** and fill the day. The Truth will speak for your life more so than the truth will speak through your words.

Sometimes we all let our mouths speak so much we forget to let our lives speak. And our lives will show others what they too crave.

As you head off to work today, let His Truth of peace, joy, compassion, mercy, and grace allow your life to speak for you in all circumstances.

Today at work, let **the Truth itself stand up** for you and fill the day with a deepened peace!

Prayer

Father, in the name of Jesus, I pray. Thank You for all You do for me so I can keep allowing my life to speak Your Truth to others. Amen.

Jimmy Davis, Jr.

Week 34, Day 1

just like smoke, it fades away

Reading

James 4:14 [NASB] Yet you do not know what your life will be like tomorrow. You are just a vapor that appears for a little while and then vanishes away.

Reflection

Last week I visited family in Memphis, Tennessee. When I was ready to go back to the hotel, I said to everyone, "I'll see you all tomorrow *if nothing happens*." Several members were perplexed by the nature of my goodbye. They wondered, what does it mean – *if nothing happens*? Was I ill? Was I worried about something? Was there a problem?

I took this opportunity to explain God does not want us to boast about tomorrow. He never promises a tomorrow. Hence, the reason I said *if nothing happens*. Well, some just laughed in relief but others knew what I was talking about. I hope it stays in their minds and hearts so they appreciate what God does promise each one today but never forget this earthly life is temporary and gone tomorrow – **just like smoke, it fades away**.

As you prepare for work this morning, you really do not know what this day will bring. So much going on with kids and family before you get to work. So many deadlines and stressors when you are at work. So much planning for the next day with both family and job.

Just remember you do not know the day or hour He will take you from this life. Any tomorrow – any extra second other than this current one – is His will, not yours. And **just like smoke, it fades away**.

Enjoy the blessings and challenges He gives you now – at home and at work. Anything else is **just like smoke, it fades away**.

Prayer

Lord, prepare me for this workday, and I will not worry about tomorrow. Let me focus on the right now despite my sketching out tentative goals for the next day and after. I do not know when You will call me Home. Let me make the most of what you give me, for I am just a vapor. Give me opportunities to teach this to my loved ones and coworkers. In Your name, I pray. Amen.

Barbara Hill

Week 34, Day 2

the extra steps needed

Reading

Matthew 5:41 [NIV] If anyone forces you to go one mile, go with them two miles.

1 Corinthians 10:24 [NLT] Don't be concerned for your own good but for the good of others.

Reflections

Some time ago, a church leader called in regards to an environmental health recommendation for the site of their new church home. As we all know, church capital campaigns take time, and having applied three years ago, the recommendation made then had long expired when they were ready to break ground. When I told her a new application was needed, she asked if something could be done about the attached fee. I talked with my supervisor to try to find a way to eliminate the fee for the church, but ultimately nothing could be done. She thanked me for trying, and she paid the fee. The next day I evaluated the property and made the updated recommendations.

Yesterday the contractor called concerning an inspection. It was apparent he was not too familiar with regulations for a church structure. Because errors could cost the congregation more money, I offered to meet him on-site to go over my expectations. While waiting for him to arrive, I chatted with a deacon who told me about the various struggles the church endured but was later blessed with the donation of additional land. I added this new information to their file and saved them much more money than a reapplication fee!

As a *Christian public servant*, it's not every day you can help a church grow. But you can take **the extra steps needed** for all citizens to make sure they gain every possible benefit. Sometimes you may not feel like it with everything on your plate – or when you're faced with an angry and demanding citizen who doesn't expect anyone to take **the extra steps needed**. But do so!

Today at work, be willing to ask that additional question or listen to a long background story. Take **the extra steps needed** to serve that citizen. Be concerned for that citizen's good, not your own. In doing so, you will glorify God!

Prayer

God, on this workday I ask You to continue to keep my mind and heart open to Your word and to learn how to be a blessing to others. These things I ask in Jesus' name. Amen.

Lakeisha Paige

Week 34, Day 3

comfort the anxiety

Reading

Proverbs 12:18 [KJV] There is that speaketh like the piercings of a sword: but the tongue of the wise is health.

Psalm 94:19 [KJV] In the multitude of my thoughts within me thy comforts delight my soul.

Reflection

A friend called me last night. Stressed out over poor communications at work. Yesterday she was told by her supervisor to put everything aside and complete 98 tasks by the end of the week. This morning, the entire work team received an email instructing them to complete all absentee management caseloads by the end of today – this was in addition to my friend's job of completing 98 tasks by Friday.

She put aside the 98 tasks and completed what she thought was her share of the absentee management caseloads. However, some team members went on doing their normal work assignments for the day, assuming for various reasons others would do their share. By late afternoon the supervisor noticed this and asked my friend to work on another stack of caseload files. Plus, she was to have it done before she went home. She asked the Lord to **comfort the anxiety** in her thoughts, and then she rearranged her after-work plans and stayed until that extra load of cases was done.

Why couldn't her supervisor just give those files to the other team members who did not do their fair share? Did my friend's *servant attitude* make her the easiest for the supervisor to target? Or did the other team members not read or understand the instructions, and the supervisor did not want to correct the communication problem at that point?

If your workplace is like my friend's, poor communication adds stress, especially in group situations. In the long-term, it needs to be addressed and corrected. But in the short-term, as a *Christian public servant*, all you can do is turn to the Lord for patience. He will **comfort the anxiety** in your thoughts, and He is there to get you through the tasks.

Today at work, do not let instructions become like a piercing sword. Just do what you are assigned to do. He will **comfort the anxiety**, and He will delight your soul!

Prayer

Lord, thank You for being my Comforter at work! Today remove my anxiety and help me cope with stress. Give me peace in knowing You are there with me in the face of poor communication. In Your name, I pray. Amen.

Renata Rankin

Week 34, Day 4

enough, enough

Reading

Proverbs 22:24 [ESV] Make no friendship with a man given to anger, nor go with a wrathful man

Ephesians 5:15-17 [ESV] Look carefully then how you walk, not as unwise but as wise, making the best use of the time, because the days are evil. Therefore do not be foolish, but understand what the will of the Lord is.

Ephesians 5:25 [ESV] Husbands, love your wives, as Christ loved the church and gave himself up for her

Reflection

A loved one called last night. Not the first time, but I pray it will be the last time without some remedy. What's going on? The man in her life abuses her. She doesn't know what to expect when she gets home at night or before she leaves the house in the morning. Her energy is drained by the time she gets to work. Her productivity is declining.

But what she told me last night took the cake. You see, this time he pushed her down the stairs and injured her ankle. I told her it must stop. She needs to care for herself – financially, emotionally, and spiritually. If she can't do her job, she will not be able to take care of the necessities of life. If she is emotionally hurt, she cannot focus on her job. And if she does not understand the Lord's will for her in this situation, then she may be spiritually foolish.

And so we prayed and talked throughout the night. Does this man love her as Christ loved the church? Is she walking wisely by being with such an angry, wrathful man? Is **enough, enough**?

Are you like her? While challenges come with all relationships, are you abused? Are you driving to work afraid of what will happen when you get home tonight? Remember God loves you so much. You deserve someone who loves you *as much as Christ loved the church.*

On your way to work today, think about God's will – not yours and not his. Is **enough, enough**?

Prayer

Lord, I come to You humbly and thank You for giving me the strength to keep going. I understand You have created me to be both loved and productive. Keep me focused on You. In Your name, I pray. Amen.

Michelle Lewis

Week 34, Day 5

God in that moment

Reading

Matthew 5:8 [KJV] Blessed are the pure in heart for they shall see God.

Psalm 51:10 [KJV] Create in me a clean heart, O God; and renew a right spirit within me.

Reflection

Last Sunday, right before church, we got blessed with a pound cake and decided to share it with everyone who attended! Since I had changed my diet, I wasn't going to eat my share. So the Holy Spirit led me to give it to a particular brother who would see his mom for the last time the next visiting day. She is dying of cancer.

Now this particular brother and I do not get along very well. So when the Holy Spirit said to give him my share, I was a bit surprised. But I checked my heart and knew I was being led to renew a right spirit within me. I took the piece of pound cake over to him.

And guess what? This brother also checked his heart, and we both saw **God in that moment**.

Check your heart before you go to work today. Is it receptive? Pure? Clean?

At work, listen for the Holy Spirit and do what is right. Make amends. Ask forgiveness. Share something. Check your heart and you, too, will see **God in that moment**!

Prayer

Father, in the name of Jesus, I pray. Create in me a clean, pure heart. I beg you to do this each morning. I want to always see You in all my circumstances. Amen.

Jimmy Davis, Jr.

Week 35, Day 1

as people, not numbers

Reading

1 Peter 4:11(a) [NLT] Do you have the gift of speaking? Then speak as though God himself were speaking through you. Do you have the gift of helping others? Do it with all the strength and energy that God supplies. Then everything you do will bring glory to God through Jesus Christ.

Reflection

As third-generation military, I remember when I first joined the Department of Veterans Affairs in my country. While my career is now taking me elsewhere, until the day I left I remained so excited being a part of an agency that cares for veterans. But I quickly noticed a culture of treating our patients impersonally. I know large agencies tend to be impersonal for a lot of reasons – insufficient budgets, limited staff, and inadequate resources to name a few. However, I really wanted to treat the patients **as people, not numbers**.

During my first week at work, a veteran came up to my desk extremely upset and shouted at me about how much time he had to wait and no one cared about his well-being. He said because I was just a young person, I had no idea what he's been through and how I wouldn't have my freedom if it weren't for him. Once he finished, I thanked him for his service and apologized for the inconvenience. I smiled and touched his hand to assure him I was listening. Well, his anger subsided, and he, too, apologized. And guess what? We began a friendly chat until it was his turn to see a physician.

Do you work in an impersonal environment? Has anger overflowed from someone you were trying to serve? Did things escalate even though it wasn't directly your fault?

Remember God has given you gifts. Because you are a *Christian public servant*, I bet He's given you the gift of speaking and the gift of helping. As taxing as the workday may be, remain humble and find ways to treat those you serve **as people, not numbers**.

Yes, at work today, use the gifts God gives you to remove a little impersonality. Do so with all the strength and energy God provides. And in the process, you <u>will</u> glorify Him!

Prayer

God, please give me humility in my heart, patience with others, and a sound mind in dealing with difficult situations. In Jesus' name, I pray. Amen.

Chameka Boswell

Week 35, Day 2

the most difficult task

Reading

John 13:34-35 [ESV] A new commandment I give to you, that you love one another: just as I have loved you, you also are to love one another. By this all people will know that you are my disciples, if you have love for one another.

1 John 4:20 [ESV] If anyone says, "I Love God", and hates his brother, he is a liar; for he who does not love his brother whom he has seen cannot love God whom he has not seen.

Reflection

I once worked as a custodian in a public school system. I was assigned to a particular school, and at the time, I was the only African-American employed in the building. I loved my coworkers! Everyone got along, and the students were wonderful! However, I got a new supervisor, and things began to change. I believe she did not like me because of the color of my skin.

This supervisor started assigning me tasks that were not a part of my job description. She insisted I do these tasks in demeaning ways. She talked about me to other coworkers, and she made every effort to make me feel out of place. While I did my best to show her love and respect, she offered nothing but hate and disrespect.

God expects us to love and respect every human being just as He does. For some reason, this seems to be **the most difficult task** in too many workplaces. How about yours?

Coworkers come with diverse backgrounds, and the people we serve arrive with many different attributes. Some people are familiar, and others can make us feel uncomfortable. Nevertheless, if we want the workplace to be *God's place*, then we must do what seems to be **the most difficult task**: love one another.

Today at work, do what seems to be **the most difficult task**: show your love to someone else! Show your love to a coworker unlike you. Tell a stranger in the elevator that you love them.

If you have hate in your heart, leave it in a trash bin out in the parking lot. When you go into your building, do what seems to be **the most difficult task** – love someone!

And tomorrow, that task may not seem so difficult!

<u>Prayer</u>

Dear Heavenly Father, I pray You touch my heart right now so I will love and not hate. In Jesus' name, I pray. Amen.

Lakisha Williams

Week 35, Day 3

no other choice

Reading

Proverbs 3:5 [KJV] Trust in the LORD with all thine heart; and lean not unto thine own understanding.

James 1:2-4 [KJV] Consider it all joy, my brethren, when you encounter various trials, knowing that the testing of your faith produces endurance. And let endurance have its perfect result, so that you may be perfect and complete, lacking in nothing.

Reflection

This has been a trying week. Our school is suffering a loss; in fact, our entire community is suffering. A child was kidnapped in a supermarket parking lot. He was later found shot to death. Children, teachers, and community members are struggling. I am so angry I can't think straight. You almost wonder if God can see what is happening.

Yet I know God sees everything. He is in control – really – in my school and in all the schools in every country. He knows what will happen today in every workplace – yours and mine. I know I must trust in His understanding, not mine, for I have **no other choice**. And I know I must endure the trials placed before me. There are workplaces around the world feeling the suffering of turmoil. Perhaps yours?

Children shot by gangs. Teens ruined by drugs. Terrorist bombs at concerts. Parents not coming home from work because something went awfully wrong. All this is real. And it makes you wonder. Yet you and I know we <u>must</u> *trust in Him and endure the trials*. We have **no other choice**.

Yes, as you go to work today, *trust in Him and endure the trials*. Whatever the trials, they are coming. But He is sitting next to you. So lean on Him – you have **no other choice**.

Prayer

Dear Heavenly Father, please put Your protection all around me, my workplace, and my community. Give focus to Your words and not what is going on in this world. Endurance, Father, give me endurance. I have **no other choice** but You. In Jesus' name, I pray. Amen.

Barbara Hill

Week 35, Day 4

wretched, pitiable, poor, blind, and naked

Reading

Revelation 3:15-17 [ESV] "I know your works: you are neither cold nor hot. Would that you were either cold or hot! So, because you are lukewarm and neither hot nor cold, I will spit you out of my mouth. For you say, 'I am rich, I have prospered, and I need nothing,' not realizing that you are **wretched, pitiable, poor, blind, and naked**."

Reflection

It's a common phenomenon in workplaces like prisons and police departments. Maybe it's also common in your work culture. While "team" is important, at the end of the day there is a tendency to want to be as self-reliant as possible. Perhaps it's the nature of working in a dangerous environment, or maybe it's just human nature, but many believe they can solve a situation with no help from anyone else.

And too often this means not asking Jesus for help – despite being **wretched, pitiable, poor, blind, and naked**. It means waiting until help is really needed before inviting Jesus into a personal relationship.

Prayer and total dependence on Jesus are essential in any workplace – as it is essential in any life. Without that dependence, you and I do our jobs in lukewarm fashion – never giving glory to God. We are spiritually dull – neither hot nor cold in our relationship with Christ.

Today at work, don't be so independent! Don't believe you don't need anyone, especially Christ. Guard against the activities that keep you from a healthy, dependent relationship with Him. Like me, you are **wretched, pitiable, poor, blind, and naked**. Like me, you are in need of everything and everyone. Like me, you are in need of Him so badly. Today at work, remember you really are **wretched, pitiable, poor, blind, and naked**. And remember He is with you.

Prayer

Father, You see me as I am – **wretched, pitiable, poor, blind, and naked**. Yet you still offer me hope! I am in need of You, Father, to help me do my job and get me through this workday. In Your Son's name, I pray. Amen.

Chris Summers

Week 35, Day 5

say nothing and just listen

Reading

1 Corinthians 10:23 [NLT] You say, "I am allowed to do anything"—but not everything is good for you. You say, "I am allowed to do anything"—but not everything is beneficial.

Reflection

Last week a brother shared his opinion about a particular passage in the Bible. Now, I know that passage well. I have studied it much longer than this brother. And yes, I have my own opinion about that passage, and my opinion is not the same as his. Yet I was led by the Holy Spirit to **say nothing and just listen**.

You see, a lot of times we don't *speak and live like Jesus* because we want nothing more than to share our own opinions or feelings. You know what I'm talking about. You hear someone express an opinion. You want to answer before listening fully – either you agree or disagree – you really want to say something. Of course, you <u>can</u> speak up right away, but it is not always good to do so. After all, if you interrupt, you may never learn something.

Let me share a secret with you. Everything I <u>could</u> say wouldn't be beneficial to the brothers around me. Isn't that also true with you and your coworkers? To *speak and live like Jesus* means you must sometimes **say nothing and just listen**.

You know, that brother truly taught me something new about that Bible passage – something I missed. And the Holy Spirit also taught me something: He does not want me talking just to hear me talk!

Today at work, *speak and live like Jesus*. But know, more often than not, this requires you to **say nothing and just listen**!

Prayer

Father, in the name of Jesus, I pray. Continue to keep me humble so I can know when to speak and when to listen. Let my words be spoken <u>only</u> when they are beneficial to those around me. Amen.

Jimmy Davis, Jr.

Week 36, Day 1

from the lie to the truth

Reading

Proverbs 19:5 [NLT] A false witness will not go unpunished, and a liar will not escape.

John 14:6(b) [NLT] I am the way, and the truth, and the life. No one comes to the Father except through me.

Reflection

The other day, I read an advertisement that was a *cry for help*. Seems this man is caught in a web of lies at work, and he needs a cover-up to save his job! He is looking for a woman to pose as his wife for an office event. He is also looking for a baby to pose as his daughter. More lies to cover-up what started as a simple lie – "family obligations" – to get a day off work.

Now that advertisement may sound funny, but it can reflect office life. We tend to exaggerate situations. We want to modify – or even make up – stories to boost our egos. In the workplace, we want to look and sound heroic despite the distance **from the lie to the truth**.

As a *Christian public servant*, being truthful is not always easy. It can be difficult to tell a client the truth about his situation. It's awkward to give negative news to a citizen about her options. It might even be threatening to tell a supervisor the truth about a proposed project or to relay an honest assessment about a colleague's work that could get him into trouble.

Do you always tell the truth at work – even about how your Sunday really went at church or the real reason why you want the next Friday off? Do you lie (fudge, forget, claim a shaky amount in mileage, or otherwise "max out" automatically) on your business travel reports? Do you tell the truth on your income tax form about all the wages you make?

Nope, it's not easy. A lot of rationalization goes on **from the lie to the truth**. But one thing is clear: God does not like liars, and when you lie there is no escape from Him knowing it.

I'm not sure what happened to that guy searching for a make-shift family to fit into his web of lies. But as you go to work today, keep in mind your goal is to be like Jesus. Following his example is not a walk in the park, but it isn't a lie.

Following Him leads to the Garden of Life! Following Him, my friend, is the only way to get **from the lie to the truth**!

Prayer

Dear Father, thank You for allowing me to be renewed in the spirit by Your Word. Help me speak the truth to my coworkers today and every day. Let my words, my actions, and my heart represent the treasure I carry in You. In Jesus' name, I pray. Amen.

Evelyne F. Altema

Week 36, Day 2

some unwholesome chatter

Reading

Ephesians 4:29 [NIV] Do not let any unwholesome talk come out of your mouths, but only what is helpful for building others up according to their needs, that it may benefit those who listen.

Reflection

Last week, I was a victim of **some unwholesome chatter**. It came in the form of office gossip. A rumor about me was spread around the floor, and it was even raised in a meeting with my manager. The rumor was untrue, and I emphatically denied the story. While the issue was resolved, I urged everyone to think twice before spreading a story.

It's easy to find yourself gossiping – especially at work. In the elevator. In the breakroom. At lunch. There's just something about talking about someone that feeds the fallen side of us. In many ways, it's like that "telephone" game children play. You remember: one child whispers into the ear of the next child in line until the last child announces the message to the entire group. The objective of the game is to pass along the message without it becoming misheard and altered. However, along the way, mistakes usually happen. Though this is a humorous game for children and the moral of the game is clear, adults are tempted to play along. But at the workplace, that telephone game is not kids' play. It leads to **some unwholesome chatter** that hurts the coworker targeted.

Today at work, remember gossip can result in real damage. When you participate in gossip, even as a funny game, it speaks to your Christian faith.

So at work today, help create a better environment for everyone. Don't let your mouth find comfort in **some unwholesome chatter**.

Prayer

Father, help me keep my lips from words that hurt and untrue stories. Instead, let me be a light in these types of situations. In Jesus' name, I pray. Amen.

Veronica Gates

Week 36, Day 3

restore, confirm, strengthen, and establish

Reading

1 Peter 5:10 [KJV] And after you have suffered a little while, the God of all grace, who has called you to his eternal glory in Christ, will himself **restore, confirm, strengthen, and establish** you.

Reflection

A couple of years ago when I was getting a haircut after work, the barber said, "In my days of living, I've learned one thing. If you are having good times, then bad times are near. And if you are having bad times, good times are just over the horizon."

To each his own, I thought. Being selfish and arrogant, in my opinion I had a good life, and it wasn't ever going to change.

And just like that, tables were turned and life as I knew it was drastically changed. Within a week, I lost my job due to the economy. I started to think I did something wrong. Maybe I was a bad individual and caused the layoff. Yes, I blamed myself for everything. The feeling of despair kept me up at night.

But then I turned to God. I prayed a lot, and in my spare time, I read the Word. I started to understand He never promised me a perfect life – "just" a life where He promises to **restore, confirm, strengthen, and establish** me. And I learned I would be OK because He has called me to His eternal glory in Christ. Yes, He promised to **restore, confirm, strengthen, and establish** me, and I knew I would be more than OK.

Well, my life is better now. Not just with a job and more money but in terms of what I gained in character and faith: humility, love, and perseverance. I no longer sit arrogantly in barber chairs after work. I no longer sit arrogantly anywhere, for that matter. I know suffering may very well come again in my journey. But I also stand with confidence in my faith. I know He promises to **restore, confirm, strengthen, and establish** me. And I know He keeps His promises.

So if you have no job to go to today, remember the suffering is temporary. He will **restore, confirm, strengthen, and establish** you. This He promises. He will keep His promise to you!

Prayer

Lord, I come to You humble and sincere. Thank You for loving me when I do not love myself and for continuing to cover me with Your grace and mercy. Guide me, Lord, so I can be the individual You have planned. In Your Son's name, I pray. Amen.

Calvin Reed, Jr.

Week 36, Day 4

simply not familiar

Reading

1 Corinthians 12:12 [NIV] Just as a body, though one, has many parts, but all its many parts form one body, so it is with Christ.

Romans 12:16(a) [NIV] Live in harmony with one another.

Reflection

My sister took her first job this week, and she is having trouble relating to coworkers of other colors and ethnicities. She is African-American, and she attended elementary and high schools where the students are primarily African-American. She just graduated from one of the historically black colleges in our country. My sister comes from a Christian family. She is well educated. But she lacks understanding of coworkers who are **simply not familiar**.

I reminded her workplace diversity fosters mutual respect among employees. I encouraged her to acknowledge the differences in others because often that leads you to find some similarities. The biggest similarity will be many coworkers are part of the Body of Christ. And our Lord wants my sister to live in harmony with those who have not yet acknowledged Christ.

If you are struggling with workplace diversity like my sister, remember what scripture says. Diversity is not just part of being human, it is a part of belonging to God.

So at work today, if you are surrounded by people who are **simply not familiar**, search deeper. Embrace the diversity of His world, His people, and His workplace.

Prayer

Head bowed, I come to You in prayer asking for strength, wisdom, and courage to embrace all those who do not look like me. Let me welcome Your image in everyone I see! In Jesus' name, I pray. Amen.

Michelle Lewis

Week 36, Day 5

disqualified in the task

Reading

1 Corinthians 9:27 [NLT] I discipline my body like an athlete, training it to do what it should. Otherwise, I fear that after preaching to others I myself might be disqualified.

Reflection

Each year the men on death row have a summer tournament! We play basketball and volleyball against each other. And each year, something strange happens. In the passion to win a ball game, some lose their passion to represent Christ. They swear and shout obscenities to players on the other team. They try to cheat and argue with the referees. Because of the choices being made, they become **disqualified in the task** of claiming Christ in the eyes of others.

Do you know someone like that? Someone at work? Perhaps it's you?

Always praying and reading the Bible, and always being the nicest person in the office. Then something comes up. It may be a work assignment, or it may be a sporting event. But it's always something that appears to be of such great value. Then that nice Christian becomes rude, angry, bitter, selfish. In the eyes of others, he can easily become **disqualified in the task** of claiming Christ.

Today at work, watch yourself. Discipline yourself. Don't let your priorities get mixed up. Others are watching you because you claim to represent Christ. You claim to be a *Christian public servant*. Do not disappoint them. Do not disappoint yourself. Do not disappoint Christ.

Today at work, do not let yourself be **disqualified in the task** of claiming Christ.

Prayer

Father, in the name of Jesus, I pray. Keep me accountable to all You have done for me and for all You have done through me. In the eyes of others – in Your eyes – I do not want to become **disqualified in the task** of claiming Christ. Amen.

Jimmy Davis, Jr.

Week 37, Day 1

leftovers to take to work

Reading

James 1:19(b) [ESV] let every person be quick to hear, slow to speak, slow to anger.

Proverbs 21:9 [ESV] It is better to live in a corner of the housetop than in a house shared with a quarrelsome wife.

Reflection

A friend called yesterday, stressed with his wife. They get into heated arguments, and he's fed up with the marriage. He is tired of her blaming him for not making enough money. His wife has a job, but she feels the husband should pay the rent and utility bills. Because of these constant arguments at night, he's having trouble focusing on his job during the day.

I reminded my friend of scripture. <u>Heated</u> communication is <u>poor</u> communication, and poor communication is <u>dishonest</u> communication. And while it is better to live in a corner of the housetop, it is best to end the quarrels by being slow to accuse and slow to anger.

Are you at work today, like my friend, with *another quarrel waiting* when you get home tonight? And from that argument, will you have **leftovers to take to work**? Like my friend, can you <u>really</u> work with such leftovers lingering in your mind and heart?

Tonight, begin the process of *Christ-centered communication* with your spouse. Both of you – learn through Christ to be quick to hear, slow to speak, and slow to anger. A life in the corner of the housetop is no Christ-life for either of you.

Yes, tonight after work, begin the healing process only a *Christ-centered conversation* can bring. Who knows? Tomorrow you just might have fewer **leftovers to take to work!**

Prayer

Lord, thank You for always watching over me and my wife in a dismayed time. Continue to place Your everlasting arms around my wife and me before we go to work and after we come home from work. Bless us with Your goodness and grace. In Your name, I pray. Amen.

William Waples

Week 37, Day 2

another number to the birthdays

Reading

Proverbs 16:31 [NIV] Gray hair is a crown of splendor; it is attained in the way of righteousness.

Proverbs 20:29 [NIV] The glory of young men is their strength, gray hair the splendor of the old.

Reflection

It seems there are two types of coworkers when it comes to birthdays. There are those who refuse to mention they are getting older. By not talking about age, especially at the workplace, they want to believe the aging process stops. Then there are others who embrace birthdays with joy and eagerly await the break-room celebration. I tend to fall into the second group. Adding **another number to the birthdays** one has should be celebrated and revered.

It's true, as age creeps in, you cannot do all you once could do. But while strength may belong to the young, those adding **another number to the birthdays** have gained tremendous wisdom and experience. Especially in the workplace, wisdom and experience should be valued.

Today at work, be one of those who believes birthdays are to be celebrated. Do not be ashamed of your age, and let no coworker be ashamed either. Gray hair is a crown of splendor and should be celebrated at work.

So order that cake for break time. A coworker is adding **another number to the birthdays**. Go ahead and celebrate that God-given age!

Prayer

Dear Lord, I am thankful I am adding **another number to the birthdays** again. You have allowed me to experience many wonders in my years. Help me find the "glory and splendor" of everyone I work with – regardless of age. Let me never run out of joy for the celebration of another year doing Your pleasing and perfect will. In Your name, I pray. Amen.

Stan Best

Week 37, Day 3

work in safety

Reading

Romans 12:12 [ESV] Rejoice in hope, be patient in tribulation, be constant in prayer.

Psalm 4:8 [ESV] In peace I will both lie down and sleep; for you alone, O Lord, make me dwell in safety.

Reflection

Lisa's a good friend who is a school bus driver. For over 30 years, she has loved that job. But in the past few years, things have changed. The older kids on the bus have become more disrespectful and disobedient. She has become the victim of verbal violence, and some have threatened her with physical violence. Oh, she reports each incident, but not much has happened. The school district can't afford security officers to ride along with her, and she's been told just to drive the bus and get the kids to their destination.

She is afraid. Yet Lisa prays each night for patience in waiting on the Lord to bring her to safety. She prays the Lord will open new and promising doors. And guess what? The Lord has heard her cry! Next school year, she's being assigned a different bus route. She will **work in safety**.

Is your work environment safe? How close are you to the threat of violence? Does it come in the form of bullying from your supervisor or a coworker? Or does harm come from those you serve? Do you go home each night afraid – thinking there is no hope for a safer tomorrow?

When your health and life are at stake, make sure you report it. But also remember God answers all prayers. He wants you to both lie down and sleep in peace knowing He promises you safety. Be faithful and understand all He requires is your patience in tribulation.

This morning, ask God for assurance that you will **work in safety** – either in your current job or a better one He is preparing. Be constant in prayer and rejoice in hope.

Our Lord will take care of you. He will make you safe.

Prayer

Dear Heavenly Father, I thank You for giving me a safe workplace. I pray You will bless everyone with the same. In Jesus' name, I pray. Amen.

Lakisha Williams

Week 37, Day 4

don't lose your footing

Reading

Psalm 73:2-3, 11-12(a) [NLT] But as for me, I almost lost my footing. My feet were slipping, and I was almost gone. For I envied the proud when I saw them prosper despite their wickedness… "What does God know?" they ask. "Does the Most High even know what's happening?" Look at these wicked people—enjoying a life of ease

Reflection

Last night I attended an athletic banquet. These are usually fun events, rewarding hard-work and seeing athletes all dressed up instead of outfitted in practice and playing wear. However, at this particular celebration, I was disheartened. Multiple program coaches chose not to attend to present the player awards. Many of these leaders make much more money than me. But that night, they were elsewhere – enjoying a life of ease. Their absence seemed arrogant, prideful, and done with calloused hearts. Nevertheless, a part of me also was envious. For I worked so hard for my players without the so-called success, awards, and provisions. Yes, at that banquet, I started to *lose my footing*, and I wished I was enjoying their life of ease.

But then I remembered something. I work for God and not for man. I strive for an eternal victory in addition to worldly trophies that accumulate dust and eventually get thrown away. I pour my heart, tears, and soul into something much more important than money or fame: helping to shape young players into a team of good citizens and beloved members of the Body of Christ. As I sat at that banquet with my players, I remembered He sees the work I am doing. He knows what's happening, and He is pleased with me.

Do you ever envy the "proud" at work? When jealousy starts to take over, **don't lose your footing**! God sees you. He knows what's happening. He is pleased with you, and He has more work for you to do.

As you prepare for work today, don't envy that life of ease so often chosen by the "arrogant." God really does know what's happening, so be careful and **don't lose your footing**!

Prayer

Father, don't let me lose my footing during the hard times and the good times – during worldly defeat and worldly victory. Help me continue to work for You in the midst of this cruel and artificial world. Give me strength, Father. Remind me who I am and to Whom I belong. Thank You for the opportunity to do Your work. I pray these things in Jesus' name. Amen.

Kathryn Saunders

Week 37, Day 5

stay in step with Jesus

Reading

1 Samuel 18:9 [KJV] And Saul eyed David from that day and forward.

John 13:15 [KJV] For I have given you an example, that ye should do as I have done to you.

Reflection

There is a brother who "attends" but does not worship in the Death Row Church. He is, let's just say, not the nicest person you would ever meet. He is cruel to other brothers, offers ridicule where comfort is needed, and takes advantage of any weakness he sees in those around him. Within our church and on Death row, he is always a divisive voice. I'm not saying he is all bad, but for the most part, it appears he does not **stay in step with Jesus**.

Another brother down the row keeps asking me why we allow this mean brother in our church? He asks me why would I even go to a church that tolerates a brother that mean? I say I don't go to church to be like King Saul. I don't go to judge or fear others or even to keep an eye on others who are sitting next to me. I go to church to **stay in step with Jesus,** and hopefully, that mean brother may someday do the same. That's what all of us in the Death Row Church need to do. That is our job as *Christian public servants* here on death row.

It's easy, especially where we work, to be like King Saul. We can quickly fall into the trap of keeping eyes on others rather than following the example of Christ. How about where you work? Do you **stay in step with Jesus,** or are you more with King Saul? Are you constantly focused on who is hurting you or on the One through which others can help you? Do you choose to protect yourself or follow His example?

As you go to work this morning, think about it. Do you want to **stay in step with Jesus**, or will you follow the example of King Saul? Choose wisely.

Prayer

Father, in the name of Jesus, I pray. Forgive me when I get out of step with Your Son. Forgive me when I want to put my eyes on people or situations I want to control. Jesus – not me or anyone else – is my example. Only through His example can I change and live. Amen.

Jimmy Davis, Jr.

Week 38, Day 1

confident through the comfort abounding

Reading

Psalm 55:22 [NIV] Cast your cares on the LORD and he will sustain you; he will never let the righteous be shaken.

2 Corinthians 1:5 [NIV] For just as we share abundantly in the sufferings of Christ, so also our comfort abounds through Christ.

Reflection

A few months ago, a coworker became pregnant with a baby boy! How wonderful, I thought, since I knew her little daughter wanted a baby brother! This was a "high risk" pregnancy, and she eventually went on bed-rest – following every bit of her doctor's orders. Most importantly, she was **confident through the comfort abounding** from our Lord.

Well, yesterday, terrible news arrived via social media. That precious newborn baby boy was delivered but quickly ascended back into heaven. I can't stop crying, and my heart is broken for that lady who works across the hallway. Yet at the same time, her postings show grace and faith. While confessing *only God knows* why her son couldn't stay, she remains **confident through the comfort abounding** from Him.

I don't know about you, but today I will hold my kids a little tighter before going to work. When I return home, I will say "I love you" a little more than before. Yet I will not forget the faith shown by my coworker in her suffering. It's true *only God knows* the why of this world, including why babies and loved ones are taken prematurely to heaven. But whatever happens, I know I must cast my cares to the Lord for He will sustain me. Yes, today and always, I will be **confident through the comfort abounding** from our Lord.

Do you know a coworker in this kind of crisis, perhaps struggling to understand the way of our Lord? Or is it you? Mourn in the loss, but pray for His grace that will certainly fall from the same heaven that takes away a loved one. He will sustain you.

As you go to work today, remember *only God knows* the timing of life. And yet, like my friend at work, be certain about God. He sustains the righteous-in-suffering. You may not understand the "why" of God, but be **confident through the comfort abounding** from Him.

Prayer

Lord Jesus, please sustain me in my suffering, as You sustain all Your people. I trust Your ways, and I know Your comfort will abound. In Your precious name, I believe and I pray. Amen.

Maureen Bereznak

Week 38, Day 2

serve Him and His people

Reading

Colossians 3:23 [GNT] Whatever you do, work at it with all your heart, as though you were working for the Lord and not for people.

Matthew 25:40 [GNT] The King will reply, 'I tell you, whenever you did this for one of the least important of these followers of mine, you did it for me!'

Reflection

My friend works at a call center for a nonprofit agency. It's important work, and senior citizens receive help from her every day. Her supervisors are encouraging, and she gets along well with coworkers. But she is not happy with her job. She received a promotion within the last year but no pay-raise. And she is growing tired of callers yelling at her when she cannot assist them. With the passing of each workday, my friend loses more motivation. To top it all off, she has applied for several jobs but has heard nothing back.

One of the worst things that can happen at work is to lose your motivation. Salary becomes the only driving force – but the less you make, the less motivation you have to do an excellent job. You start looking at the clock to see how much time is left before breaks, lunch, and going home. You stop looking at the clock to see how much time remains to help others as a *Christian public servant*.

Scripture teaches our real boss is the Lord and our real task is to **serve Him and His people**. You and I have no option but to obey Him, and so we must find ways to do this – either in the same job or in a new job.

If you are heading to work this morning without motivation to **serve Him and His people** with all your heart, think twice. You have no option – if you want true success in your current job or true success leading to another job – you must follow His Word. Motivation comes not from salary or raise, and it doesn't come from encouraging supervisors and friendly coworkers. It certainly does not come from grateful citizens. All these things help with motivation, but all these things can easily pass away before the hour to leave the office.

Today at work, don't serve for worldly reasons. Serve with all your heart. Obey scripture and **serve Him and His people**. You will find motivation – for this job and the next!

Prayer

Dear Lord, thank You for being my motivation at work. I promise to serve You and Your people throughout the day. In Your name, I pray. Amen.

Brianna Gibson

Week 38, Day 3

a Christian communicator

Reading

James 1:19(b) [NIV] be quick to listen, slow to speak and slow to become angry

Reflection

I'm a single mother raising two children, working full-time, and in graduate school at night. It's not easy, believe me. Too often the stress builds up, and this can affect home, workplace, and classroom.

Scripture says communication is important. But *communication through Christ* is not the same as communication through secular means. It's not a *quid pro quo*. It's not trying to out debate someone. It doesn't consist of shouting and angry outcries.

Scripture requires me to be **a Christian communicator**. This means I must show an obedience to listening when it comes to conversations with God. Being **a Christian communicator** means being slow to speak when it comes to seeing and understanding the needs of my children. Being **a Christian communicator** means I need to be really slow to anger, including when it comes to my workplace and classroom. Scripture gives a prescription for checking my emotions and freeing me from the bounds of my situation.

Are you under stress? Are you like me – a single parent with a full-time job and enrolled in night school? Sure, you are doing important things that will improve your family and advance your career. But are you **a Christian communicator**? Or are you willing to communicate just like everyone else in the secular world?

As you go to work today, think about what scripture says about communication. Listen well, then speak, and check your anger. Be **a Christian communicator**.

Prayer

Father, help me learn how to communicate by listening to You, my children, those in my workplace, and those in my classroom. Teach me how to measure my words so I can deflate my emotions. Help me to cope through these stressful times. In Jesus' name, I pray. Amen.

Veronica Gates

Week 38, Day 4

a friend unknown

Reading

John 15:13 [NIV] Greater love has no one than this: to lay down one's life for one's friends.

Luke 10:36-37 [NIV] "Which of these three do you think was a neighbor to the man who fell into the hands of robbers?" The expert in the law replied, "The one who had mercy on him."
Jesus told him, "Go and do likewise."

Reflection

A few summers ago, I had the honor to stand at the National Cemetery at Omaha Beach in Normandy, France. As I looked from the cliffs at the beach those men had to cross and the white crosses of those who did not make it, I came to understand the true meaning of "hero." Those who "lay down" their lives for me – **a friend unknown** – they are true heroes.

And of course, Jesus tells about the Samaritan who helped a stranger victimized by robbers. Jesus does not describe this man as a hero, for he did not lay down his life, but simply as a neighbor offering mercy to a stranger – **a friend unknown**.

So when I hear coworkers and supervisors pontificate about the sacrifices they must make for their agency – well, you'll have to forgive me if look the other way. We have developed a real talent in convincing others how greatly we sacrifice – acting as if that somehow makes us heroes. And boasting is never an attribute of being a Good Samaritan. As *Christian public servants*, we must understand the meaning of real sacrifice and the meaning of real mercy, and therefore, we should never participate in talk that belittles those meanings.

As you go to work today, think of all the amazing sacrifices made by true heroes – including today's heroes protecting us from terrorists. Then think of all the offerings of mercy that could be performed on this very day – gestures of mercy that can stem the tide of hatred in the world and in your neighborhood. Finally, remember God doesn't expect you to be a hero today. But He wants you to be a Good Samaritan every day.

Today at work, don't complain. Don't pontificate. Don't cross the street to avoid being either a hero or a neighbor. Look for ways to sacrifice for others so they can gain a small idea of the great love that has been shown to you. Do this for just one person at work – **a friend unknown**.

Now, go and do likewise.

Prayer

Dear Lord, I thank You for heroes and neighbors. Thank You for being both Hero and Neighbor to me, showing Your great love that saved a sinner like me. Help me each day show that love to others, not just friends but enemies, as a hero or as a neighbor. In this way, may others come to know that great love for themselves and always call You Friend! In Your name, I pray. Amen.

Stan Best

Week 38, Day 5

a nevertheless spirit

Reading

Matthew 26:39(b) [NIV] My Father, if it is possible, may this cup be taken from me. Yet not as I will, but as you will.

Reflection

As I read and study, I find so many people in the Bible who had **a nevertheless spirit** of obedience to God. You know, people who followed God regardless of the detail and regardless of the consequence. Moses, Noah, David, Daniel, and Paul come to my mind. And then, of course, there was Jesus. The *worldly part* of Jesus did not want to die. (Who does?) But the *spiritual part* of Jesus knew even death was in God's hands. Even in preparing for death, He lived a life of obedience – not worldly will but *spiritual will*. Jesus was going to do whatever God wanted Him to do, regardless of the pain involved.

And so it should be with us.

Every day you and I are put in situations we don't want. We see things we wish we didn't. We hear things we can't block from our ears. Settings beyond our comfort zones.

As a *Christian public servant*, don't let circumstance control your action. Don't let the world dictate your outcome. Don't let fear lead your way.

So at work today, you may not be where you want to be. You may be way out of your comfort zone. That's OK. Just be obedient to God regardless of all else. Listen to Him always. Keep **a nevertheless spirit** in your heart and in your soul.

And when you do, coworkers and those you serve will begin to see Him. Through you, my friend, others will experience the one true God. Yes, if you keep **a nevertheless spirit** of obedience to God, others will begin to hear His will – not theirs!

Prayer

Father, in the name of Jesus, I pray. Keep me humble. Give me opportunities today to do Your will, not mine. Amen.

Jimmy Davis, Jr.

Week 39, Day 1

sooner than what you think

Reading

Matthew 23:12 And whoever shall exalt himself shall be abased; and he that shall humble himself shall be exalted.

Reading

While the public service is so very different than the business sector, we do have one thing in common: the art of *networking*. "Here's my business card." "Connect with me on LinkedIn!" "Befriend me on Facebook." "Hook up via Twitter."

Sound familiar?

We live in a world of networking, a culture of self-promotion. This happens everywhere, and we all do it. Me? As an elected public servant, some call me the "king of networking." I have over 9,000 "close personal" friends on Facebook and many more Twitter contacts.

If you're like me, you love to connect with other public servants to help those we serve – and that makes networking a good thing. But too often we may use networking solely to promote ourselves. I know I sometimes do. That is what most MPA programs teach appointed public servants, and the internet is filled with web pages offering workshops on "networking" for elected officials.

As *Christian public servants*, elected and appointed, we need to keep things in perspective. Do we exalt God and help others in our networking, or do we use it selfishly? What kind of image and reputation are you building? Scripture tells me I need to be humble, and if I am, I will be exalted. Am I as humble as I must be to please Him?

Here's an idea. Today let's all engage in a little reverse networking – let's network others who humbly do not network themselves. Let's advance others who are <u>unable</u> to advance themselves.

You know **sooner than what you think** your business card will be lost. LinkedIn and Facebook will be technological relics. Yes, **sooner than what you think** people will have only memories of how you conducted yourself. Will they reflect fondly on your reputation of networking and advancing coworkers and the people you served?

And **sooner than what you think**, perhaps even today, they will exalt you for exalting others.

Networking? On the market? Looking for that promotion? Need that merit raise? Want to move up in your professional society? That's fine. Like me, you may also be a king or queen of networking. Perhaps that's necessary.

But as this work-week begins, let's practice a little reverse networking. Our Lord promises your success. You will be exalted!

Prayer

Lord, shape me into a humble servant today. Engage me in quietly doing my best work. Calm me in knowing it will be recognized by those *You* choose to recognize it. If others feel the need to exalt me, that is fine, but let me not exalt myself. Challenge me to advance the works and reputations of others. Today at work, let me practice a little reverse networking. Let me humble myself for You. Amen

Matt Whitman

Week 39, Day 2

felt, present and abides within

Reading

Acts 4:31-32 [ESV] And when they prayed, the place in which they were gathered together was shaken, and they were all filled with the Holy Spirit and continued to speak the word of God with boldness. Now the full number of those who believed were of one heart and soul, and no one said that any of the things that belonged to him was his own, but they had everything in common.

Reflection

Scripture tells us about a very powerful moment in the life of His church. Oh, how it must have felt to be there! To feel His presence! To know He was abiding within everyone in that room!

When the Spirit of God is **felt, present, and abides within** the believer, the community of God is perfected by divine grace. The heart and soul are changed into a oneness. Nothing, including *the blessings of Christ*, belongs to one person or one group or one nation. Everything, including *the blessings of Christ*, belongs to everyone – red and yellow, black and white; poor and rich; illiterate and educated; liberal and conservative; Marxist and capitalist; all nations and regions in this world.

This oneness in Christ can also happen in your workplace. Just imagine what oneness would look like there! Think what might be accomplished if the Spirit of God is **felt, present, and abides within** each coworker and the citizens you serve!!

It all begins with prayer and a gathering together. Before work begins? During a 15-minute work break? At lunch? After work?

And it all begins with you. Then one other. Then others around you.

Yes, it all begins with prayer and a gathering together. Yes, it all begins with you. And when the Spirit of God is **felt, present, and abides within** your workplace, everything changes!

Today, will you invite Him into your workplace? If you do, your workplace will certainly shake!

Prayer

Father, let me be bold today at work in glorifying You. I want to feel the presence of the Holy Spirit throughout the workday. I want the Holy Spirit to abide within all hearts and souls where I work. I want my workplace to shake with You. In Your Son's name, I pray. Amen.

Chris Summers

Week 39, Day 3

pass the test before you can serve

Reading

1 Timothy 3:10 [NLT] Before they are appointed as deacons, let them be closely examined. If they pass the test, then let them serve as deacons.

Reflection

Last Sunday, my pastor preached a powerful message titled "God proves you before He promotes you." As scripture confirms, you must **pass the test before you can serve**. That is what good leadership requires – whether in the capacity of church deacon or agency manager. You must **pass the test before you can serve**.

Are you tired of your job assignment? Feel stuck at your current rank? Are you eagerly awaiting the opportunity for promotion? Or are you only part-time and want to become full-time? Perhaps you are an intern hoping a position will open with your name on it?

Remember *God loves good human resource management*. He knows serving at a higher level requires knowledge and experience to do the job right. He favors performance assessment so abilities can be judged.

Today at work, don't grow tired of what you do. Don't just wait eagerly for an opportunity. *Work hard – very hard* – to show others you can do more if asked. Rest assured, God is with you on this venture. But whatever door He wants to open, He wants you to be prepared.

Both God and good managers are on the same page: **pass the test before you can serve**.

Prayer

Dear Heavenly Father, please help me pass Your test and the tests of my supervisor at work. I want to be obedient to You, Father. I want to be obedient to You in all places including my workplace. In Jesus' name, I pray. Amen.

Barbara Hill

Week 39, Day 4

with godly confidence

Reading

John 16:33 [ESV] I have said these things to you, that in me you have peace. In the world you have tribulation. But take heart: I have overcome the world.

Reflection

Knowing Jesus has overcome the world should give us tremendous relief. It allows you and me to respond to the world's influences that create doubt concerning the Way. The peace of God is our assurance to act always **with godly confidence**.

Yet it's difficult always to conform to the Way, isn't it? There are so many tribulations, including at work; so many efforts by the world to overcome you.

Just think about the worldly temptations you will face today. What will challenge you on the way to work? What will tempt you at work? What will you face when you leave work?

Take heart! Jesus overcame those same tribulations. And it is only through Jesus you can have peace – peace going to work, peace while at work, peace returning home from work.

So go to work today **with godly confidence**. His peace is offered. You can overcome the world!

Prayer

Father, remind me throughout this workday what Your Son overcame in this world. Bless me with the peace that comes only from Him. Give me strength to work **with godly confidence**. In Jesus' name, I pray. Amen.

Chris Summers

Week 39, Day 5

stay focused on the task

Reading

Hebrews 11:7 [KJV] By faith Noah, being warned of God of things not seen as yet, moved with fear, prepared an ark to the saving of his house; by the which he condemned the world, and became heir of the righteousness which is by faith.

Reflection

There is a brother on Life Row who refuses to listen to what God can do for him. Growing up, he was hurt by members of a church. He was abused by family members who claimed to love Jesus. He is on Life Row *without Christ*, yet God continues to direct me to this brother. For several years now, I have tried and tried. But it seems like bringing Christ to this brother is a hopeless task.

Lots of times, God asks me to do things – venture into situations – I feel are hopeless. But then I think of what God asked Noah to do. I remember the faith Noah showed in his obedience – even though he *moved with fear*. So I am learning to **stay focused on the task** God wants me to do. I am learning how to *move with fear* with Him by my side. And so I stay concentrated on that brother who does not know Christ.

Is God asking you to do the hopeless at work today? Is there a situation that is impossible? A project that requires a miracle? A coworker who settles for a lot less than Christ? And is God asking you to help?

Today at work, look a lot less at what seems hopeless. You may *move with fear*, but just **stay focused on the task** God has given you. Don't worry about what you can't see or understand. Like Noah, you will show righteousness. And like Noah, you will get a sneak view of God's bigger picture.

Prayer

Father, in the name of Jesus, I pray. Keep me focused so I can be an example of You. Let me move in Faith while I move in fear. Amen.

Jimmy Davis, Jr.

Week 40, Day 1

let others see

Reading

Matthew 5:16(b) [NIV] let your light shine before others, that they may see your good deeds and glorify your Father in heaven.

Reflection

A friend went to a grocery store after work. Because of the time of day, there were many people shopping and all wanted to get home as quickly as possible. Naturally, the checkout lines were long. A woman, unknown to my friend, pushed past those in front to get next to my friend. There she told my friend she had been watching her throughout the store and believed my friend to be a Christian. She then asked if my friend would pray over her because something was wrong. Well, my friend took the time to pray over this woman, and then they both went on their ways.

Some people in the checkout line were bothered. After all, prayer stopped my friend from loading up the conveyor belt. It kept the cashier from scanning my friend's items and putting them into sacks. It kept her from inserting the chip into the machine for payment. And it was true, that prayer took a few minutes of everyone's time.

But my friend didn't care. She decided to follow Him and **let others see** her light shine. She wasn't arrogant, nor was she slothful in doing it. But she wasn't shy or afraid to **let others see** her good deed and glorify her Father in heaven.

Today someone will need you as a Christian. This may be at work, on the way to work, or after work. It may be in someone else's workplace. That person will need you to step out of your comfort zone and bring our Lord a bit closer.

Will you step out? Will you shy away from Christ?

Today, **let others see** you shine. Your good deed will affect their good deeds, and Father will be glorified by all!

Prayer

Lord, forgive me for those times when my light is too dim. Give me strength to ever increase the wattage of Your Spirit in me. In Your name, I pray. Amen.

Alan Cox

Week 40, Day 2

looking for peace and security

Reading

Psalms 91:1-2 [KJV] He that dwelleth in the secret place of the most High shall abide under the shadow of the Almighty. I will say of the LORD, He is my refuge and my fortress: my God; in him will I trust.

Reflection

Yesterday in the break room, someone brought up the horrible act of terrorism that took place a few months ago. You remember, don't you? A young man walked into a church and opened fire on believers as they were ending their service. Someone at our lunch table mentioned0 it seems there is nowhere safe anymore, not even in church!

Everyone is **looking for peace and security**: children in their parents; wives in their husbands and vice versa; each one of us in our jobs; everyone in their governments. All our references are shaken, and no one can find peace or security.

Someone at the table proclaimed God is our only help in finding peace. If we are truly looking for security, it can only be found by choosing to dwell in Him. And dwelling doesn't just mean living under His wings. It means living with the strong intimacy of God, leading a real life of prayer, and reading daily the Word. It means taking prayer, the Word, and His intimacy to the world.

Spend a few minutes of your workday in silent prayer for peace. Yes, there is great confusion all around, but as a *Christian public servant*, you and I are called to promote harmony in our families, workplaces, and communities – harmony in our governments – anywhere we can make a practical difference.

Today, invite a coworker or citizen to join you in dwelling in God's peace. If you are **looking for peace and security**, it can only be found with Him..

Prayer

Dear Father God, thank You for reminding me fear has no place in my life. Help me find the time to pray at work, and bless me with the will to share Your Word and peace with someone else. In the name of the *One who makes the wind and the waves stand still*, I pray. Amen.

Evelyne F. Altema

Week 40, Day 3

struggle against the crowd

Reading

Luke 23:4, 24-25 [NIV] Then Pilate announced to the chief priests and the crowd, "I find no basis for a charge against this man." ... So Pilate decided to grant their demand. He released the man who had been thrown into prison for insurrection and murder, the one they asked for, and surrendered Jesus to their will.

Reflection

We all **struggle against the crowd**. After all, we live in a world where everyone is on display and constantly evaluated for what we look like, how we talk, what we say and post, and even what we don't say and post. This is especially true for Christians at work. We **struggle against the crowd** whenever a crowd gathers.

It's easy to get worn-down and just give in to the crowd. That's what Pilate did. He knew there was no basis for the charges against Jesus, and yet in a moment of weakness, he gave in to their demands and granted the warrant to execute the King of the Jews.

Now you might think you would have done better than Pilate. Yet I will confess I have failed miserably sometimes in my **struggle against the crowd**. I have not stood up to the break room jokes, to the frequent character assassinations of coworkers, to decisions made simply to treat citizens as customers and not as brothers and sisters. To go along with others after work just for the sake of comfort, ease, and popularity. In my **struggle against the crowd**, I know I have failed Jesus.

Yet I am reminded Jesus turns our broken failures into the greatest love story. If Pilate refuses to crucify him and had not turned him over to the crowd in the square, the course of our salvation would have looked dramatically different. So as I continue to **struggle against the crowd**, I realize God knows my mistakes and sees my failures. He plans for my moments of weakness, just as He did with Pilate's weakness. My failures play a role in someone else's story. My destiny is, therefore, closely linked to those around me. And I know God can work someone's failures into my success story.

Today at work, as you **struggle against the crowd**, take comfort in knowing God can work your failures into another's success. He can work another's failures into your success. It is not your responsibility to figure it out. Just know you are convicted yet repaired by Him!

Prayer

Father, I thank You for all You do for me. I thank You for my mess and for working through me. Give me strength to struggle against the crowd but forgiveness when I fail. In Jesus' name, I pray. Amen.

Kathryn Saunders

Week 40, Day 4

that bad attitude day

Reading

Ephesians 4:31[NLT] Get rid of all bitterness, rage, anger, harsh words, and slander, as well as all types of evil behavior. Instead, be kind to each, tenderhearted, forgiving one another, just as God through Christ has forgiven you.

Reflection

Yesterday my supervisor temporarily transferred me to another task that was not part of my job description. Being unfamiliar with this assignment, I thought about everything that could go wrong. Despite catching on after an hour or so, I remained angry. I treated everyone coldly and, in a few instances, impolite. By noon the look on my face revealed to one and all I was having **that bad attitude day**.

At lunch, a coworker sat me down, and we prayed God would remove all negativity from my heart. Before lunchtime was over, I realized God did not approve of my behavior. As the afternoon began, I apologized to my coworkers and supervisor. And guess what, I fell in love with my new task assignment and hope I can do these tasks again!

The workplace brings out a lot of emotions. When things don't go your way, it doesn't mean you can take it out on others. After all, having **that bad attitude day** can easily lead to a poor reputation and bad assessment – the kind you really don't want. It also displeases your Lord.

Today at work, if negativity starts to enter the equation, pray before things develop into **that bad attitude day**. Bitterness, rage, anger, and harsh words are not worth it – neither in your workplace nor in His kingdom. So be kind, tenderhearted, and forgiving – just as Christ is to you!

Prayer

Dear God, thank You for this workday. Let no negativity enter my heart. In Jesus' name, I pray. Amen.

Lakisha Williams

Week 40, Day 5

seemingly never-ending process

Reading

Isaiah 40:31(a) [NKJV] But those who wait on the LORD shall renew *their* strength

Reflection

I wait on a lot of things. I bet you do, too. The older we get, the more patient we become in *the waiting game*. I wait on the cell to open each morning so I can do my job as a runner here on Life Row. You wait for the coffee to brew before you get dressed for work. I wait on the ice bucket to arrive so I can cool down the brothers a bit. You wait on the air conditioner to start up when you get to work. I bet we both wait for some of our meals. Yes, the older we get, the better we wait.

But how patient are you in waiting on the Lord? The less patient you are, the more tired you get. Suddenly you have little or no strength left. Am I right?

Waiting on the Lord is a **seemingly never-ending process** – not because He does not love you, but because he wants to renew your strength. How else will you be strong enough for that new job? For that promotion? For that important task He needs you to perform? The **seemingly never-ending process** of waiting on the Lord not only strengthens you, it also strengthens those around you.

Are you waiting for something special to happen at work today? Don't forget all the time it takes in His **seemingly never-ending process** will provide the needed strength.

So at work today, be patient – only He can renew your strength!

Prayer

Father, in the name of Jesus I pray. Thank You for renewing my strength as I wait on You. Amen.

Jimmy Davis, Jr.

Week 41, Day 1

lunchtime with God

Reading

Proverbs 15:33 [KJV] The fear of the LORD is the instruction of wisdom; and before honor is humility.

Reflection

There are many ways workers spend their lunch break. Most days, I spend mine with a salad and the computer screen displaying some learned article or course text. The time spent feeds both my body and mind.

One afternoon I was munching along and reading an article with the main message "Who you are is how you lead." The article asked the reader to identify words or phrases that best define who you are. In response, I found myself thinking, "What makes God happy? Do I appreciate God's creation around me?" And finally, "What makes me happy?"

Before I even realized it, I was spending **lunchtime with God**!

While the article's aim was to help others produce their best at work, I realized God's Word gives me the best self-help and professional development. In fact, including God in my day-to-day work is the only way I can do my best.

So are you making God happy on this workday? I know some days being a good *Christian public servant* just takes a little more time and effort. It's not always easy to make Him happy.

Today, why not spend **lunchtime with God**? The time spent will not only make God happy, it will help you do your best for the remainder of the workday.

Prayer

Father, please never let me get so full of myself or the analytical philosophies of professional self-help I can't see Your hand and guidance in all things. Let Your Spirit guide me to become a better person and leader. Please keep me uncomplicated, humble, and ready to serve all so You receive the glory. I pray this in Jesus' name. Amen.

Patricia A. Maley

Week 41, Day 2

quietly by the wayside

Reading

Philippians 1:6, 4:13 [KJV] Being confident of this very thing, that he which hath begun a good work in you will perform it until the day of Jesus Christ... I can do all things through Christ which strengtheneth me.

Reflection

I was almost overcome by fear the first day I entered the office. Can I really do this job? Yet as days turned into weeks and weeks turned into months, I discovered that not only could I perform my job duties, I could perform them well! My fears fell **quietly by the wayside**, but I must confess I had help.

My help? I was comforted by the Holy Spirit as He led me to scripture. There I found Christ is working in all believers and anything is possible if done through Him. Yes, scripture says you and I can do all things through the strength of Christ!

So my fears fell **quietly by the wayside** as the Holy Spirit enabled me to prepare and do my job. I've come to know He, not I, performs the work needed in me. I have come to know I'm not on my own in the workplace. I confess I have help. I am hidden in Christ Jesus, and it is He who stands with me in all tasks I prepare to do.

Are you fearful at work? Have an intimidating assignment? Must give an introduction or a speech? Or are you entering a new office like I did? Remember Christ Jesus is with you. He offers the grace and strength you need to prepare for the daily work and perform the duties well.

As you prepare for the tasks of the day, cast out your fears and leave them **quietly by the wayside**. Today at work, you, too, have help!

Prayer

Father, I need Your help in everything I do – especially in my job. Thank You for Your grace and Your strength in preparing me for this workday. Through you, I am ready to enter the office! In Christ Jesus' name, I pray. Amen.

Sureldie Williams

Week 41, Day 3

building His kingdom

Reading

II Chronicles 9:22-23[NKJV] So King Solomon surpassed all the kings of the earth in riches and wisdom. And all the kings of the earth sought the presence of Solomon to hear his wisdom, which God had put in his heart.

Matthew 24:35 [NKJV] Heaven and earth will pass away, but My words will by no means pass away.

Matthew 6:19-21 [NKJV] Do not lay up for yourselves treasures on earth, where moth and rust destroy and where thieves break in and steal; but lay up for yourselves treasures in heaven, where neither moth nor rust destroys and where thieves do not break in and steal. For where your treasure is, there your heart will be also.

Reflection

One of the great things I get to do, as part of my work, is to travel as an international accreditation mentor and evaluator. Recently I was in Mongolia, famous for Genghis Kahn who conquered more of the earth's land surface than any other conqueror in history. What people do not know is he also created a very efficient system public service to run his far-flung empire. Under his rule, paper currency was introduced, religious tolerance was permitted in his court, and trade flourished. Looking at the grasslands in Mongolia, I can imagine Genghis Kahn riding with his army across the plains. Little has changed, and outside of the cities, Genghis would recognize much of contemporary Mongolia *– except his kingdom has taken the path all earthly kingdoms ultimately take. He is dead, and his kingdom is gone.*

Solomon, like Genghis Kahn, built a kingdom, but for all his wisdom, it passed away too. Jesus, on the other hand, is alive and still **building His kingdom** through His followers. Every *Christian public servant* must keep **building His kingdom** daily by the way we live and conduct ourselves through our work. The "kingdoms" you and I work for will someday pass away – but what we do for our Lord will not fade if we focus on **building His kingdom**.

As you go about your workday, remember what you do must have more than just an impact on the here and now – it must have *an impact on eternity*. The paperwork will perish someday, but the lives you impact for Christ will bear fruit for eternity.

Today, keep **building His kingdom** in your workplace.

<u>Prayer</u>

Lord, thank You for building a kingdom that will not end. Help me be a part of building that kingdom today in some small way through the work You have called me to do. In Jesus' name, I pray. Amen.

Kevin Cooney

Week 41, Day 4

the perfect bond of unity

Reading

Colossians 4:12(b), 14 [HCSB] put on heartfelt compassion, kindness, humility, gentleness, and patience, accepting one another and forgiving one another if anyone has a complaint against another… Above all, put on love—**the perfect bond of unity**.

Reflection

Ah, somewhere in the world, it's summertime! It is warm and beautiful. In a perfect world, that kind of weather brings friends together for picnics, outdoor events, and quiet dinners at outdoor cafés. One can feel the love, kindness, and acceptance of one another. But sometimes spending too much time with other people creates tensions. Long past arguments and grudges resurface, new arguments emerge, and all arguments seem to come as dessert with the topping of gossip and back-handed compliments. Even the most beautiful evening can be ruined when "that person" shows up.

Scripture reminds us to be at peace with everyone. If you and I can't do that with those closest to us on a warm and beautiful day or night, how can we form **the perfect bond of unity** with those not so close to us. Specifically, how can we ever expect to bravely put on love during the trials and tribulations of interacting with those found in the workplace?

Wherever you live and regardless of season, reestablish the bonds of love with others. As *Christian public servants*, community must be the foundation of all your interactions – including the workplace. That kind of community is only built on love, honesty, and support. Then throughout the rest of the year, you will not feel so distant from others. And *feeling distant is easiest in the workplace*. Today at work, renew those decaying bonds around you. A community of love – **the perfect bond of unity** – is a blessing on or off work and in every season!

Prayer

Dear Lord, thank You for blessing me with communities of love – with friends, family, and coworkers. Regardless of the season, help me be thankful for these communities throughout the entire year – just as I am grateful for the bond of unity I have with You for eternity. In Your name, I pray. Amen.

Joshua Nierle

Week 41, Day 5

love others in return

Reading

1 John 4:19 [NIV] We love because he first loved us.

Reflection

There is this new brother down the row. Quiet. Shy. Practically built a wall around himself. But one day last month, I was the "runner" for the row – you know, the brother who gets the celled brothers ice cubes and water. Well, this new brother stopped me outside his cell, and he started to talk. After a few minutes of idle chatting, he started to talk about himself: how bad he was, the murder that got him to death row, and how his family and gang on the outside choose not to write or answer his phone calls. And so we talked for quite a while, with the other brothers being patient in receiving their requests as they knew what was happening. I told him everything he has done in the past is not what he can do today. I said, "Our Lord loved you first, and now you must go and **love others in return**."

I had to make my rounds, as other brothers were waiting, but I told this brother I'd be back. And when I went back, I surprised him with some chips and a cold drink of water. We talked some more, but this time about me – the bad things I did in my free-world life and how Christ took a hold of me once I got here on Life Row and empowered me with His love. Then this brother said, "Jimmy, I love you." I told him I loved him, and he put his hands through the bars so he could hug me. And I hugged him back. When I stepped from his cell gate, I could see Jesus' love in his smile. This brother had learned to **love others in return**.

I don't know much about where you live and work, but it can't be too much different than where I am. Is it? Here, men do not smile much. They certainly don't hug. And they don't show love. Is that not the case at your workplace? But as Christians, we must **love others in return** for the love Jesus first gave us.
As you go to work today, remember Jesus first loved you. You must **love others in return**. And your workplace is a good place to start!

Prayer

Father, in the name of Jesus, I pray. Thank You for Your love. Now I need to pass it on! Amen.

Jimmy Davis, Jr.

Week 42, Day 1

a simple yes or no

Reading

Matthew 5:37 [ESV] Let what you say be simply "Yes" or "No"; anything more than this comes from evil.

John 8:31(b)-32 [ESV] If you abide in my word, you are truly my disciples, and you will know the truth, and the truth will set you free.

Reflection

There was a time I liked listening to the news driving to work each morning. But increasingly I'm bothered by all the spin. Oh, I know the problems we face are quite complex. There are so many gray areas; very little of the world is denotative. Yet we seem to have grown comfortable with *rationalization, partial truth, and alternate facts*. It doesn't matter what the issue is, whether in your country or in my community, and no philosophy or ideology has a monopoly on spin. But when did we get so mesmerized by it?

Maybe spin has always been there. This may be why Jesus addresses the issue of swearing falsely and giving incomplete testimony. Quite possibly, this is why He teaches all is needed is **a simple yes or no**. For if you and I live in His Word, we will know the truth, and the <u>truth</u> – not *rationalization, partial truth, and alternative facts* – will set us free.

As a *Christian public servant*, you <u>are</u> judged by what you say. Many hope your words come from evil. And the more words you use, the greater the chances those words will be steamed in *rationalization, partial truth, and alternate facts*.

If you practice **a simple yes or no** at work today, telling the truth concisely yet completely as His Word leads you, then your spin will go away. And the spin used by others may just follow. And soon, perhaps the spin of the whole world will follow suit. Who knows, soon the news driving home from work might just abide in His Word. And it <u>will</u> set us all free!

Prayer

Father God, today at work, let me abide in You. Let me remove my own *rationalization, partial truth, and alternate facts*. Let the truth in You set others free – in my workplace and throughout the world. In Jesus' name, I pray. Amen.

James D. Slack

Week 42, Day 2

take God with you

Reading

1 Peter 5:7 [GNT] Leave all your worries with him, because he cares for you.

Deuteronomy 31:6 [GNT] Be determined and confident. Do not be afraid of them. Your God, the Lord himself, will be with you. He will not fail you or abandon you.

Reflection

This summer I've moved 15 hours from home to take an internship in my nation's capital. The path I'm on is where I want to be, and so I was eager to begin this adventure. However, when I moved in and settled down into the routine of work, the excitement started to diminish. It wasn't anything about the job. It was just I started to feel like a "small-town boy" in a big city. This feeling of being in a strange place seemed overwhelming. Although everyone at the office was nice to the "new kid," I felt alone.

Then I realized something. As a child of God, I have the luxury of <u>never</u> being alone. Scripture reminds me I will <u>not</u> be abandoned – if I acknowledge God's presence within me every day. And guess what? My confidence started to build, and the excitement is back!

Do you have an internship? Have you started a new position with a different agency? Are you working in a strange city? A new job is always exciting, offering both challenges and opportunities. Each day will be filled with unique struggles and the busyness of work. Remember it is important to **take God with you** on the new adventure. After all, He cares about <u>you</u>!

Yes, today leave your worries with Him. You will <u>not</u> feel alone at work – if you **take God with you**!

Prayer

Almighty Lord, thank You for never abandoning me through challenging times. Please help me use this ultimate love You have shown me to show love and compassion to others in need. In Your Holy name, I pray. Amen.

Stephen W.G. Chavez

Week 42, Day 3

how will you spend your time

Reading

Ephesians 5:15-17 [ESV] Look carefully then how you walk, not as unwise but as wise, making the best use of the time, because the days are evil. Therefore do not be foolish, but understand what the will of the Lord is.

Reflection

I always approach my evenings with the same good intentions. I plan to study my Bible, read the paper or a good book, spend time with my wife and kids, and maybe watch a bit of TV. On Wednesday night, of course, there is church supper. I leave work looking forward to these activities.

Yet, unfortunately, it's difficult to do the things I look forward to. I find myself either distracted by the news on TV or consumed by the work I take home. Suddenly I realize the entire evening is sort of, well, wasted.

As a *Christian public servant*, I have a responsibility to understand how the Lord wants me to spend my time – at work and when I get home. Consequently, I need to make sure work life does not bleed too much into home life. To do so would be a selfish use of my time because it would not honor the will of my Lord.

After work tonight, **how will you spend your time**? Will you spend it glorifying the Lord with the Word and with family? Will you be blessed with time to help your son with homework? Blessed with time to go to your daughter's soccer game – without using your iPhone? Will the church supper be a part of your plan?

So after work, **how will you spend your time**? Do not be foolish. Understand what the Lord wants. Know the days are evil.

Prayer

Dear Lord, help me treat my time preciously and judiciously so I may honor You by always following Your will. In Your name, I pray. Amen.

Paul Theroux

Week 42, Day 4

put aside the inconsequential

Reading

Deuteronomy 6:6-7 [NIV] These commandments that I give you today are to be on your hearts. Impress them on your children. Talk about them when you sit at home and when you walk along the road, when you lie down and when you get up.

Reflection

Driving to work each morning, I have a million things running through my head. Where to have lunch. Get the oil changed. What to shop for after work. What movie to watch tonight. The weekend to-do list. But how much of this *stuff* really matters? How much of it leads to a focus on God?

You know God commanded the Israelites to take His Commandments and place them on their hearts. They were to think constantly of Him so He would be the most important thing in their lives. There would be no time to worry. They were to **put aside the inconsequential** things in life. He delivered them from Egypt, kept them in the desert, and prepared the Promised Land. He wanted them to focus only on Him because He would provide everything else for them.

The amazing thing is He wants you and me to do the same today. We get so wrapped up in the trivial things we sometimes forget to stop and focus on Him and His Word. He can and will provide everything for us – from time to perform our daily tasks at work to time to worship Him. Even time to rest our weary bodies.

So before you leave for work today, write down everything you want to remember. Then on your way to work, **put aside the inconsequential** list of this day. Some things are important, sure, but not as important as focusing on God. Yes, **put aside the inconsequential** this morning! Focus on Him and see what He can and will do in your workday and in your life.

Prayer

Lord, thank You for reminding me I am to focus on You in all things and in all situations today. Let me press Your Word onto my heart. In Your name, I pray. Amen.

Gilbert O. Craven

Week 42, Day 5

become a slave to all

Reading

1 Corinthians 9:19 [NLT] Even though I am a free man with no master, I have become a slave to all people to bring many to Christ.

Reflection

So many free-world brothers come here each week to share Jesus with the brothers on Life Row. They take off work, use vacation days, and drive for hours while paying for their own gas. And sometimes they must turn around once they get here because of a lock-down. Still, they make those weekly trips with joy and peace. Each free-world brother has **become a slave to all** of us on Life Row so many might come to Christ.

Before you get out of your car to start the workday, set it in your heart to **become a slave to all** so many might come to Christ. A coworker you know needs Him today.

Will you **become a slave to all** at work today?

Prayer

Father, in the name of Jesus, I pray. Give me the confidence to **become a slave to all**, to gain more sisters and brothers in the Family of Your Son, Jesus Christ. Amen.

Jimmy Davis, Jr.

Week 43, Day 1

win favor and a good name

Reading

Proverbs 3:1(b)-4 [NIV] keep my commands in your heart, for they will prolong your life many years and bring you peace and prosperity. Let love and faithfulness never leave you; bind them around your neck, write them on the tablet of your heart. Then you will **win favor and a good name** in the sight of God and man.

Reflection

So often it's difficult to be kind when faced with meanness, rudeness, or anger in the workplace. But Solomon instructs us to keep God's commands in our hearts because when we do we will add peace and prosperity to our lives.

I know this is not an easy thing to do, but kindness – love and faithfulness – cannot be absent from the work life of each *Christian public servant* if you and I expect to have peace.

As this workweek begins, **win favor and a good name** in the sight of God, your coworkers, and those you serve. Practice love and faithfulness in your workplace. Bind them around your neck. Write them on your heart.

Today at work, **win favor and a good name** through His kindness to one and all.

Prayer

Father, I thank You for Your commands. Through them, I find peace and prosperity. Let me take love and faithfulness to work today. Let me show kindness to my coworkers and the people I serve. In Your Son's name, I pray. Amen.

Linda Chambers

Week 43, Day 2

follow through

Reading

Ruth 1:16 [NIV] But Ruth replied, "Don't urge me to leave you or to turn back from you. Where you go I will go, and where you stay I will stay. Your people will be my people and your God my God."

Reflection

Could you blame Ruth if she had returned to her home where everything was familiar? Me neither! Yet she decided to stay with Naomi. And what she declared is important because it sheds light on her success in ultimately finding Boaz. Ruth knew she needed someone (Naomi) to hold her accountable and encourage her. She also needed a plan to set in motion her success. Ultimately, she needed an oath with God. There would be days of temptation to turn back, but Ruth would have the strength to **follow through** on her decision.

We make decisions at work each day. But when push comes to shove, it's not always easy to **follow through** – especially when it counts. So much can happen between point A and point B. Altered deadlines. New issues. Revised budgets. Somewhere along the line, we can falter and turn back.

As *Christian public servants*, you and I must be like Ruth. We need to have the highest level of determination to **follow through** on all tasks at work. And we also need to trust God and surround ourselves with the right people – coworkers who will hold us accountable and call us out if we start to stray from the purpose and decision.

Whatever daunting work-tasks you face today, do as Ruth did: create an inner circle, plan, and make a covenant with God. Do as Ruth did, and you will be able to **follow through** on anything this workday has to offer.

Prayer

Father, I thank You for placing tasks before me and for providing supervisors and coworkers who hold me in support. Give me strength in moments of weakness and hold me accountable for the greatness within. Continue to do Your work in me and through my work. In Jesus' name, I pray. Amen.

Kathryn Saunders

Week 43, Day 3

that desert called no job

Reading

Psalm 63:1,3 [ESV] O God, you are my God; earnestly I seek you; my soul thirsts for you; my flesh faints for you, as in a dry and weary land where there is no water... Because your steadfast love is better than life, my lips will praise you.

Reflection

Someone I know lost her job about a year ago. It wasn't anything she did; the state just had to cut the budget, and her agency was eliminated. She worked over 20 years in that office, and now she had to find other work. The problem was there were no jobs to be had, and even part-time jobs at fast-food restaurants were not hiring. She quickly lost her apartment, and with no family, she stayed at our home a few nights. But she left to drive around the region to find work. She became homeless and lost contact with everyone else.

Then I saw her yesterday, and I hardly recognized her. Yet she smiled when I approached and greeted me like a brother. You see, she has not given up hope. Rather than turning to the seamy side of life – or worse, contemplate suicide – she quickly realized Who she needs from the first day she landed in **that desert called no job**. It may sound silly, but she found water where there was no water. And it is only God's steadfast love that keeps her going.

I wish I could say my friend is out of **that desert called no job**. She has found a room in a homeless apartment building, and she volunteers at a church dedicated to serving the homeless. She is now seriously considering a ministry serving the homeless. She has hope and always has had hope because of God's steadfast love.

Today, I hope you are not in **that desert called no job**. But if you are, remember Who you thirst for. Remember for Whom your flesh faints. I'm sorry to say miracles don't always happen overnight. Your time in **that desert called no job** may be longer than you think. And it may be hard to understand His steadfast love is better than what you were doing before and His love is better than what you will be doing after. But have faith His love is better.

If you are in **that desert called no job,** force your lips to praise Him. For your soul will not thirst and your flesh will not want. He promises you this and much more. And He keeps His promises.

Prayer

Father God, I pray for all who find themselves in **that desert called no job**. I know I was once there for a seemingly long time. But I also know my soul did not thirst and my flesh did not want. My lips will praise You throughout my life. In Your Son's name, I pray. Amen.

James D. Slack

Week 43, Day 4

chasing the wind

Reading

Ecclesiastes 1:17 [NLT] So I set out to learn everything from wisdom to madness and folly. But I learned firsthand that pursuing all this is like **chasing the wind**.

Revelation 16:15 [NLT] Look, I will come as unexpectedly as a thief! Blessed are all who are watching for me, who keep their clothing ready so they will not have to walk around naked and ashamed.

Reflection

I had lunch with an old friend yesterday. We've known each other for three decades – since graduate school. Over the years, my friend has made a tremendous impact on his profession. He's written so many articles and books. And he has dedicated so much time and effort to ensure the success of his students. And now he is retiring.

What was supposed to be a celebratory lunch turned out quite differently. After ordering our meals, my friend confided in me. The week before, he was diagnosed with a inoperable stage 4 cancer. With or without treatment, he has less than a year to live.

He confessed his anger and shame – spending all those decades in his work and not going to be able to enjoy retirement. You see, he put off doing so many things with his family throughout his career. Oh, there was love, but he felt his time was "better spent" putting career first. And so he missed countless events in the lives of his kids. He hardly knows his grandchildren. And all those trips with his wife were never taken so he could attend "important" conferences.

My friend now grasps, throughout his career, he was worried about **chasing the wind**. Focusing on work advancement while not investing in other things he thought could easily be made up sometime in the future. And only now he realizes he missed so much with his family.

Today at work, think hard and long about **chasing the wind**. While job and career are important – sometimes even crucial – in no way do they substitute for what really counts in this life – the love of God and enjoyment of the love-blessings He bestows.

So do not take work home tonight. Go to that ballgame with your son. Take in a movie with your daughter. Walk with your spouse. Listen, listen, love, love. The Lord will come for you shortly, unexpectedly, and you don't want to be caught naked and ashamed.

Tonight when you leave work, stop **chasing the wind**.

<u>Prayer</u>

Father God, You will come for me unexpectedly. Let me have no regrets for what really counts in this life. Let me be prepared. In Your Son's name, I pray. Amen.

James D. Slack

Week 43, Day 5

not to judge

Reading

John 12:47 If anyone hears my words but does not keep them, I do not judge that person. For I did not come to judge the world, but to save the world.

Reflection

A couple of months ago, I was really down. It seemed so many brothers around me were angry and getting into fights. Even the brothers involved in our church were arguing. Many of the correctional officers seemed bent on cracking down on all brothers, regardless of any wrong-doing. I needed some guidance, and fortunately, that came from one of my spiritual mentors.

I was reminded of scripture. If Jesus came **not to judge** the world but to save it, who am I to judge those who do not keep His Words? I understood (again) my job is **not to judge** but to keep spreading His Words.

I took that advice. Rather than watching the wrongs and failings of my brothers, I started to watch God working in their lives – God working in the lives of my brothers in major ways! Also, I enjoyed the gift God gave me of seeing some of His seeds growing, spread by me through His Words! And who knows, I may be blessed by a harvest or two before my life is over!

Today at work, there may be Christian coworkers not keeping His Words. Take a deep breath and remember you are **not to judge.** Your purpose at your job is to keep spreading His Words.

And if you have trouble doing that today at work, find a spiritual mentor who can remind you of the job you really have in your workplace!

Prayer

Father, in the name of Jesus, I pray. Thank You for continually convicting my heart when I begin to judge others. Thank You for Your constant reminder my job today is to show You to others. Amen.

Jimmy Davis, Jr.

Week 44, Day 1

reminders of His love

Reading

Daniel 2:21(a) [ESV] He changes times and seasons;

Isaiah 43:19 [NIV] See, I am doing a new thing! Now it springs up; do you not perceive it? I am making a way in the wilderness and streams in the wasteland.

Reflection

Nature reflects God's creative character. Just look at trees. In the fall season, they show an elaborate array of colors while, in spring, trees display the light greens of new life. The summer season, of course, brings out their full green. Through the beauty of these colors, God provides **reminders of His love**. Yet even in winter – a season of wilderness and wasteland – there remains hope for the start of a new season. And in this hope God is also providing **reminders of His love**.

As believers, we are like trees reacting to each new season. The barren winter may come unannounced bringing devastation to one's work and career. There will be setbacks and even layoffs. There may even be false accusations of misconduct leveled against the believer at work. A project may fall flat. These things may seem like a colorless wilderness or wasteland.

Regardless of trial and season, you and I must never forget the **reminders of His love**. We must have hope the winter season is soon to pass. As *Christian public servants*, we must not only have hope during times of trial in our own careers, but we must also offer that same hope to others – we must be like streams in the wilderness.

Are you struggling at work today? Are you struggling to find a job? Maybe a coworker is in a colorless wilderness. If so, just look about. Certainly, He is giving all sorts of **reminders of His love**. Let your hope be renewed as God changes times and seasons.

Prayer

Lord, guide me through the trials of career. Let me always remember You are making a way for me in the wilderness and You are the stream in the desert; the colors of spring, summer, and fall! In Jesus' name, I pray. Amen.

Chip Harrell

Week 44, Day 2

both neighbors and enemies

Reading

Matthew 5:43-44, 47 [HCSB] You have heard that it was said, Love your neighbor and hate your enemy. But I tell you, love your enemies and pray for those who persecute you, so that you may be sons of your Father in heaven... And if you greet only your brothers what are you doing out of the ordinary?

Reflection

I love the experience of being part of a small group study. During our meetings, though, it dawned on me most of our comments centered directly on having to constantly deal with non-Christians in the workplace. The comments then devolved into complaints and criticisms of "others."

Discouragement is a by-product of the differing worldviews when interacting with non-Christians. It is easy to become focused on trying to change them rather than on how we can be an influence in their lives with the love of Christ. We are called to love **both neighbors and enemies**. This command holds true whether our enemies change their behavior or not.

In your workplace during times of discouragement, stop for a minute and remember the emphasis in the verse "love your enemies" is on *you and your actions*. You are to love unconditionally, **both neighbors and enemies**, as Christ unconditionally loves you. This is an action that can never be perfected but is a goal to strive toward. The more obstinate your enemies, the greater you will be able to love them – and that is a blessing not only for us but for **both neighbors and enemies**.

Today in your workplace, choose to be a blessing. Love **both neighbors and enemies**.

Prayer

Dear Lord, thank You for giving me the capability to unconditionally love others as You first loved me. Help me never forget *love is an action* and it must be constantly improved upon. When I feel the impossibility of taking part in unconditional love, remind me of Your grace and Your love, and how honored I am to take part in Your eternal goodness. In Your name, I pray. Amen.

Joshua Nierle

Week 44, Day 3

a disconnect with the Spirit

Reading

Galatians 6:8 [NIV] Whoever sows to please their flesh, from the flesh will reap destruction; whoever sows to please the Spirit, from the Spirit will reap eternal life.

Reflection

After work in the summertime, do you volunteer to help kids? A coach in sports? A teacher in Vacation Bible School? A Scout leader? Helping on a youth mission trip? A chaperone of some sort?

I work with a lot of kids over the summer. Most of them are a pleasure, but a few are terrors. Amongst our coaching group, we discuss how difficult some kids are and how parents are to blame. I think to myself, "I'm going to be a better parent. My kids won't act this way."

But then I stop. I can't imagine a parent intentionally raising a child to be "difficult." No parent wants to create a brat. No mom or dad tries to produce an emotionally unstable child. At least I pray not!!

Scripture reminds us to sow seeds of the Spirit, not seeds of the flesh. Maybe some parents just plant the wrong kind of seeds in their children's lives. And maybe – just maybe – volunteers like you and me do the same. I mean, how often do we let our emotions run wild in front of kids? How often do we do things for the instant gratification and don't understand why we have such pain and frustration later? And how often do we have minor meltdowns when kids do not do what we ask?

So maybe it's not just some kids who are in trouble. Maybe they are just following what they see us doing – parents and summer volunteers. They hear what we say about others. They feel when we have **a disconnect with the Spirit**.

When you leave work today, think about what kind of volunteer you will be. Remember kids will feel your words. They will mimic your behavior. If you have **a disconnect with the Spirit**, they will think it's OK for them to have the same.

The kind of seeds you sow is just as important <u>after</u> work as it is during work. This is especially true when you volunteer with children's programs. It's not just parents – it's volunteers who have an impact on what seeds take root in a child.

Tonight at that Scout meeting or sports practice or on that mission trip, make sure you do not demonstrate **a disconnect with the Spirit**. You and that child must reap eternal life!

<u>Prayer</u>

Father, I need Your Spirit. Help me turn from seeds of destruction to seeds of life. Free me from the bondage I am spreading to others – at work with adults and when I volunteer with children. Clean out the weeds. Plant new seeds. Bring fresh growth. In Jesus' name, I pray. Amen.

Kathryn Saunders

Week 44, Day 4

a peacemaker at work

Reading

Matthew 5:9 [NIV] Blessed are the peacemakers, for they will be called children of God.

Reflection

Coming out of Sunday school, my cousin pulled me over to vent about her employees. She is the CEO of a small nonprofit, and it seems some of her employees keep asking for advancements in their paychecks. Last Friday, it got to the point she blew up. In the harshest of tones, she informed them it just wasn't appropriate for them always to ask for advancements.

Now, I was shocked to hear such a harsh tone from my cousin who is always the godliest person I know. And she seemed to forget most of her employees make just a little above minimum wage and they are mostly single parents. They are just trying to make ends meet.

And so I reminded her of all this. I also told her Jesus expects her to be **a peacemaker at work**. I encouraged her to apologize first, and then begin a conversation about advancements and money management.

Well, she did just that. Today she apologized for her tone, and a conversation ensued that benefited all at the table – including my cousin. She became **a peacemaker at work**!

Jesus expects <u>you</u> to be **a peacemaker at work** today. That doesn't mean caving into whims. But it does mean you must try to find a way to satisfy needs. It means your employees and coworkers <u>should</u> know you as *a child of God*.

Prayer

Dear God, thank You for expecting me to resolve issues at work. Guide my thoughts and my tongue, Father, so I may be called one of Your children. In Jesus' name, I pray! Amen.

Renata Rankin

Week 44, Day 5

something to be remembered for

Reading

Acts 9:17 [NIV] Then Ananias went to the house and entered it. Placing his hands on Saul, he said, "Brother Saul, the Lord—Jesus, who appeared to you on the road as you were coming here—has sent me so that you may see again and be filled with the Holy Spirit."

Reflection

A brother in the free-world told me of a grandmother who is trying to leave a legacy for her eight grandchildren. She takes them to ballgames and amusement parks. She takes them out to dinner almost every day. She even takes them with her on month-long vacations. Yet she has never taken them to church.

We all try to leave a legacy – **something to be remembered for**. Even here on Life Row, the brothers write letters to family members and call them as much as they can. But through all the words, how many brothers talk about Christ? Scripture reminds us our legacy is to tell people about Jesus. Ananias' job was to welcome Paul into the Christian family – despite his past. See, Ananias' legacy spoke through the life of Paul. And what a legacy that was!

Is your job today so much different than Ananias? Is there a coworker who needs to be transformed from Saul to Paul? Is there someone at work who you can welcome into the Christian family – despite their past record? Ananias left a true legacy – **something to be remembered for** – and so can you.

Today at work, don't just be friends with people. Do more than just go to lunch or do nice things for that coworker. These are important, but is that the legacy you really want when you are at the foot of the Throne? Welcome that coworker into the Christian family – change Saul into Paul. Leave a true legacy – **something to be remembered for**! And this weekend when you are with loved ones, don't be like that grandmother. Just as at work, leave a true legacy – **something to be remembered for**!

Prayer

Father, in the name of Jesus, I pray. Thank You for my Ananias who changed me from Saul to Paul. Let me build a legacy for You by being Ananias to someone else. Amen.

Jimmy Davis, Jr.

Week 45, Day 1

God's answer, not yours

Reading

John 14:14 [NLT] Yes, ask me for anything in my name, and I will do it!

2 Corinthians 12:8-9(a) [NLT] Three different times I begged the Lord to take it away. Each time he said, "My grace is all you need. My power works best in weakness."

James 4:3 [NLT] And even when you ask, you don't get it because your motives are all wrong—you want only what will give you pleasure.

Hebrews 11:6(a) [NLT] And it is impossible to please God without faith.

Reflection

I've known coworkers to bring a lot of concerns to the workplace: fears about health issues, problems about family, needs for salary raises, desires for peace in the workplace or a new job or an old job or a promotion in the current job. Some even want "ungodly" things, like to block a competing project, humiliate another coworker, or the failure of an unwanted supervisor. Many pray and seek prayer warriors at the workplace to help God hear their cries. Each time something goes "right," we proclaim God answers prayers – all of them – if you ask through Christ. Yet each time the prayer request heads south, we lament God did not hear any one pray.

You know over half the prayers sought in the Bible were not answered in the affirmative. Even Paul's prayer for health relief was denied on three different occasions. And there are a lot of reasons why prayer requests are denied: our selfishness, to keep us weak, to keep us humble like Paul, to reject our wrong motives, or because God may have other plans for you and me.

When you pray at work or when you invite coworkers to be prayer warriors on your behalf, remember God really does answer all prayers – even those that seem to head south – if asked through Christ. But it is **God's answer, not yours**. And His answer will come from His unfathomable wisdom, not your simple rationalization.

So whether you are praying about health or that new job or that project, remember to pray humbly and with the right motives. Yet still, the answer may not be to your liking. But know it will be **God's answer, not yours**. And that must be OK with you – *if you claim faith in His Son.*

Prayer

Father God, on this workday and all workdays, I pray for Your answers, not mine. I claim faith in Your Son. It is in His name, I pray – always. Amen.

James D. Slack

Week 45, Day 2

all too familiar with that same sin

Reading

Romans 2:1 [ESV] Therefore you have no excuse, O man, every one of you who judges. For in passing judgment of another you condemn yourself, because you, the judge, practice the very same things.

Philippians 2:3(a) [ESV] Do nothing from selfish ambition or conceit ...

Romans 12:15(b) [ESV] ... weep with those who weep.

Reflection

Can it be said any clearer than in *Romans* 2:1? Remember the old saying "it takes one to know one?" Well, Paul says the same thing. When you identify the sin of another, you are saying "I am **all too familiar with that same sin**."

Yes, I know how difficult it is at work when a core part of your job requires judgment – assessing a task or project, conducting annual performance appraisals, auditing the books, or taking disciplinary action. It is not our nature to judge – primarily because we do it so poorly in this world!

But if your job calls for judgment, do not get confused. Scripture really is quite clear. Judge humbly without accusation. Do not seek to find personal sin. Do not let selfish ambition creep in. And show empathy – weep with those you critique.

Remember if one finger is pointing at a coworker, four fingers are pointing right back at you. And conceit will force you to admit you are **all too familiar with that same sin**.

Instead, show empathy – weep with those you had to critique.

Prayer

Father, I ask for empathy when I must judge another at work. Keep my eyes away from ambition, and keep my heart filled with Your grace. In Your Son's name, I pray. Amen.

Chris Summers

Week 45, Day 3

acknowledge the God you serve

Reading

James 1:12 [ESV] Blessed is the man who remains steadfast under trial, for when he has stood the test he will receive the crown of life, which God has promised to those who love him.

Reflection

It's a busy day at work, and many of my coworkers have called-out for various reasons. Usually, the team consists of six, including a supervisor. But for the past two days, there has only been another worker and me to perform all the duties of the team. The other employee is new and is not completely familiar with the responsibilities and duties of the job.

And so telephones continue to ring. Citizens continue to approach the counter. And mail full of requests has yet to be opened.

When work seems overwhelming, you must take a deep breath and **acknowledge the God you serve**. The Lord will never put more on you than you can bear, and it is important you continue to let your light shine. Your hard work will never be unrewarded, and if you seek your Father, *anything is possible.*

Yes, today at work, **acknowledge the God you serve**. Seek your Father, and *anything is possible.*

Anything!

Prayer

Eternal Father, keep me serving Your people. Knowing my help comes from You, I seek You when the pressures of the job weigh me down. I ask for Your aid and support to continue my work knowing You see all and will reward me for my faithfulness. In the name of Jesus, Your Son, I pray. Amen.

Deyonta T. Johnson

Week 45, Day 4

for all the hurt and all the joy

Reading

John 11:35 [NIV] Jesus wept.

Reflection

Why do you weep? If you're like me, you weep for all sorts of reasons. Unmet expectations. Being sad, hurt, frustrated. Being fired or not getting that one job you really wanted. An illness bringing pain to body, mind, and soul. A disease shortening retirement plans. However, you and I also weep when we are overwhelmed with joy about a wedding or many anniversaries, encouraged by career success, proud of job accomplishments, blessed by family and friends. Yes, we weep for a lot of reasons.

Scripture tells us Jesus wept because he loved Lazarus. But He wept for much more than what meets the eye. Jesus wept for us – thousands of years before we were born. And Jesus still weeps for you and me – **for all the hurt and all the joy** we face.

What a Savior! He weeps for the same things we do. He has indeed walked it out. His heart knows what it's like to have no words, just tears. He knows what it's like to have unmet expectations. He knows what it's like to be overwhelmed with joy in the midst of a blessing. What does that tell us?

When you go to work today, remember Jesus is weeping for everything that happens to you. That very positive performance appraisal – He is weeping for joy! That promotion you did not get – He is weeping for your hurt. In the breakroom, whether you talk about the upcoming marriage of your youngest child or the problems you're having with dental implants – He is weeping.

Today at work, be comforted in knowing He is weeping for you – everything about you – **for all the hurt and all the joy** you face. Remember Jesus loves you so much, He weeps for you. And He is there with you through it all!

Prayer

Lord, thank You for tears that cleanse my soul. Thank You for Your great love in every situation. I pray to be more like You. I pray to weep for everyone I see. In Your name, I pray. Amen.

Kathryn Saunders

Week 45, Day 5

first praise from Him

Reading

John 12:42-43 [KJV] Nevertheless among the chief rulers also many believed on him; but because of the Pharisees they did not confess him, lest they should be put out of the synagogue: For they loved the praise of men more than the praise of God.

Reflection

I am blessed to interact with a lot of correctional officers in here, and the vast majority are believers. But while they believe in Jesus, some do not confess Him – due to others they work with. For the most part, these officers are not ashamed of Jesus. But like elsewhere, some are concerned about what others think and do not want to stir things up.

Scripture reminds us many – even leaders – believed in Jesus, but many also did not confess Him – due to wanting to fit in. Just like where I live and work, some were more worried about first seeking praise from others than seeking **first praise from Him**.

How about where you work? How about you at work? Does the need for praise from coworkers outweigh seeking **first praise from Him**?

Today at work, don't worry about the praise of others. Just find ways to *believe* and *confess*. Find ways to show you *believe* in Christ. But also find ways to *confess* He is your Savior. Through your words and actions, *confess* you belong to Him. Through your behavior, *confess* He is the Deliverer from all evil.

Today at work, *believe* and *confess*. Don't worry about stirring things up. Look not first for praise from others. Have strength and confidence to seek **first praise from Him**.

Your workday will be better than you think!

Prayer

Father, in the name of Jesus, I pray. Continue to stir up my faith, not just to believe, but to confess Your Son Jesus to others – no matter what. Amen.

Jimmy Davis, Jr.

Week 46, Day 1

the gifts God bestows

Reading

Galatians 3:28 [NIV] There is neither Jew nor Gentile, neither slave nor free, nor is there male and female, for you are all one in Christ Jesus.

Reflection

The great part about being a *Christian public servant* is we encounter so many of God's children. All have different backgrounds, talents, ideas, and opinions. Each contributes with **the gifts God bestows** on him or her.

With such diverse personalities assigned to the same projects, sometimes tensions can exist. Sure, there's going to be disagreements on how to complete the project. But with our separate ideas and opinions, we can come together and make compromises, creating better plans as a team to improve our community. The *Christian public servant* plays a key role in this aspect. After all, is that not one of **the gifts God bestows** on us?

God's plan calls for you to work with others and make great things happen – no matter the differences among coworkers. Your task is to be the light shining in the dark areas of disagreement. You can bring harmony into the workplace.

Today, as you leave for work, say a little prayer for the Holy Spirit's assistance in preparing you for the stresses that will arise. Remember God put others in your path to help you and for you to help. Also remember the Creator made you unique – unique with **the gifts God bestows**.

Now, go share your gifts and make the workday a little brighter!

Prayer

Father God, thank You for yet another day to serve You and my community. Please watch over me and help me think more clearly through my daily stresses. Remind me to be open to new ideas and opinions – the gifts You bestow in others – so I may make my workplace more harmonious. I ask this in Your Son's name. Amen.

Meredith Pulsford

Week 46, Day 2

He will reward you

Reading

Ephesians 2:8-9 [NIV] For it is by grace you have been saved, through faith – and this is not from yourselves, it is a gift of God – not by works, so that no one can boast.

Reflection

There are gifted coworkers who appear to be perfect and receive all the praise and support from management. They always get everything right the first time, and life seems easy for them. Yet you work tirelessly trying to accomplish the same thing, doing the same job, but never receiving any recognition. That can be frustrating, right?

As a *Christian public servant,* you should be an example of excellence and character in the workplace – but also realize *your worth is not in your job* or in the recognition received. Your worth is in the finished work of Christ, provided through grace, as you exercise faith. As your efforts become focused on glorifying Him, **He will reward you** in return.

Today at work, give your best. Honor your supervisor's requests. Encourage your coworkers. Bless the citizens you serve with compassion. And thank God for the gift of a job. Your attitude and spirit will be noticed, and **He will reward you** for your faithfulness. Not because of what you have done, but because of what He has done through you.

Prayer

Lord, You blessed me in so many ways. Continue to show favor in my deeds for You, and help me to grow more and more in faith and awe of You. Thank You for all You continue to bless me with In Your name, I pray. Amen.

Sara Garth

Week 46, Day 3

a small bucket of bigotry and hate

Reading

Matthew 13:23 [NIV] But the seed falling on good soil refers to someone who hears the word and understands it. This is the one who produces a crop, yielding a hundred, sixty or thirty times what was sown.

Mark 4:11(b)-12 [NIV] The secret of the kingdom of God has been given to you. But to those on the outside everything is said in parables so that, they may be ever seeing but never perceiving, and ever hearing but never understanding; otherwise they might turn and be forgiven!

Reflection

Around the coffee pot at work today, you may be consumed by talk of recent political events. Your country may be different than ours, but here there seems to be so much bigotry and hatred being expressed and endorsed. Neo-Nazis, KKK, white nationalists – in our country many claim the Bible and His salvation. Yet their hate is directed toward others who claim the same Bible and even the same Savior. *How could that be?*

Jesus warns about hearing the Word without understanding it. When you read just <u>what</u> you want to read, you lose accountability with God. The soil sours – <u>you</u> sour – and Satan uses you to hate. You become a slave to the manipulation of parables or to the prejudice of a misguided pastor or to the shouts of the crowd in a torchlight parade. You become accountable to Satan. The crop then yields nothing of value – just **a small bucket of bigotry and hate**.

Wherever you live, whatever crisis is infecting your nation, remain accountable to God. Being angry is fine – God understands anger – even His Son grew angry at times. But you need to <u>understand</u> the Word, not just read it. Understand what Jesus would do in your situation. Understand what Jesus wants <u>you</u> to do in the face of bigotry and hatred.

So today at the coffee pot, *be of good soil*. Understand what Jesus wants of you. Be accountable only to Him. Satan will <u>not</u> win. And your seeds will yield much more than **a small bucket of bigotry and hate**!

Prayer

Father, in the name of Jesus, we pray. Give us eyes to read the Word and hearts to understand the Word. Let us do what You want us to do with our anger and with our love. Around all discussions today at work, let us be of good soil that yields much value to Your glory. Amen.

Jimmy Davis, Jr.
James D. Slack

Week 46, Day 4

through or out of

Reading

Psalm 138:7-8 [ESV] Though I walk in the midst of trouble, you preserve my life; you stretch out your hand against the wrath of my enemies, and your right hand delivers me. The Lord will fulfill his purpose for me; your steadfast love, O Lord, endures forever. Do not forsake the work of your hands.

Reflection

Are you going through a difficult time at work? Coworkers or a supervisor working directly against your good efforts? Been reprimanded? Have you lost your job?

Know this: Jesus will deliver you **through or out of** the difficult circumstance. He may want you to stay in that job, or He may have need of you elsewhere. Either way, the Lord is using you to fulfill His purpose. It is His steadfast love that brought you here, and He will not forget you – because you are the work of His hands.

So before you get to work today, realize Jesus is using you to accomplish His will. And count on Jesus to deliver you **through or out of** whatever mess you're in. He will not forsake the work of His hands. He will not forsake you!

Prayer

Father, I am scared – always worried about what will come today at work. Afraid of the wrath of my coworkers and supervisor. Comfort me, Father. Remind me You will preserve me; Your right-hand will deliver me. You will fulfill Your purpose for me. In Your Son's name, I pray. Amen.

Chris Summers

Week 46, Day 5

keep walking in love

Reading

Exodus 4:10 [NIV] Moses said to the LORD, "Pardon your servant, Lord. I have never been eloquent, neither in the past nor since you have spoken to your servant. I am slow of speech and tongue."

Ephesians 5:2(a) [NIV] and walk in the way of love, just as Christ loved us

Reflection

As I work as a "runner" in the halls on my row, I come across a lot of situations where I am attacked, used, and devalued. I could get angry and hateful, but I must **keep walking in love** – even when it hurts and even if it would be easier to retaliate. I must obey right away.

You see, if I delay being obedient to Christ – if I would first respond with hate – it would stop the love of Christ. My disobedience to His love would limit His glory, His joy, and most important, the purpose and plan He has for that person shouting at me. So I don't want to be like Moses who delayed doing what God wanted because he did not feel eloquent. I don't want to think of any reason why I should delay my obedience. So I must **keep walking in love**.

Now, your workplace is not like mine in so many ways. But still, I bet there is a coworker who ticks you off. There are citizens you serve who try to devalue you. Your boss may attack you.

Today at work, do not delay being obedient to showing God's love. Do not interfere with His plans because your feelings get hurt. He's given you everything needed to carry out His will.

Regardless of what happens at work today, you must **keep walking in love**.

Prayer

Father, in the name of Jesus, I pray. Thank You for giving me everything I need to love as You love me when I am doing my work. I promise I will obey directly and immediately. I want to glorify only You. Amen.

Jimmy Davis, Jr.

Week 47, Day 1

demonstrating love for God

Reading

Proverbs 21:23 [NIV] Those who guard their mouths and tongues keep themselves from calamity.

Luke 23:24 [NIV] Jesus said, "Father, forgive them, for they do not know what they are doing."

Reflection

The break room at work can be filled with all sorts of conversations – talk about progress on a project, what you might do after work, things going on around your house, and other various topics. At times, these conversations may not be productive. You know, gossip, rumors, criticisms of others. – and the list goes on.

In my break room, one coworker is always complaining about her ex-husband. It seems with every break she tells everyone about her most recent contact with him. He wants forgiveness and reconciliation. But, she wants no part of it and is openly judgmental of him. This person is unloading all her baggage to anyone who will listen. Her actions clearly are not **demonstrating love for God**.

You know it's hard not to bring baggage to the workplace – much less speak about it to coworkers. Yet sometimes that very baggage reflects more than your relationship with another person – it may reflect your relationship with God. You and I need to ask whether our actions are **demonstrating love for God**.

Scripture tells us to be guarded in what we say. The Word also says we should not judge. We are to stand against Satan and his demons and pray for and forgive people. God commands us to forgive even when it is not requested.

Today at work, whether you are in your office or the break room, guard what you say. Reflect on God and His Word. If you find yourself judging someone, even if that someone has hurt you, STOP! Leave judgment to God. Encourage others by being the example of forgiveness.

Be the one **demonstrating love for God**. It will make the workplace a better place.

<u>Prayer</u>

Father God, I stretch my hands to you asking for continued guidance. I need You now more than ever, Lord. Keep me in Your arms and direct my path so I no longer allow the enemy to move for me. Allow me to guard my tongue and be forgiving of others as You, Lord, have forgiven me. Help me to demonstrate my love for You. In Jesus' name, I pray for your grace and mercy. Amen.

Michelle Lewis

Week 47, Day 2

I could do more

Reading

1 Peter 4:10 [ESV] As each has received a gift, use it to serve one another, as good stewards of God's varied grace.

Acts 20:35 [ESV] In all things I have shown you that by working hard in this way we must help the weak and remember the words of the Lord Jesus, how he himself said, 'It is more blessed to give than to receive.'

Reflection

I recently decided to help a friend going through a tough divorce. I offered to take her children to school which was followed with a request to watch them overnight while she worked. I agreed hesitantly until further help was requested. However, wanting more time with my own family, I began to pull back and declined requests for more help. My spirit troubled me though. I realized how blessed I was and, after prayer, decided **I could do more** and offered help.

As *Christian public servants,* you and I are sometimes called to go above and beyond in serving others. While this help may come at an "inconvenience" to us, it can be a real blessing to those in need. In the workplace, it might even mean saying "**I could do more**" to provide others with the help they need.

At work, the mantra of "**I could do more**" could bless a supervisor or coworker in amazing ways as they feel the touch of Christian love upon their lives. The blessing received in return will continue to encourage you as you live your life for Christ who gave His all.

Prayer

Dear God, I ask You to continue guiding me in Your light. I ask You to help me to do Your will. Make me into a steward of grace and help me to give unto others as You have given to me, Lord. Amen.

Logan Dickens

Week 47, Day 3

work to-do list

Reading

Matthew 16:24-25 [ESV] Then Jesus told his disciples, If anyone would come after me, let him deny himself and take up his cross and follow me. For whoever would save his life will lose it, but whoever loses his life for my sake will find it.

Reflection

Like many people, I have a continually full **work to-do list**. Recently, as I examined that list, it occurred to me nowhere on it was a reminder to serve Jesus today or to put Him above my needs.

How did I let myself get so busy at work I do not remember my Lord? Where is Jesus in my workday? Do I serve Him in my workplace each day? If so, what have I specifically done for my Lord today? If Jesus is my best friend, how will I get through my workday without Him?

From that moment on, I resolved to put Jesus at the top of my **work to-do list** – permanently!

Like you, I have a job that is sometimes stressful and always busy, and there are many days I can feel overwhelmed. Nevertheless, it is important I always remember my most important task at work is serving Jesus.

Before you start your tasks today, check your **work to-do list**. Is He on the list? Is He at the top?

Prayer

Dear Lord, help me to always remember my most important task is serving You first and advancing Your kingdom. Help me to deny myself and put You first in everything I do at work today. In Jesus' name, I pray. Amen.

Paul Theroux

Week 47, Day 4

in a most unlikely place

Reading

Genesis 28:16 [ESV] Then Jacob awoke from his sleep and said, "Surely the Lord is in this place, and I did not know it."

Acts 13:1,52 [ESV] And the disciples were filled with joy and with the Holy Spirit.

Reflection

Many years ago, I had the opportunity to visit some brothers in a place which most of the outside world forgets about – prison. Even though these men were incarcerated, I realized we had much in common. These men made mistakes, and some of those mistakes were horrific. However, God's love became very clear during that visit. Together with the brothers, I rejoiced in the splendor of God and His presence revealed **in a most unlikely place**.

How often do you celebrate the presence of God, and for that matter, do you celebrate His presence in the place where you work? Is God there with you even as you fill out paperwork, sit at the computer, answer that phone call, or meet with that citizen? It can be so easy to overlook the fact the Spirit is with you always – even **in a most unlikely place**.

Today at work, acknowledge the presence of God wherever you are and remain focused on Him. You will come into His presence in every room in your building – even **in a most unlikely place**.

Prayer

Lord, thank You for never leaving me. Your presence surrounds me and guides my steps each and every day. I pray today I will be able to see your glory in my life, so the world around may as well. Help me to honor You with my every action. In the precious name of Jesus. Amen.

James D. Slack

Week 47, Day 5

that special righteousness

Reading

James 1:20 [NLT] Human anger does not produce the righteousness of God's desire.

Reflection

Where I live and work, righteousness can sometimes be hard to find. It's there, but you really need to search for it. Anger, however, can be found just down the row. If you are not careful, anger can be found in your own cell. Anger can block both vision and relationships. It can block the heart and, more importantly, **that special righteousness** of God's desire.

As a *Christian public servant*, regardless of where you live and work, it is your job to keep a check on anger. Because of who you are and Who you represent, anger produces the wrong image of our Heavenly Father.

Today at work, produce **that special righteousness** of God's desire. Do so even when others have wronged you, even when others don't do as they say, and even when others show hate.

If you do this, you will show others what God really wants. Let **that special righteousness** flow from your heart. The results will bless many and please Him.

Prayer

Father, in the name of Jesus, I pray. Thank You for Your righteous love of me. Let me show Your desires to others today. Amen.

Jimmy Davis, Jr.

Week 48, Day 1

delight in

Reading

Jeremiah 29:11 [NIV] For I know the plans I have for you, declares the LORD, plans to prosper you and not to harm you, plans to give you hope and a future.

1Timothy 4:12 [NLT] Don't let anyone think less of you because you are young. Be an example to all believers in what you say, in the way you live, in your love, your faith, and your purity.

Reflection

My good friend and coworker belittles her accomplishments so as not to offend those around her. She was first in her family to go to college. She worked hard and made the dean's list, was inducted into a National Honor Society, graduated a semester early, and was accepted into graduate school. And now, with an MPA degree, she has an excellent job and is doing well. These are her successes. And she deserves to **delight in** her accomplishments. So I took her on a weekend vacation to honor all her hard work. She cried because she didn't believe she deserved to be celebrated. But she started to realize, even though not everyone has walked the same path or experienced the same successes, these remain her moments and trophies to **delight in** God. And each success is a way God takes **delight in** telling her she is on the right track. God is using her to show others they can do anything with Him.

As a *Christian public servant*, recognize God has ordered your steps. Every big or small success at work or school is a part of the plan He has for you. Remain humble, but **delight in** His blessings. Each accomplishment is a stepping stone on your journey ordained by God.

Today realize what my friend and coworker now knows. As you go to work, **delight in** the tasks God has trusted you with. At work, **delight in** the plans He has for you. Then come home with **delight in** your heart at having discovered He is with you each step throughout the day!

Prayer

Dear God, thank You for guiding my steps and leading me on this journey. I **delight in** the opportunities You have blessed me with. By following Your will, I can accomplish many things. Use me as a vessel to show others they can achieve their goals. I am honored to glorify You. In Jesus' name, I pray. Amen.

Logan Dickens

Week 48, Day 2

the rest God has set aside

Reading

Genesis 2:3 [NIV] Then God blessed the seventh day and made it holy, because on it He rested from all the work of creating that He had done.

Proverbs 19:23 [NIV] The fear of the Lord leads to life; then one rests content, untouched by trouble.

Psalm 62:5 [NIV] Yes, my soul, find rest in God; my hope comes from him.

Reflection

It seems like the more days tick off during the week, the more restless and tired I become. I "go and go" at work only to realize, at times, the progress made is for naught. After work, I run all over creation doing things with my family yet never spend any quality time with them. It is just "go here" and "go there". The weekend comes and I am so spent I forget to take **the rest God has set aside**. Can you relate?

You know we only have to turn to the Word to get the appropriate guidance. Scripture reminds us God made the seventh day holy, and most importantly, He rested. Scripture is mindful He wants us to rest, too!

The most important time you and I have, aside from spending time with Him in His house, is when we take **the rest God has set aside**. But when we take our weekends to "rest" in our own selfish way, we negate time to truly recharge with Him. After each day of work, do not forsake your time alone with Him. On Sundays, do not neglect to gather with the body of Christ to learn, refresh, recharge, and prepare your heart for another workweek.

This coming weekend, take **the rest God has set aside**. Then you will truly be able to serve Him and others better come Monday morning!

Prayer

Lord, thank You for showing me where I need to focus my time. Thank You for the constant reminder You love me and I need to rest. I pray this in Your Son, Jesus', Holy name. Amen.

Gilbert O. Craven

Week 48, Day 3

become truly free

Reading

Galatians 5:1, 13 [NIV] It is for freedom that Christ has set us free. Stand firm, then, and do not let yourselves be burdened again by a yoke of slavery…You, my brothers and sisters, were called to be free. But do not use your freedom to indulge the flesh; rather, serve one another humbly in love.

Reflection

Have you ever noticed how much we all look forward to holidays? It doesn't matter the season of the year, you can always tell when a coworker is getting ready to go on vacation. He seems lighter somehow, like just the thought of getting away is liberating.

Why not? It seems during the rest of the year people are shackled to their jobs. Often the pressures of the everyday grind just get to them, and they cannot see the freedom right before them. The *Christian public servant* has a responsibility to share that freedom with others and to share in a responsible way. Scripture reminds us we must not use freedom to indulge in worldly anticipation. Rather, we are to use the freedom Christ gives us to humbly love and serve one another.

It is in the serving of others you **become truly free**. You are no longer just an employee working on a menial task. You now have a mission – His mission – and that mission brings freedom.

Today at work, don't let the pressure place its "yoke" on you. For the sake of all you come in contact with today, love others humbly and show others what it means to **become truly free**.

Yes, a vacation is nice. But today, stand firm for Him at work and **become truly free**.

Prayer

Dear Lord, I am free because You have redeemed me. Help me not waste the high price You paid for me. Help me reach others who are bogged down at work. Help me live free for others and as a witness of what a life in You is all about. In Your name, I pray. Amen.

Stan Best

Week 48, Day 4

choose not to harm the faith

Reading

1 Corinthians 10:23-24, 31 [ESV] "All things are lawful," but not all things are helpful. "All things are lawful," but not all things build up. Let no one seek his own good, but the good of his neighbor… So, whether you eat or drink, or whatever you do, do all to the glory of God.

Reflection

Going out after work with colleagues and coworkers can be fun and, perhaps, productive, but it can also test the will of any follower of Christ. While it may be a welcome opportunity to stray from your diet and that second or third alcoholic drink may be a welcome opportunity to let your hair down, remember others are watching. Some wait for you to trip on your faith. You want to have fun like everyone else, but in doing so, *you don't want to hurt the faith-building of someone just starting to look to Christ.*

Scripture verifies this predicament is nothing new. The ancient Christians of Corinth knew the eyes of others may interpret one's eating and drinking as worshipping things other than Christ. Like you, the Corinthians wanted to have fun, but they learned to **choose not to harm the faith** of the on-looker.

So when you go out with coworkers, do as your brothers and sisters in Corinth did so long ago. Have fun, but don't make selfish decisions. Have fun, but remember just because you "can" doesn't mean you should. Have fun, but make sure your behavior glorifies God and edifies others for Jesus. Have fun, but build others up.

Yes, have fun and let your hair down. But **choose not to harm the faith** of those around you.

Prayer

Father, especially when having fun with coworkers, let me always glorify You and let my behavior teach others about Jesus. Let me be more concerned with the helpful and less with the legal. Let me seek not my own good, but the good of the coworker watching me. Let me **choose not to harm the faith** of a coworker who looks at me in the hope of seeing Christ for the first time. In Your Son's name, I pray. Amen.

Chris Summers

Week 48, Day 5

something deeper than religion

Reading

Galatians 5:6 [MSG] For in Christ, neither our most conscientious religion nor disregard of religion amounts to anything. What matters is something far more interior: faith expressed in love.

Reflection

As a *Christian public servant*, all I have is faith. Faith in Jesus. Faith in His love. Faith in His protection. Yes, here on Life Row, faith is all I really have.

Are you any different? In your life and in your workplace, is there anything more you really have than faith in Jesus? I don't think so.

Yet as *Christian public servants*, it is our job to use our faith to express love to those around us. It is difficult to do this where I am, but is it any easier for you to express love to those in your workplace?

Today at work, show others **something deeper than religion**. It really doesn't matter if you wear a symbol of Him around your neck or have a Bible lying on your desk. Your faith in Jesus is not based on what happens today. Circumstances or feelings do not matter. What does matter is something far deeper inside you – the love of your Heavenly Father within you.

Go to work today with an attitude of love based on your faith. Express that love to everyone. Show them **something deeper than religion**. Show them Christ.

Prayer

Father, in the name of Jesus, I pray. Continue to increase my faith in You so I can express to others that love you put inside of me. Amen.

Jimmy Davis, Jr.

Week 49, Day 1

it leads to hope

Reading

Matthew 27:46(b) [NIV] Jesus cried out in a loud voice, "Eli, Eli, lema sabachthani?" (which means "My God, my God, why have you forsaken me?").

Romans 5:3(b)-4 [NIV] We also glory in our sufferings, because we know that suffering produces perseverance; perseverance, character; and character, hope.

Reflection

Last year I read with indifference a report about the skyrocketing price of an allergic reaction drug. Despite many people suffering because of the prohibitive cost, it was easy for me to feel indifferent since I never had an allergic reaction. Then I had a reaction to my blood pressure medicine. I spent three days in the hospital suffering on a breathing machine.

In a world of technological marvels, it's easy to think we should never suffer. Commercials make it seem there is a drug for anything that ails you. No one wants to suffer, and everyone tries to avoid it. Yet scripture says suffering has a beneficial effect: **it leads to hope**.

As you travel to work today, pay attention to all the suffering. People limping or walking with canes along the sidewalk. That man in a wheelchair in the convenience store. Think about the suffering you don't see. Those with families trapped by storm and water. The young coworker dying of cancer. The older lady in accounting who just lost her husband. The person down the hall with diabetes and fearing blindness comes next.

And then think of me. I now know the suffering of those who have allergic reactions. Think of yourself: have you suffered in life? And then think of Jesus and how His suffering gave you eternal life of no suffering.

As you go to work, remember suffering teaches caring. Suffering leads to empathy and empathy to love. Ultimately, **it leads to hope**. His hope – of never being forsaken. Yes, **it leads to hope**.

Prayer

Dear Lord, forgive my indifference. On the way to work today, let me be empathic of others who suffer. Help me help those in pain. Let me learn the lessons taught in my suffering, and allow hope to spring eternal from You, oh Lord. In Your name, I pray. Amen.

Stan Best

Week 49, Day 2

when darkness approaches

Reading

Hebrews 10:35[NIV] So do not throw away your confidence; it will be richly rewarded.

1 John 2:11(a) [NIV] But anyone who hates a brother or sister is in the darkness and walks around in the darkness.

Revelation 7:9(b) [NIV] there before me was a great multitude that no one could count, from every nation, tribe, people and language, standing before the throne and before the Lamb.

Reflection

Recently racial slurs were written on message boards at one of my country's military academies. In response, the Commandant called together all cadets, faculty, and officers and talked about how they, as human beings, must be outraged at such behavior. He said the appropriate response to evil ideas is better ideas. And his better idea was this: do not throw away confidence in civil discourse about the power of diversity.

The Commandant was certainly taking a risk – given all the present challenges to our faith and civilization. After all, it's so easy to turn away **when darkness approaches**. It's too easy to forget someday we will see the light of His diversity before the Throne and before the Lamb. And so, it's one thing to clean the message boards. It's one thing to quietly investigate to find the author of those racial slurs. But it's quite another thing for the Commandant to raise the issue of bigotry to a moral level – a level demanded by Christ.

As *Christian public servants*, we must also respond at a moral level **when darkness approaches**. Have confidence in the breakroom to engage in a conversation about the power of diversity – the diversity you see today and the diversity you will surely see before the Throne and before the Lamb. Have confidence to speak up at lunch and in meetings – as Christ demands.

Today at work, have the courage to be like that Commandant. Do not be silent **when darkness approaches**. Have courage to respond as Christ demands. And you will be richly rewarded!

Prayer

Jesus, You love all the children – red and yellow, black and white and brown. Loving less is darkness. Give me strength to remember who will be before the Throne and before the Lamb. And let me join them in this world and the next. In Your name, I pray. Amen.

Larry H. Hanson

Week 49, Day 3

accomplishments sought for envy

Reading

Ecclesiastes 4:4 [NIV] And I saw that all toil and all achievement spring from one person's envy of another. This too is meaningless, a chasing after the wind.

Matthew 5:16 [NIV] let your light shine before others, that they may see your good deeds and glorify your Father in heaven.

Reflection

I once worked at a gambling casino where the unofficial policy was to reward higher performance appraisal scores to employees willing to give more than what they receive from the company. Sacrifice was an important attribute. But once proving your willingness to sacrifice, it became easier to move up the ladder of success.

So I tried my best to sacrifice, mainly because I was as desperate as anyone else to keep a job. Yet when I succeeded, I found a larger problem: I was despised by coworkers I jumped ahead of, and the few who were once my bosses, well, they hated me when I became <u>their</u> boss.

Do you work in an environment like I once did? Where employees are "asked" to do all sorts of things – take odd shifts or work fewer hours – and not complain, just to show they are team players? Is there jealousy of those who do better in that kind of rat-race?

Scripture says **accomplishments sought for envy** are meaningless in His eyes. Good performance is important, yes, but in glorifying God (even in a casino workplace like mine), good deeds will not be done for greed or from ambition. Instead, shine your light, letting all coworkers know your relationship with Christ is far more important than what you sacrifice to an employer. If not that way, you are just chasing after the wind.

As you work today, remember Who you work for. Don't choose **accomplishments sought for envy**. Show your good deeds in the proper light, His light, and others will not resent you.

Prayer

Lord, You are the light that shines within me. Thank You for the lessons You provide about desperation and greed. Allow me to be Your servant because, within Your love, I will never be desperate – I will never be greedy, and I will never envy. In Your Son's name, I pray. Amen.

Calvin Reed, Jr.

Week 49, Day 4

Christian ways to help the team

Reading

1 Thessalonians 5:14(b)-15 [ERV] warn those who will not work. Encourage those who are afraid. Help those who are weak. Be patient with everyone. Be sure that no one pays back wrong for wrong. But always try to do what is good for each other and for all people.

Reflection

A friend called last night. She was having difficulties at work earlier in the day. Her team was given a task to be completed by the time they went home. The team agreed on the outcome, but it was hard to gain consensus on how to complete the project. You see, everyone had their own way of doing things, and the team found it hard to agree on which approach to take. For a while, the team wasn't much of a team.

Scripture says a lot about teamwork. How to be supportive and how to be nurturing. It even gives guidance on how to be corrective. Patience is key in finding **Christian ways to help the team**. Not that you should do someone's job along with your own, but God can guide you in warning those who are not pulling their weight.

While it's easy to get frustrated, my friend took a deep breath and remembered scripture. Then she prayed. She got the team to focus on the goal and the outcome of the project. She got the team to focus on what completing the project would mean to the people they were helping. She found **Christian ways to help the team**. Everyone had input, and everyone accepted specific tasks. And the project was completed well before the end of the day!

As you go to work today, remember it takes more than "just" prayer. It takes more than "just" scripture. You must find **Christian ways to help the team** complete projects. And finding His way to task completion is just as close as prayer and scripture! Now, do good for each other and for the people you serve.

Prayer

Dear Father, as I go about my workday, help me work in harmony with others and in harmony with You. I give You praise, Father, in all the accomplishments of the day. In Jesus' name, I pray. Amen.

Arnekeya Fisher-Coleman

Week 49, Day 5

walk in God's steps

Reading

Ecclesiastes 7:8 [KJV] Better is the end of a thing than the beginning thereof: and the patient in spirit is better than the proud in spirit.

Reflection

When I work the row as a runner, it is easy to become proud in spirit. After all, I am the only one out of his cell. Everyone else is stuck in a 5' x 8' confinement 23 hours a day where it is hot in the summer and cold in the winter. So it's great to be able to exercise a little as I walk, to stretch without hitting the walls, and to just be "out." Plus, the brothers depend on me to bring them ice in the summer and to heat up drinks in the winter. Yes, when I am a runner, it is easy to believe I am important. Very important. It is easy to become proud in the spirit where I work – as I skip to my own steps.

But scripture reminds us it is better to **walk in God's steps** than it is to walk in our own. When we go by our own steps, we become prideful. This leads to saying or doing something hurtful and turns others from Jesus. But when we **walk in God's steps**, we become patient in spirit. We wait for God to show us where the next step goes.

When you are at work today, will you be arrogant or will you be patient? Will you think only of the beginning, or will you think about the end?

Will you walk in your steps, or will you **walk in God's steps**?

Prayer

Father, in the name of Jesus, I pray. Thank You for every step you bless me with today. Let me be ever patient and wait on Your steps. Amen.

Jimmy Davis, Jr.

Week 50, Day 1

may not return home tonight

Reading

Mark 4:39 [KJV] And he arose, and rebuked the wind, and said unto the sea, Peace, be still. And the wind ceased, and there was a great calm.

John 15:13 [KJV] Greater love hath no man than this, that a man lay down his life for his friends.

Reflection

Most of us go to work without having to put our lives on the line. Sure, you and I are servants of God in our own workplaces and, as such, are *Christian public servants*. Yet there are some who go to work for God and know they **may not return home tonight**.

First responders across the world work in danger to save others. They do so amid disasters – earthquakes, fires, hurricanes, and the like. First responders understand they **may not return home tonight**. They recognize the stakes and still accept the responsibilities.

As you drive to work today, remember the first responders in your community. They exemplify the role played in God's plan. They accept the chance of death when the winds are not yet rebuked and the seas are not yet peaceful. They are God's hands and feet in creating calm during and after the disaster. They do so knowing they **may not return home tonight**.

Each workplace is unique, and each Christian worker follows the plan of God. Yet some follow Him knowing they **may not return home tonight**. Today at work, find one to thank.

Prayer

Father God, thank You for inspiring those who risk everything for others. Let them all return home tonight. In Your Son's name, I pray. Amen.

James D. Slack

Week 50, Day 2

providing influence

Reading

1 Corinthians 10:33 [KJV] Even as I try to please everyone in every way. For I am not seeking my own good but the good of many, so that they may be saved.

Reflection

I am not an avid tennis fan, passionate hunter, or a proficient automobile mechanic. Yet I know enough about each of those interest areas to carry a conversation because I chose to learn about them. I didn't choose to learn about them because I was necessarily interested in them. I learned about them during different periods in my career as I was trying to build relationships with my supervisors, coworkers, and subordinates.

I have found learning what is "pleasing" to someone becomes a currency that allows you into their sphere of influence. That currency leads to relationship. That relationship then allows communication and when you have communication flow, you have the ability to provide influence to the other person.

As a *Christian public servant,* whether you are leading a workplace effort or guiding someone toward the principles of Christ, you are **providing influence**. As good servant-leaders, it is not about satisfying self but about **providing influence** that will lead others to success and, more importantly, a relationship with Jesus.

At work, who are you pleasing (influencing) today?

Prayer

Father, use me as an instrument of change, as an instrument of influence, and as an instrument of Your grace. Lead me with Your wisdom to opportunities of service this day. In Jesus' name, I pray! Amen.

Bill Dudley

Week 50, Day 3

pause to seek Him first

Reading

Matthew 6:33-34 [KJV] But seek ye first the kingdom of God, and his righteousness; and all these things shall be added unto you. Take therefore no thought for the morrow: for the morrow shall take thought for the things of itself. Sufficient unto the day is the evil thereof.

Reflection

Did you ever run out of work to do? Me neither. The work keeps coming and coming. One day, with everything hitting me at once, I found myself about to turn in a project report that wasn't as polished and complete as it should have been. With a quick prayer for guidance, the Holy Spirit prompted me to remember today's scripture. I knew I had given the project my best, but I also knew my best was not enough. And so I decided to sleep on it.

The next morning, refreshed with prayer and private time with our Lord, I reread the memo from my supervisor. It turns out my stress caused me to misread it. The project report wasn't due for another week! God refocused me because I gave **pause to seek Him first**.

You and I face daily deadlines along with insufficient time and limited resources for completion of assignments and tasks. Regardless of the kind of workplace, the stress and anxiety can really build up. We need to take time and give **pause to seek Him first**. We must be mindful God will provide for our needs in the workplace, just as He does in all other realms of our lives.

As you begin work today, do not stress and do not fear what may come later in the day or even tomorrow. Just give **pause to seek Him first** and the right things will be added to your day!

Prayer

Heavenly Father, thank You for providing my needs each day. Grant me faith to continue to trust You first before I focus on the problem or issue at hand. Give me peace knowing You are always with me – including in my workplace – and You will continue to meet my needs. I know You will never leave me nor forsake me. In Jesus' name, I pray. Amen.

TaQuesha Brandon

Week 50, Day 4

in true relationship

Reading

Hosea 6:6 [NIV] For I desire mercy, not sacrifice, and acknowledgment of God rather than burnt offerings.

Matthew 5:23-24 [NIV] Therefore, if you are offering your gift at the altar and there remember that your brother or sister has something against you, leave your gift there in front of the altar. First go and be reconciled to them; then come and offer your gift.

Reflection

Have you ever met someone who gives God a bad name? A citizen you serve in your job? A coworker? Maybe it's you? Boasting of being in church all the time but having no mercy or care for others. Those around know it, and it makes the title – a *Christian public servant* – a poor epithet.

God wants you and me to be **in true relationship** with those around us. However, we seem to get so busy we may sometimes forget the very thing God wants. Sure, He wants our love, but He also wants us to love and care for one another. Instead of shouting in the public square so we can be right, You and I should spend time with others and get to know them better.

When you are at work today, focus on being **in true relationship** with someone. If you do this, perhaps the office stress will decrease. Maybe you will find a person in need. Or maybe, you will find that person in the greatest of need.

Today at work, finding true worship with God begins with you being **in true relationship** with others. Be reconciled and be blessed!

Prayer

Dear Lord, help me to stop and spend time building true relationships with the people I pass by at work each day. You created me to watch out for others, not to shout against another. I pray for godly love to be my brother's and sister's keeper and, in so doing, worship You better. In Your name, I pray. Amen.

Stan Best

Week 50, Day 5

that coworker no one likes

Reading

1 John 4:8 [NIV] Whoever does not love does not know God, because God is love.

Reflection

Once my job was to babysit my nephew when he was a toddler. He would always point to what I was eating, and he wanted some. Though he didn't have teeth, I still gave him a little taste because I loved him. If I didn't love my nephew, I suppose I might not have given him a taste of those treats. But I loved him, and I wanted my nephew to know me through my love.

So what about that person working next to you? No, not the one you really like. You know, the one <u>not</u> like my nephew – the one no one likes. What if he knows nothing about the God you serve? What if she doesn't have a clue about the love of God or even how to love God? How is that coworker supposed to know God? And what if that coworker died leaving work?

Today's scripture is about believers – not non-believers, not yet-to-be-believers, not baby believers. It is about you and me – mature believers in Christ. It reminds us about the responsibilities of love. It proclaims God <u>is</u> love, and therefore, you and I must love if we are to know God. We must love – even **that coworker no one likes**.

So at work today, remember God really <u>is</u> love. Before the workday ends, love **that coworker no one likes**. When you do, you will know God. And so will that coworker.

Prayer

Father, in the name of Jesus, hear my prayer. Thank You for Your awesome love, and for showing me how to share it with others. Amen.

Jimmy Davis, Jr.

Week 51, Day 1

better than the mighty

Reading

Proverbs 16:32 [KJV] He that is slow to anger is **better than the mighty**; and he that ruleth his spirit than he that taketh a city.

Reflection

I was **better than the mighty** today. Yes, sir – I always wanted to be, and today I was! No arrogance about it, just plain biblical truth. So as not to confuse you, let me explain.

I was in a planning meeting, and everyone wanted their idea or agenda to get funded. As you can imagine, this kind of meeting went on much longer than needed. The arrogance of some began rubbing on my last nerve. I wanted to shout *"make a decision!"* But I did not. Instead, I prayed and thanked God for the many ways He has blessed me. I controlled my spirit, and that makes me, according to God's word, mightier than one who "taketh a city." Yes, in that planning meeting, I became **better than the mighty**!

Now, if you think I think I am somebody special, let me assure you – I am! Not because I was mighty today, but because a mighty God loved me so much and reached into my life. Jesus changed me, and the Holy Spirit gives me the strength to control my spirit. I am only **better than the mighty** when He is in control.

Today at work, what challenges face you? Who is driving you to the edge of losing control? Let God provide the calmness of His Spirit and make you **better than the mighty.**

Yes, on this workday, you can be somebody special because you have a mighty God who loves you and wants to reach into your life! So you, too, can be **better than the mighty** – if He is in control.

Prayer

Thank You, heavenly Father, for the power of Your Spirit. Thank You for changing my heart and for giving me the strength to live according to Your word. Thank You for the mighty works You choose to perform through me throughout my workday. Use me for Your glory. In Jesus' name, I pray. Amen.

Bill Dudley

Week 51, Day 2

stillness... quiet... peace...

Reading

Job 3:26 [HCSB] I cannot relax or be still; I have no rest, for trouble comes.

Reflection

stillness... quiet... peace... My heart longs for serenity, yet I find I have no rest.

Budget cuts reduce staffing until everyone is working at least a job-and-a-half. Over time – a requirement rather than a choice. Morale is low. Everyone is just – so – tired. The only comfort I have is the hope my staff really sees me working as hard as they. It feels absurd to suggest they or I should take time during the day for reflection when I know such precious time simply doesn't exist. Leadership includes crisis management, but dear Lord, there must be more! I mean, it cannot only be a reactive process.

stillness... quiet... peace... Insisting these words become of integral value for today will help assure I have the focused-center to be a good administrator. Making these words become of integral value for my staff's day will certainly help them tackle the impossible tasks I must lay before them.

And when I <u>finally</u> secure the resources they need to do their jobs, I will be mindful of their need for such things as time-off, real vacations, and even professional development!

But for today, I promise I will find each a few minutes of unexpected **stillness... quiet... peace...**

How about you? What integral values will help shape your workday? Stress? Anxiety? Fear? Or will you drape at least part of the workday in **stillness... quiet... peace...**

Prayer

Father, show me how to be still today – quiet and in peace – to allow You to transform me into who and what You call me to be. Help me learn not to borrow trouble and to be faithful to Your word. In Jesus' name, I pray. Amen.

Stephanie L. Bellar

Week 51, Day 3

waited with worry

Reading

Isaiah 26:4 [KJV] Trust in the LORD forever, for the LORD GOD is an everlasting rock.

Psalm 75:6 [KJV] Promotion comes neither from the east, nor from the west, nor from the south.

Reflection

I remember optimistically applying for a higher level job within my organization. I knew I could handle the essential functions; heck, I surpassed the qualifications. Excited about my impending promotion, I mentioned it to a coworker who replied, "I *hope* you get the job."

Hope? Did he say *HOPE*?? Wasn't this job <u>mine</u>? I mean, it practically had *my name on it*!

I started to wonder: Did I really meet the qualifications? Could I actually perform the essential functions? Did I have the right combination of leadership skills and management tools? I was in the midst of an *internal battle of doubt*. For three weeks I **waited with worry.**

Then I came to my senses. I prayed, and I no longer **waited with worry.** It was in God's hands, not mine or the hiring staff or anyone else in my organization.

At work, have you ever had an *internal battle of doubt*? Have you ever **waited with worry**?

Trust in the Lord, and know <u>nothing</u> comes out of the east, west, or south.

Prayer

Lord, I stand before You as Your servant. I want to advance in my workplace. If it is Your will, bless me with what I want. I trust You know best. In Jesus' Name, I pray. Amen.

Matthew Pough

Week 51, Day 4

teach like Jesus

Reading

Matthew 22:35-40 [NIV] One of them, an expert in the law, tested him with this question: "Teacher, which is the greatest commandment in the Law?" Jesus replied: "'Love the Lord your God with all your heart and with all your soul and with all your mind.' This is the first and greatest commandment. And the second is like it: 'Love your neighbor as yourself.' All the Law and the Prophets hang on these two commandments."

Reflection

Jesus was and is a wonderful teacher! In answer to a potentially complicated question, He made the lesson in this reading so simple for us—*love God and love others*.

Love is the basis of a godly public service – whether in government, armed forces, police and fire departments, the classroom, or nonprofit organizations. We defend, improve, and advance our community because we love it and its citizens. It doesn't mean we should ignore wrong and embrace sin, but it does mean we must love both stranger and friend equally with all our hearts, souls, and minds.

This is what Jesus teaches, and we are all in His classroom.

Today at work, what might result if you invest in loving God and loving others? Oh, the miracles that would happen in your workplace!

Today at work, try to **teach like Jesus**!

Prayer

Dear Lord, I need You today. I want to be so in love with You and to truly show love to others at work. Help me be more like You, to teach like You, to do like You. Help me in this journey. Show me the way of love, to see others as You see them. In Your name, I pray. Amen.

Kathleen Patterson

Week 51, Day 5

now an ambassador

Reading

2 Corinthians 5:20(a) [NLT] So we are Christ's ambassadors; God is making his appeal through us.

Reflection

Every day I wake up I ask the Lord to give me His wisdom and strength to walk in love and mercy with others – even when it hurts.

Why do I offer that prayer? Because I no longer represent me – Mr. Jimmy Davis, Jr. I am **now an ambassador** – an ambassador for Christ.

And if I am **now an ambassador**, I must have His wisdom and strength to make His appeal to others. I need His wisdom to appeal to the ones around me who can be so difficult to forgive and love. I need his strength when I represent Him to the old me: the one I find hardest to forgive and love. The one who tries to show up again every now and then.

No! I no longer represent Mr. Jimmy Davis, Jr. Now I have another job. I am now on His payroll. I am **now an ambassador** – an ambassador for Christ.

Today at your work, forget your name tag. Forget the uniform you may wear. Forget the brand of car you drove to work. Forget your status or job title – whether it be worker or officer or boss. Forget you are a Mr. or Mrs. or even a Dr.

Today, do not represent you at work. Accept the job with Him. You are **now an ambassador** – an ambassador for Christ!

Prayer

Father, in the name of Jesus, I pray. Give me Your grace so I can go anywhere or go nowhere and make Your appeal to others. Amen.

Jimmy Davis, Jr.

Week 52, Day 1

microphone for God

Reading

1 Corinthians 16:8-9 [NIV] I stay on at Ephesus until Pentecost, because a great door for effective work has opened to me, and there are many who oppose me.

Ephesians 4:29 [NIV] Let no corrupt communication proceed out of your mouth, but that which is good to the use of edifying, that it may minister grace unto the hearers.

Reflection

Have you ever wondered how the apostles communicated in order share the Good News about Jesus? How did they reach the world? How did they do this without communication tools like public address systems, phones, email, social media, faxes, and other communication tools? In other words, what was their **microphone for God**?

Well, I believe it was their behavior. The example each apostle set in everyday situations, as well as in the most trying times, was the best **microphone for God**. How each treated one another, cared for the sick, helped the poor, and sought out the downtrodden – it got everyone's attention. Yes, because of the example of sharing Christ's love through the way they lived, they spoke loudly in an edifying manner.

Today at work, you and I, as the new apostles – *Christian public servants* – are called to be the standard bearers of the **microphone for God**. We are the ones who need to speak and deliver the message of the Good News by the manner in which we perform our jobs and interact with God's children. You and I can show compassion and empathy for coworkers and those we serve. We can take the extra measures to live the example of sharing Christ's love. Yes, at work today, won't you lead others to Christ? In your own way, won't you become a **microphone for God**?

Prayer

Heavenly Father, please help me follow the example of the apostles and spread the Good News to others in my workplace. Help me effectively communicate to others by the way I work and live my life. Help me be Your microphone. I pray this in Jesus' Name. Amen.

Barbara Hill

Week 52, Day 2

do not exchange God's standards for job values

Reading

Psalm 119:133-134 [ESV] Keep steady my steps according to your promise, and let no iniquity get dominion over me. Redeem me from man's oppression, that I may keep your precepts.

Reflection

Sadly, most workplaces do not represent the moral standards of God. Profit so easily gets in the way, and politics often block the way. Then there are the contradictory challenges of productivity, equity, and compassion. Oh, there are many reasons why too many workdays end without application of God's moral standards.

You know the Bible is the moral guide for your workplace – a setting that seems to oppress godly behavior and Christian thought at every turn. That is why you must deliberately apply the Word, seasoned with God's grace, in all situations and every decision.

Today at work, **do not exchange God's standards for job values**, for the day is way too short. Instead, stand strong in demonstrating God's truth. Lead by God's Word and His Spirit.

Yes, at work today, keep steady your steps, and **do not exchange God's standards for job values**. He promises no inequity will gain dominion over you!

Prayer

Lord, I pray for Your protection and Your encouragement as I await the fulfillment of Your promise. Let me find ways to apply Your moral standard in my workplace. Keep steady my steps. In Your name, I pray. Amen.

Chris Summers

Week 52, Day 3

change the label

Reading

2 Corinthians 5:17(b) [NLT] anyone who belongs to Christ has become a new person. The old life is gone; a new life has begun!

Reflection

I was once the type of person who never let someone cross me twice. Oh, as a Christian, I believed in forgiveness. But I also believed a person's actions defined who he was. If you stole from me, I labeled you a thief – no additional questions asked. This is how I protected myself – knowing others could never **change the label** I gave them.

Well, a coworker changed all that! When I first met her, she was a workplace gossiper. She knew everyone's business, and to spice things up, she would even throw in a few untrue details. I learned very early what came from this coworker's lips was probably fabricated and most likely not worth my energy to listen.

But one day she wanted to talk to me during break. Knowing I was a Christian, she said she wanted to get saved. I really didn't believe her. And I even thought about talking her out of it. I told her it was a big commitment. She had to change her entire life. She listened and said, "I know."

A few weeks later, I saw her having lunch in the break room. As I walked in, she was talking to a few other coworkers. I assumed she was up to her old gossiping tricks. But as I approached, I notice the Bible on her lap. I heard her speaking. *She was talking about Jesus*! Was she new? Could Jesus change her?

He could and, in fact, He did! Just like He changed me and continues to change me. Just like He saved you. He saved my coworker and taught me something about labeling because she was a new creature.

Are you negatively labeling a coworker? Realize she is not so far out of the reach of Christ. Realize you are not far out of His reach, either. And know deep in your heart Christ can **change the label** on anyone – including sinners like you and me.

Today at work, remember Christ can **change the label** on anyone. And new life will begin!

Prayer

Heavenly Father, thank You for making me a new creature. You have labeled me "forgiven." And I must label others no longer. In Jesus' name, I pray. Amen.

Crystal Featherston

Week 52, Day 4

based on much more

Reading

Joshua 1:8 [KJV] This book of the law shall not depart out of thy mouth; but thou shalt meditate therein day and night, that thou mayest observe to do according to all that is written therein: for then thou shalt make thy way prosperous, and then thou shalt have good success.

Reflection

I woke up yesterday morning reflecting on what I had to do. Get to work, check the email, respond to emails, make phone calls, work on cases, interview clients, write reports, maybe take a lunch break, fight with the electronics that never seem to work, write more reports, and finally leave work. I felt discouraged just thinking about my day.

Work seems to be a never-ending to-do list. Nothing ever seems to be finished. Unfortunately, that means I often define success as accomplishing one task, not adding another three items to my to-do list, or just making it through another chaotic day. If I accomplish anything, I feel successful and my ways have been prosperous. However, many days I leave the office feeling unsuccessful and discouraged.

In the chaos, I so often forget God does not define my prosperity and success through what I accomplish at work on a daily basis. He does call me to work hard, but my prosperity and successfulness in life are **based on much more**.

Today at work, meditate on laws of the Lord and strive to obey them. Then, and only then, will you understand true prosperity and find your day to be successful – even if your entire to-do list is not accomplished. Yes, meditate on His laws, and you will find your value is **based on much more**!

Prayer

Lord, the way to success is only through You! Help me remember that truth today as I prepare for another busy day at my workplace. Lead me to a level of prosperity that can only be found in Your Word, and help me remember accomplishing my to-do list does not define my success. In Your name, I pray, Amen.

Reagan Hinton

Week 52, Day 5

seeing what God is doing

Reading

Luke 10:41-42 [NKJV] And Jesus answered and said to her, "Martha, Martha, you are worried and troubled about many things. But one thing is needed, and Mary has chosen that good part, which will not be taken away from her."

Reflection

One day a brother confronted me about how I was ministering to someone else here on Life Row. We sat down, and I listened to his concerns. When he finished, I explained what I was doing. It was clear this brother did not know what God was doing in me and what path He was directing me to follow. Like Martha, he didn't understand – so he just made a quick judgment.

There's a lesson here for all of us.

When you see someone doing something different, do not make a quick judgment, speculating about what you don't understand. Instead, focus on **seeing what God is doing** in that person. He may be messing up, but then again, he may be following God.

And how about where you work? Have you been making quick judgments about a coworker or supervisor? If so, stop it! Just be patient and focus on **seeing what God is doing** – in yourself and that other person.

And if you do this, like Mary, you will not be worried nor troubled throughout the day!

Prayer

Father, in the name of Jesus, I pray. Help me to keep focused on what You want in me so I can help advance Your kingdom. Give me patience to see what You want in others so I do not get in Your way. Amen.

Jimmy Davis, Jr.

About the Contributors

Alexander, Deanna, M.A. – Week 4, Day 4
    County Supervisor
    Milwaukee County
    Milwaukee, Wisconsin USA

Altema, Evelyne F. – Week 20, Day 2; Week 22, Day 1; Week 28, Day 4; Week 36, Day 1; Week 40, Day 2
    Language Assessment Services
    Government of Canada
    Quebec, Quebec Canada

Arbitter, Angela, M.P.A. – Week 21, Day 1; Week 24, Day 4; Week 29, Day 2
    International Justice Mission
    Gulu, Uganda

Baker, Gigi – Week 32, Day 2
    Legislative outreach Secretary
    Legislative Outreach Office
    Pennsylvania House of Representatives
    Harrisburg, Pennsylvania USA

Ballard, Dawnielle – Week 4, Day 2
    Health Partner Resolution Specialist
    CareSource
    Youngstown, Ohio USA

Bayer, Paul, M.A. – Week 8, Day 2; Week 20, Day 3; Week 28, Day 2
    Paralegal
    Pittman & Anderson Real Estate Legal Service
    Norfolk, Virginia USA

Bednarczuk, Michael, Ph.D. – Week 10, Day 3; Week 23, Day 2
    Assistant Professor & Chair
    Department of Public Administration
    Belhaven University
    Jackson, Mississippi USA

Bellar, Stephanie L. – Week 51, Day 2
    Professor
    Department of Political Science
    University of Central Arkansas
    Conway, Arkansas USA

Bereznak, Maureen – Week 38, Day 1
    Research Analyst
    Health Care Committee & Professional Licensure Committee
    Pennsylvania House of Representatives
    Harrisburg, Pennsylvania USA

Best, Stan – Week 4, Day 1; Week 12, Day 2; Week 15, Day 2; Week 18, Day 2; Week 26, Day 1; Week 29, Day 1; Week 37, Day 2; Week 38, Day 4; Week 48, Day 3; Week 49, Day 1; Week 50, Day 4
    Training Manager
    Apprentice School
    Newport News Shipbuilding
    Newport News, Virginia USA

Boisselle, David, D.S.L. – Week 3, Day 1; Week 9, Day 3; Week 15, Day 1
    President & CEO
    Agape Leadership Consulting, LLC
    Chesapeake, Virginia USA

Boswell, Chameka – Week 35, Day 1
    MPA Candidate
    Belhaven University
    Jackson, Mississippi USA

Brandon, TaQuesha, M.P.A. – Week 28, Day 1; Week 50, Day 3
    Robertson School of Government
    Regent University
    Virginia Beach, Virginia USA

Carr, Erica – Week 33, Day 4
    Psychosocial Rehabilitation Coordinator
    Weems Community Mental Health
    Bay Springs, Mississippi USA
    MPA Candidate
    Belhaven University
    Jackson, Mississippi USA

Chambers, Linda – Week 43, Day 1
    Senior Deputy Treasurer
    Town of Gordonsville
    Gordonsville, Virginia USA

Chavez, Stephen W.G. – Week 42, Day 2
    Legislative Intern
    Office of Senator Roger Wicker
    Washington, D.C. USA
    Undergraduate
    Department of Policy Leadership
    Trent Lott Leadership Institute
    University of Mississippi
    Oxford, Mississippi USA

Christian, Courtney, M.A. – Week 4, Day 3
    City Administrator
    Leesville, Louisiana USA

Cooney, Kevin, Ph.D. – Week 1, Day 1; Week 5, Day 1; Week 8, Day 1; Week 11, Day 1; Week 19, Day 1; Week 21, Day 4; Week 23, Day 3; Week 25, Day 2; Week 41, Day 3
    Co-editor
    The Christian Public Servant
    Visiting Professor
    Ritsumeikan Asia Pacific University
    Beppu, Japan

Cox, Alan – Week 13, Day 2; Week 25, Day 4; Week 40, Day 1
    Development Specialist
    City of Toledo
    Toledo, Ohio USA

Craven, Gilbert O., M.A. – Week 42, Day 4; Week 48, Day 2
    Civil Engineering Technician
    Naval Facilities Engineering Command Atlantic (NAVFALANT)
    U.S. Department of Defense
    Norfolk, Virginia USA

Crone, Loren, Lt. USN – Week 30, Day 4
    Chaplain
    Marine Corps Base Quantico
    U.S. Department of Defense
    Quantico Station, Virginia USA

Davis, Jimmy, Jr. – Weeks 1-52, Day 5; Week 46, Day 3
    Z-557 Unit N-10
    Death Row
    W.C. Holman Correctional Facility
    Alabama Department of Corrections
    Atmore, Alabama USA

Dickens, Logan, M.P.A. – Week 12, Day 1; Week 47, Day 2; Week 48, Day 1
    Special Projects Analyst
    Virginia Department of Medical Assistance Services
    Richmond, Virginia USA

Dudley, William (Bill), M.P.A. – Week 1, Day 1; Week 1, Day 3; Week 6, Day 4; Week 9, Day 1; Week 50, Day 2; Week 51, Day 1
    Co-editor
    The Christian Public Servant
    Worship Pastor at Beacon Baptist Church
    Logistician
    U.S. Department of Defense
    Virginia Beach, Virginia USA

Featherston, Crystal, M.P.A. – Week 52, Day 3
    Management & Budget Analyst II
    Department of Budget & Management
    City of Virginia Beach
    Virginia Beach, Virginia USA

Fisher-Coleman, Arnekeya – Week 49, Day 4
    Client Benefit Specialist
    CANOPY Children's Solutions
    Jackson, Mississippi USA
    MPA Candidate
    Belhaven University
    Jackson, Mississippi USA

Garnes, LaShonda, M.P.A. – Week 22, Day 2; Week 23, Day 4; Week 26, Day 2; Week 30, Day 2; Week 33, Day 3
    Business Operations Manager
    Public Works & Utilities
    City of Wichita
    Wichita, Kansas USA

Garth, Sara, M.A. – Week 46, Day 2
    Robertson School of Government
    Regent University
    Virginia Beach, Virginia USA

Gates, Veronica – Week 36, Day 2; Week 38, Day 3
    MPA Candidate
    Belhaven University
    Jackson, Mississippi USA

About the Contributors   353

Gibson, Brianna – Week 38, Day 2
    Family Service
    Hinds County Human Resources Agency
    Jackson, Mississippi USA
    MPA Candidate
    Belhaven University
    Jackson, Mississippi USA

Graham, Samantha Pineiro, M.P.A. – Week 31, Day 3
    J.D. Candidate
    Law School
    Regent University
    Virginia Beach, Virginia USA

Green, John – Week 31, Day 1
    City Council Member
    City of Hoover
    Hoover, Alabama, USA

Griffing, Noah, M.P.A. – Week 3, Day 3; Week 19, Day 4
    Worldwide Flight Services
    Belgrade, Montana USA

Hankle, Dominick D., Ph.D. – Week 30, Day 3
    Professor and Chair
    Psychology Program
    College of Arts & Sciences
    Regent University
    Virginia Beach, Virginia USA

Hanson, Larry W. – Week 20, Day 4; Week 49, Day 2
    City Manager
    City of Valdosta
    Valdosta, Georgia USA

Harrell, Chip, M.A. – Week 27, Day 3; Week 44, Day 1
    J.D. Candidate and President
    Student Bar Association
    School of Law
    Regent University
    Virginia Beach, Virginia USA

354 About the Contributors

Henry, Samuel, M.A. – Week 27, Day 1
    Deputy
    Training, Readiness and Exercises
    U.S. Transportation Command
    Norfolk, Virginia USA

Hill, Barbara – Week 2, Day 3; Week 34, Day 1; Week 35, Day 3; Week 39, Day 3; Week 52, Day 1
    Teacher Assistant
    Jackson Public Schools
    Jackson, Mississippi USA
    MPA Candidate
    Belhaven University
    Jackson, Mississippi USA

Hill, Phoenecia, M.P.A. – Week 2, Day 1
    Indexing and Enrolling Assistant
    Virginia House of Delegates
    Richmond, Virginia USA

Hinton, Reagan, M.A. – Week 52, Day 4
    International Justice Mission
    Gulu, Uganda

Johnson, Deyonta T. M.P.A. – Week 45, Day 3
    Street Law Program Assistant
    Norfolk Court Service Unit
    Virginia Department of Juvenile Justice
    Norfolk, Virginia USA

Jordan, Keith – Week 6, Day 2; Week 31, Day 2
    Food Safety Specialist, Senior
    Virginia Department of Agriculture and Consumer Services
    Virginia Beach, Virginia USA

Kay, Jessica, DCJS Certified – Week 6, Day 3
    Senior Operations Supervisor
    Emergency Communications and Citizen Services
    City of Virginia Beach
    Virginia Beach, Virginia USA

Kelly, Ruth E. – Week 16, Day 2
    2nd Ward Commissioner
    City of Grand Rapids
    Grand Rapids, Michigan USA

Knight, Joanna, MPA – Week 32, Day 1
    Robertson School of Government
    Regent University
    Virginia Beach, Virginia USA

Lacourse, Lyse – Week 30, Day 1
    Administrative Coordinator
    Office of the Chief Actuary
    Office of the Superintendent of Financial Institutions
    Government of Canada
    Ottawa, Ontario Canada

Lantz, Jonathan, M.P.A – Week 11, Day 2
    Intern
    City of Chesapeake
    Chesapeake, Virginia USA

Lassiter, Lou – Week 3, Day 2
    Assistant County Administrator
    Chesterfield County
    Chesterfield, Virginia USA

Lewis, Michelle – Week 34, Day 4; Week 36, Day 4; Week 47, Day 1
    CEO/Executive Director
    Kicks N More Unltd Boutique
    Jackson, Mississippi USA
    MPA Candidate
    Belhaven University
    Jackson, Mississippi USA

Long, F. Long, Jr. ETC, USCG, Ret. – Week 10, Day 1
    Reverend
    Equipment Specialist
    Surface Forces Logistics Center
    U.S. Coast Guard
    Baltimore, Maryland US

Maley, Patricia A., AICP – Week 8, Day 3; Week 41, Day 1
    Senior Planner
    Planning, Design and Review
    City of Wilmington
    Wilmington, Delaware USA

Meconnahey, Christopher Sean, M.P.A. – Week 7, Day 1
    Contract Specialist
    Department of the Navy
    U.S. Department of Defense
    Virginia Beach, Virginia USA

Miller, Brandon, M.A. – Week 1, Day 2
    Associate Editor
    Grand View Media
    Birmingham, Alabama USA

Monnin, Rachael, J.D. – Week 6, Day 1
    Law School
    Regent University
    Virginia Beach, Virginia USA

Neal, Brooke, M.P.A. – Week 22, Day 3
    Donor Relations and Program Development for Childbirth
    PATHS International
    Virginia Beach, Virginia USA

Nierle, Joshua, M.A. – Week 28, Day 3; Week 41, Day 4; Week 44, Day 2
    Robertson School of Government
    Regent University
    Virginia Beach, Virginia USA

Paige, Lakeisha – Week 34, Day 2
    Environmental Health Program Specialist
    Mississippi State Department of Health
    Jackson, Mississippi USA
    MPA Candidate
    Belhaven University
    Jackson, Mississippi USA

Patterson, Eric, Ph.D. – Week 7, Day 4
    Dean
    Robertson School of Government
    Regent University
    Virginia Beach, Virginia USA

Patterson, Kathleen, Ph.D. – Week 51, Day 4
    Professor
    School of Business and Leadership
    Regent University
    Virginia Beach, Virginia USA

Peavy, Tammy L. – Week 1, Day 1
   Co-editor
   The Christian Public Servant
   State Fire Marshal's Office
   State of Mississippi
   Jackson, Mississippi USA

Pincus, Stephen, M.P.A.– Week 1, Day 1; Week 14, Day 1; Week 23, Day 1
   Co-editor
   The Christian Public Servant
   Battalion Chief – retired
   Newport News Fire Department
   Newport News, Virginia USA

Pough, Matthew, M.P.A. – Week 51, Day 3
   Security Professional
   U.S. Department of Defense
   Atlanta, Georgia USA

Pulsford, Meredith, M.P.A. – Week 5, Day 4; Week 9, Day 4; Week 46, Day 1
   Operations Officer
   Norfolk Police Department
   Norfolk, Virginia USA

Rankin, Renata – Week 34, Day 3; Week 44, Day 4
   Disabilities Adjustor
   MS Disability Rights
   Jackson, Mississippi
   MPA Candidate
   Belhaven University
   Jackson, Mississippi USA

Reed, Calvin, Jr. – Week 12, Day 4; Week 36, Day 3; Week 49, Day 3
   MPA Candidate
   Belhaven University
   Jackson, Mississippi USA

Roberts, Gary E., Ph.D. – Week 5, Day 2; Week 24, Day 1; Week 25, Day 1; Week 26, Day 4; Week 29, Day 4
   Professor & Director
   Master of Public Administration Program
   Robertson School of Government
   Regent University
   Virginia Beach, Virginia USA

Saunders, Kathryn – Week 10, Day 2; Week 15, Day 4; Week 16, Day 3; Week 17, Day 2; Week 21, Day 2; Week 22, Day 4; Week 26, Day 3; Week 27, Day 2; Week 29, Day 3; Week 33, Day 2; Week 37, Day 4; Week 40, Day 3; Week 43, Day 2; Week 44, Day 3; Week 45, Day 4
    Head Soccer Coach
    Texas Southern University
    Houston, Texas USA

Shultz, David, M.A. – Week 7, Day 3
    EDDMU-6
    Transitioning Naval Officer
    Virginia Beach, Virginia USA

Slack, James D., Ph.D., Ph.D. – Week 1, Day 1; Week 10, Day 4; Week 13, Day 1; Week 13, Day 4; Week 14, Day 2; Week 18, Day 1; Week 24, Day 3; Week 31, Day 4; Week 42, Day 1; Week 43, Day 3; Week 43, Day 4; Week 45, Day 1; Week 46, Day 3; Week 47, Day 4; Week 50, Day 1
    Co-editor
    The Christian Public Servant
    Professor
    Jackson State University
    Jackson, Mississippi USA

Smith, Greg, M.A. – Week 1, Day 1; Week 11, Day 3
    Co-editor
    The Christian Public Servant
    Johnson County (Kansas Sheriff's Office
    Executive Director
    Kelsey Smith Foundation
    Overland Park, Kansas USA

Somerset, Graham – Week 24, Day 2
    Auditor
    Department of the Army
    U.S. Department of Defense
    Joint Base Langley-Eustis
    Newport News, Virginia USA

Standorf, Wendy, PHR, IPMA-CP – Week 7, Day 2; Week 8, Day 4; Week 17, Day 4; Week 18, Day 3; Week 32, Day 3
    Director
    Human Resources
    City of West University Place
    West University Place, Texas USA

About the Contributors 359

Steele, Valerie, M.P.A. – Week 14, Day 3; Week 16, Day 1
    Manager
    Natchez Trace Stables Foundation
    Jackson, Mississippi USA

Summers, Chris – Week 2, Day 4; Week 9, Day 2; Week 12, Day 3; Week 13, Day 3; Week 16, Day 4; Week 18, Day 4; Week 19, Day 2; Week 20, Day 1; Week 27, Day 4; Week 35, Day 4; Week 39, Day 2; Week 39, Day 4; Week 45, Day 2; Week 46, Day 4; Week 48, Day 4; Week 52, Day 2
    Chaplain
    W. C. Holman Correctional Facility
    Alabama Department of Corrections
    Atmore, Alabama USA

Theroux, Paul, MPA – Week 42, Day 3; Week 47, Day 3
    Maintenance Program Manager
    Naval Base Norfolk
    U.S. Department of Defense
    Norfolk, Virginia USA

Van Straten, Stephanie – Week 33, Day 1
    School of Medicine
    Past President
    Student Surgical Society
    University of Witwatersrand
    Johannesburg, South Africa USA

Waples, William – Week 1, Day 4; Week 2, Day 2; Week 37, Day 1
    Investigator
    Jackson Public Schools
    Jackson, Mississippi USA
    MPA Candidate
    Belhaven University
    Jackson, Mississippi USA

Waugh, Linda – Week 3, Day 4; Week 14, Day 4; Week 21, Day 3
    Editor/Graphic Artist
    Briarwood Presbyterian Church
    Birmingham, Alabama USA

Waugh, Jonathan, Ph.D. – Week 3, Day 4; Week 14, Day 4; Week 21, Day 3
    Professor & Chair
    Department of Cardiopulmonary Sciences
    School of Public Health Professionals
    Samford University
    Homewood, Alabama USA

Williams, Lakisha – Week 35, Day 2; Week 37, Day 3; Week 40, Day 4
    Personal Care AID
    Ability Works
    Jackson, Mississippi USA
    MPA Candidate
    Belhaven University
    Jackson, Mississippi USA

Williams, Sureldie – Week 41, Day 2
    Administrative Support Staff
    an agency in the
    Hampton Roads area, Virginia USA

Whitaker, Chris – Week 25, Day 3
    Writer/Editor
    Flowood, Mississippi USA

Whitman, Matt – Week 39, Day 1
    Deputy Mayor
    City of Halifax
    Halifax, Nova Scotia Canada

Wilson, Ronald – Week 5, Day 3; Week 11, Day 4; Week 15, Day 3; Week 17, Day 3; Week 19, Day 3; Week 32, Day 4
    Development Review Coordinator
    Franklin County
    Rocky Mount, Virginia USA

Winge, Greg R. M.S.W. – Week 17, Day 1
    C.S.A. Program Director
    Office of Children's Services
    Franklin County
    Rocky Mount, Virginia USA

Subject Index

a Christian communicator – Week 38, Day 3
a disconnect with the Spirit – Week 44, Day 3
a friend unknown – Week 38, Day 4
a gentle and quiet spirit – Week 6, Day 3
a griper or a gleaner – Week 16, Day 1
a half-stick of gum – Week 7, Day 5
a Jesus change – Week 12, Day 5
a list for you – Week 26, Day 3
a name really matters – Week 29, Day 1
a nevertheless spirit – Week 38, Day 5
a peacemaker at work – Week 44, Day 4
a perfect workday – Week 4, Day 4
a promise to preserve – Week 12, Day 3
a simple yes or no – Week 42, Day 1
a slow suicide – Week 32, Day 4
a small bucket of bigotry and hate – Week 46, Day 3
accomplishments sought for envy – Week 49, Day 3
acknowledge the God you serve, Week 45, Day 3
all kinds of nasty weather – Week 24, Day 1
all too familiar with that same sin – Week 45, Day 2
an office-party heart weighed down – Week 10, Day 1
another number to the birthdays – Week 37, Day 2
anything less than sharpening – Week 18, Day 3
as bad as the bully – Week 16, Day 4
as if it were home – Week 15, Day 2
as people, not numbers – Week 35, Day 1
asking then listening – Week 5, Day 3
balance the storm – Week 25, Day 5
based on much more – Week 52, Day 4
be more like Him – Week 5, Day 4
be still and seek God's presence – Week 11, Day 2
be strong & stay focused – Week 2, Day 4
become a slave to all – Week 42, Day 5
become truly free – Week 48, Day 3
believe it, see it and feel it – Week 1, Day 1
begin afresh each morning – Week 31, Day 4
better than the mighty – Week 51, Day 1
blessed enough to know – Week 4, Day 5
both neighbors and enemies – Week 44, Day 2
building His kingdom – Week 41, Day 3
bring love to work – Week 3, Day 1

capture the beauty – Week 27, Day 3
change as a bad thing – Week 31, Day 3
change the label – Week 52, Day 3
chaplains do not carry rifles – Week 30, Day 4
chasing the wind – Week 43, Day 4
choose not to harm the faith – Week 48, Day 4
Christian ways to help the team – Week 49, Day 4
comfort the anxiety – Week 34, Day 3
confident through the comfort abounding – Week 38, Day 1
cut the ropes – Week 29, Day 5
deeper than eyes can see – Week 10, Day 2
delight in – Week 48, Day 1
demonstrating love for God, Week 47, Day 1
disqualified in the task – Week 36, Day 5
do anything to help – Week 2, Day 2
do justice today and be content with enough – Week 16, Day 2
do not exchange God's standards for job values – Week 52, Day 2
doing the rules right not just rote – Week 18, Day 4
don't lose your footing – Week 37, Day 4
drink from His cup – Week 5, Day 5
enough, enough – Week 34, Day 4
enough of who – Week 26, Day 2
even more is required – Week 26, Day 1
even the wicked – Week 8, Day 1
even when it causes division – Week 4, Day 1
everything will work out – Week 1, Day 2
excited for the vision – Week 33, Day 2
facing mighty mountains today – Week 16, Day 3
fail with grace – Week 26, Day 4
faith, love, and hope – Week 20, Day 4
far more precious than jewels – Week 32, Day 2
fear may be conquered – Week 31, Day 1
felt, present, and abides within – Week 39, Day 2
filled to the brim – Week 14, Day 5
finds paths of integrity – Week 8, Day 3
first praise from Him – Week 45, Day 5
fix both eyes on what is unseen – Week 29, Day 2
focus on God – Week 28, Day 3
follow through – Week 43, Day 2
foot slipping away – Week 32, Day 1
for all the hurt and all the joy – Week 45, Day 4
forgive even without an apology – Week 4, Day 2
frail human biases – Week 2, Day 3
from the lie to the truth – Week 36, Day 1
gain the more – Week 30, Day 5
get out of God's way – Week 21, Day 5

go beat myself up – Week 1, Day 3
God has blessed you – Week 23, Day 3
God in that moment – Week 34, Day 5
God's answer, not yours – Week 45, Day 1
God's intended results – Week 30, Day 2
guide, advise, and watch over – Week 17, Day 1
hamster wheel – Week 5, Day 2
help keep the advantage – Week 22, Day 5
He will reward you – Week 46, Day 2
His encourager of hope – Week 24, Day 4
hold onto peace – Week 26, Day 5
how will you spend your time – Week 42, Day 3
I could do more, Week 47, Day 2
idle talk about things – Week 6, Day 1
if the reckoning is right – Week 10, Day 4
in a bullying culture – Week 14, Day 2
in a true relationship – Week 50, Day 4
in-Christ – Week 20, Day 5
in His hand – Week 20, Day 3
in someone else's shoes – Week 33, Day 4
in the most unlikely places – Week 47, Day 4
it leads to hope – Week 49, Day 1
it's the how that counts – Week 31, Day 5
joy in the work – Week 5, Day 1
just a fleeting memory – Week 23, Day 1
just like smoke, it fades away – Week 34, Day 1
just really bad company – Week 17, Day 2
just to replenish – Week 21, Day 1
just wait silently for His advice – Week 6, Day 5
keep walking in love – Week 46, Day 5
leave a legacy for Christ – Week 19, Day 5
leave the day with integrity intact – Week 13, Day 2
leftovers to take to work – Week 37, Day 1
let it go – Week 23, Day 4
let others see – Week 40, Day 1
like a candle in front of a firehouse – Week 11, Day 1
like sparks flying upward – Week 11, Day 4
like spring rain and sunshine – Week 17, Day 3
like the watchman in the Bible – Week 25, Day 2
line up with God's word – Week 15, Day 5
live by His standard – Week 27, Day 2
live without fear – Week 14, Day 4
live well, live full, and live free – Week 19, Day 3
look back with regret – Week 21, Day 4
looking for a job – Week 2, Day 1
looking for peace and security – Week 40, Day 2

love others in return – Week 41, Day 5
lunch food that really matters – Week 22, Day 1
lunch time with God – Week 41, Day 1
make it grow – Week 3, Day 2
make something that lasts – Week 20, Day 1
may not return home tonight – Week 50, Day 1
microphone for God – Week 52, Day 1
move mountains through faith – Week 25, Day 3
need to give pause – Week 33, Day 3
no other choice – Week 35, Day 3
not going to be easy – Week 9, Day 5
not to judge – Week 43, Day 5
not your home – Week 9, Day 2
now an ambassador – Week 51, Day 5
one seat open – Week 24, Day 3
open to recognize Him – Week 31, Day 2
overcome evil with good – Week 28, Day 1
pass the test before you can serve – Week 39, Day 3
paths straight – Week 30, Day 1
pause to seek Him first – Week 50, Day 3
pray for your supervisor – Week 28, Day 2
prey to your I-mode – Week 16, Day 5
prosper the mission and achieve success – Week 7, Day 4
providing influence – Week 50, Day 2
put aside the inconsequential – Week 42, Day 4
quietly by the wayside – Week 41, Day 2
regardless of circumstances – Week 12, Day 4
reminders of His love – Week 44, Day 1
restore, confirm, strengthen, and establish – Week 36, Day 3
riches in your heart – Week 22, Day 4
save yourself from the corruption – Week 7, Day 3
say nothing and just listen – Week 35, Day 5
see the goodness – Week 6, Day 4
seeing what God is doing – Week 52, Day 5
seemingly never-ending process – Week 40, Day 5
seize the day for Christ – Week 8, Day 5
serve Him and His people – Week 38, Day 2
show someone the kindness of God – Week 1, Day 5
simply not familiar – Week 36, Day 4
sin in the situation – Week 3, Day 4
some kind of new – Week 21, Day 2
some unwholesome chatter – Week 36, Day 2
something deeper than religion- Week 48, Day 5
something that shows His love – Week 24, Day 2
something to be remembered for – Week 44, Day 5
sooner than what you think – Week 39, Day 1

specks in coworkers' eyes – Week 23, Day 2
spice things up – Week 28, Day 4
start over and push on – Week 14, Day 1
stay focused on the task – Week 39, Day 5
stay in step with Jesus – Week 37, Day 5
stillness…quiet…peace… - Week 51, Day 2
stop blocking the Light – Week 18, Day 5
struggle against the crowd – Week 40, Day 3
suffer grief in all kinds of trials – Week 32, Day 3
teach like Jesus – Week 51, Day 4
take a stand for righteousness – Week 19, Day 1
take God with you – Week 42, Day 2
taken captive by the world – Week 11, Day 3
that bad attitude day – Week 40, Day 4
that coworker no one likes – Week 50, Day 5
that desert called no job – Week 43, Day 3
that kind of prosperity – Week 20, Day 2
that one most-awful workday – Week 12, Day 1
that other workplace document – Week 13, Day 1
that special righteousness – Week 47, Day 5
that uncomfortable feeling – Week 8, Day 2
that which has no wisdom – Week 3, Day 3
the antidote – Week 19, Day 2
the beautiful life still holds – Week 33, Day 1
the best food – Week 10, Day 5
the culture of bullying – Week 18, Day 1
the door to one of the vending machines – Week 23, Day 5
the extra steps needed – Week 34, Day 2
the furrow you cut in the field – Week 6, Day 2
the gifts God bestows – Week 46, Day 1
the hands and feet of Jesus – Week 8, Day 4
the kingdom of God within – Week 9, Day 3
the most difficult task – Week 35, Day 2
the need of the moment – Week 10, Day 3
the only life preserver you need – Week 15, Day 3
the perfect bond of unity – Week 41, Day 4
the politics of His love – Week 9, Day 4
the rest God has set aside – Week 48, Day 2
the right attitude – Week 32, Day 5
the road followed – Week 28, Day 5
the rules of the road – Week 12, Day 2
the same question Jesus asked – Week 21, Day 3
the scariest verse in the bible – Week 22, Day 3
the spiritual lens He gives – Week 22, Day 2
the truth itself stands up – Week 33, Day 5
the urgency of hope – Week 13, Day 4

the wrong standards and lenses – Week 6, Day 3
things simply not known – Week 27, Day 4
this kind of workplace violence – Week 1, Day 4
this new plain power – Week 11, Day 5
this really simple question – Week 13, Day 3
through eyes of grace – Week 27, Day 5
through or out of – Week 46, Day 4
to beat the truth – Week 9, Day 1
training as continual education – Week 18, Day 2
trust Him and live by faith – Week 7, Day 1
trust the Artist of that canvas – Week 29, Day 3
try to please someone, Week 2, Day 5
using only one ear rather than two – Week 17, Day 4
waited with worry – Week 51, Day 3
walk away to find a way – Week 17, Day 5
walk in God's steps – Week 49, Day 5
walk out the calling – Week 14, Day 3
walking it out – Week 15, Day 1
well able-no matter what, Week 3, Day 5
what makes organizations successful – Week 7, Day 2
when darkness approaches – Week 49, Day 2
where He begins – Week 15, Day 4
where the real treasure is found – Week 25, Day 4
why do we work – Week 30, Day 3
with godly confidence – Week 39, Day 4
with hearts in unity of cause – Week 24, Day 5
with intentional words – Week 4, Day 3
with road rage – Week 27, Day 1
win favor and a good name – Week 43, Day 1
work in safety – Week 37, Day 3
work problems beyond your control – Week 29, Day 4
work to-do list, Week 47, Day 3
wretched, pitiable, poor, and naked – Week 35, Day 4
you really can feed them all – Week 13, Day 5
your forgiveness quotient – Week 25, Day 1
value true wisdom – Week 19, Day 4

www.ingramcontent.com/pod-product-compliance
Lightning Source LLC
Chambersburg PA
CBHW072131220426
43664CB00013B/2213